YOU NEED THIS BOOK IF:

1. YOU HAVE CREATED A LITERARY, ARTISTIC, OR MUSICAL WORK, AND/OR,
2. YOU WANT TO COMMERCIALLY EXPLOIT SUCH A WORK, AND/OR,
3. YOU WANT TO KNOW ABOUT COPYRIGHT AND THE NEW ACT.

THIS BOOK CONTAINS:

Scholarly historical articles. Pages 1-35

The new Act of October 19, 1976, generally effective on January 1, 1978. Pages 41-102

Instructions concerning copyright notice and registering works. Pages 139,140,143,172,173

Aspects of copyright discussed by the Supreme Court. Pages 178, 196, 217, 226

Aspects of copyright discussed by the Copyright Office. Pages 103,110,115

Practical aspects of copyright exploitation. Pages x-xv, 122-135, 147-148

MORE? SEE THE REST OF THE BOOK!

Author Walter E. Hurst, an attorney, has written *THE RECORD INDUSTRY BOOK, THE MOVIE INDUSTRY BOOK,* and other books on the entertainment industry. Mr. Hurst has taught classes about copyright at Columbia College, UCLA Extension, College for Recording Arts, and the UWLA School of Law.

Illustrator Don Rico of the "Golden Age of Comics", illustrated *YOUR INCOME TAX COMIC BOOK, MUSIC/RECORD BUSINESS & LAW,* and other books of the Seven Arts Press, Inc. Entertainment Industry Series.

OTHER BOOKS BY THE AUTHOR(S):

The Record Industry Book

The Music Industry Book

The Publisher's Office Manual

The U.S. Master Producers & British Music Scene Book

The Movie Industry Book

The Managers, Entertainers & Agents Book

Film/TV Law (Your Introduction To Film/TV Copyright, Contracts & Other Law)

Film Superlist: 20,000 Motion Pictures In The United States Public Domain

Music/Record Business & Law (Your Introduction To Music/Record Copyright, Contracts & Other Business & Law)

Motion Picture Distribution (Business &/Or Racket?)

How To Be A Music Publisher

Your Income Tax Comic Book

How To Start A Record Company or Independent Production Company

How To Register A Trademark

POSTER

The Entertainment Industry Money Flow Chart

CASSETTES

Music Industry Series
Motion Picture Industry Series
Copyright Series
Supreme Court Series
Sherlock Holmes Series
O. Henry Series
Fairy Tales Series
Other Series

A 7Arts Press
Entertainment Industry Book

COPYRIGHT

HOW TO REGISTER YOUR COPYRIGHT & INTRODUCTION TO NEW & HISTORICAL COPYRIGHT LAW

BY

WALTER E. HURST

ILLUSTRATED BY DON RICO

Authors of MUSIC-RECORD BUSINESS AND LAW and MOTION PICTURE DISTRIBUTION

AUTHORS | SONGWRITERS
PHOTOGRAPHERS | ARTISTS
PRODUCERS | PUBLISHERS
Books & Periodicals | MOVIES
STUDENTS & TEACHERS | RECORDS

SHARON MARSHALL, Editor

Foreword by: SHARON MARSHALL
Introductions by: LEO KULKA, IRWIN ZUCKER, JIM HUGHES
Cover & Illustrations by: DONATO RICO

We would like to express our appreciation to ASCAP for allowing us to reproduce some of the material which is contained in this book.

Our special thanks to the following people for their assistance in compiling this book: MATTHEW GENTRY, AL BERGMAN, TOM MARUZZI, MARSHALL GENTRY, DAVE DIXON, RICHARD BERNSTEIN, JACK SHAPIRO, TOM JOHNSON, STEVE KENDIS, MAKEE BLAISDEL, JOE YORE, MICHELE RICO, JOHN CHARNAY and SUE KNOX.

©COPYRIGHT. HOW TO REGISTER YOUR COPYRIGHT & INTRODUCTION TO NEW & HISTORICAL COPYRIGHT LAW

Library of Congress No. 77-75588
Hurst, Walter E.
©Copyright. How To Register Your Copyright & Introduction To New & Historical Copyright Law
(The Entertainment Industry Series, vol. 13)
Standard Book No. -0911370-29-3 Hardcover
-0911370-30-7 Paper

This is Volume 13 of The Entertainment Industry Series.
U.S. ISSN 0071-0695

For additional copies of this book, mail $10.00 in cash, check or money order to:

SEVEN ARTS PRESS, INC.
6605 Hollywood Boulevard, Suite 215
Hollywood, CA 90028

This book is dedicated to men of the noblest professions and the noblest of trades: Walter Derenberg (author, teacher and attorney) and Alan Siegel (bookseller), and George L. George (book reviewer).

"Every man who knows how to read has it in his power to magnify himself, to multiply the ways in which he exists, to make his life full, significant and interesting."

- Aldous Huxley

This publication is designed to provide accurate and authoritative information in regard to the subject matter covered. It is sold with the understanding that the publisher is not engaged in rendering legal, accounting or other professional service. If legal advice or other expert assistance is required, the services of a competent professional person should be sought.

- From a Declaration of Principles jointly adopted by a Committee of the American Bar Association and a Committee of Publishers and Associations.

WARNING - It is quite possible that:

1. There may be errors in this book;
2. You may interpret something in this book differently from the way we meant it;
3. Something which was correct when this book was written is not correct at the time you read it;
4. The law may change after we write this book.
5. Future editions may contain corrections, if we have learned of errors.

FOREWORD

COPYRIGHT - how the word scared me. COPYRIGHT LAW - how complicated it appeared to me.

I dreaded the thought of reading a complicated book on copyright. But, overcoming my dread, was my desire to make money for myself and my husband by commercially exploiting my husband's creations.

When I read the historical portions of this book, I was facinated by the thought that two centuries ago our Founding Fathers considered copyright, when they wrote The Constitution of the United States.

I read easy to understand circulars of the Copyright Office. I studied the fabulous illustrations by Don Rico, whose illustrations simplify and clarify the entertainment industry in other books of the Entertainment Industry Series.

Then slowly, one word at a time, I read the new Copyright Law. I read an ASCAP written comment on the new act.

Each part of this book helped me understand the fantastic theory behind copyright: that the law should benefit <u>creators</u>, and those persons who spend time and money <u>trying</u> to <u>distribute</u> the work of creators, and the <u>public</u>.

I now have a much better understanding of copyright, Copyright Office procedures, and how to make money for my beloved copyrightable work creator (my husband), for creators who assign copyrights for business reasons, and for myself.

....Sharon Marshall
Editor

INTRODUCTION

Professor Walter E. Hurst lectures students at the College For Recording Arts in San Francisco about the theoretical aspects of copyright, about registration of claims of copyright with the Copyright Office, about songwriters' common law and statutory copyrights, about copyright assignments and copyright licenses.

A knowledge of copyright which the reader obtains from © COPYRIGHT is essential for persons dealing with legal or business aspects of the music publishing, recording and related industries.

Everyone should know how to obtain copyrights, how to register copyrights, how to commercially exploit copyrights.

....Leo Kulka, Dean
College For Recording Arts

San Francisco, California

I was amazed how your book, © COPYRIGHT is structured for the average reader who may want general or detailed information on the recent law changes.

I found it very easy to absorb and certainly found the book comfortable for my "arm chair" leisure reading.

....Jim Hughes
Para-legal student
Los Angeles City College

Los Angeles, California

© COPYRIGHT - It's great, it's great!

....Irwin Zucker
AS I Z IT
President, Book Publicists Of
Southern California

Hollywood, California

CONFLICTING COPYRIGHT INTERESTS

"There is, therefore, no kind of property which is so dependent on the help of the law for the protection of the real owner."

......R. R. Bowker

"Special Libraries association and its individual members would prefer continuation of the long recognized concept that the preparation of a single copy consitutes fair use."

....Frank E. McKenna, Executive Director
Special Libraries Association

"Scholars should be paid for their scholarship... but when this principle is translated into payment for scholarship whose access is via the photocopy machine, there is a strange objection to payment....proposal-ten percent of the net cost of reprography should go to the copyright proprietors of the intellectual property being photocopied.

....Professor Albert P. Blaustein
Rutgers University School of Law

"Baseball's basic position on the merits of the copyright issue remains as follows: A. Unrestricted cable transmission of Baseball games could seriously dilute the value of Baseball's television revenues and devastate home game attendance in both Major League and Minor League cities...C. Unrestricted cable carriage could destroy the Minor League system."

....Bowie Kuhn, Commissioner of Baseball

AUTHOR'S LETTER TO READER

Dear Gentlepersons:

I love copyright.

I love the level of civilization which we have reached with copyright.

I love learning, listening, speaking, teaching, writing and publishing.

This 13th book in The Entertainment Industry Series is a labor of love.

After the basic manuscript was prepared, the next steps concerned typing, typography, rubber cement, paying, and getting the book ready for the printer. The printer's job is to print, bind, and deliver copies to the publisher.

The publisher sends out review copies for reviewers, buyers for bookstores, and others who can decide whether they will bring the book to the attention of potential acquirers of copies of the book.

I look forward to receiving royalties for my work.

Receiving money for creating a work of love is a high form of happiness.

If I am lucky, there will be a big demand for future editions, which will bring later copyright developments to the attentions of readers.

That's part of my story as a creator.

I do wish to you a lot of luck, happiness, recognition and money in your life as creator, as commercial exploiter, and as user of copyrights.

I hope this book will help you dream, do, push, and receive.

......Walter E. Hurst
Hollywood, California

STEP 1
COPYRIGHT INITIALLY BELONGS TO THE CREATOR
Reference: 17 USC 201
Ownership of Copyright
This Book: See Page 68

STEP 2
COPYRIGHT NOTICE IS PLACED ON WORK TO BE REPRODUCED.
COPYRIGHT by WALTER E. HURST
©MCMLXXVII by Walter E. Hurst
How? Where? When? WORDS AND MUSIC by Wm. Storm Hale
©MCMLXXVII by Room Seven Music
The ENTERTAINMENT INDUSTRY MONEY FLOW CHART
©MCMLXXX by 7ARTS PRESS, Inc.

STEP 3
THE WORK (WHICH CONTAINS THE COPYRIGHT NOTICE) IS REPRODUCED
©
COPYRIGHT
by
WALTER E. HURST
HOW? WHERE? WHEN?
WORDS AND MUSIC
by Wm. Storm Hale
©.MCMLXXVII
ROOM SEVEN
The ENTERTAINMENT INDUSTRY
MONEY FLOW CHART
© MCMLXXX
by 7 ARTS PRESS, INC
The
Reference for Copies 17 USC 101
Definition "COPIES."
Our Page 42

STEP 4
THE COPIES (CONTAINING THE COPYRIGHT NOTICE) ARE PUBLISHED.
("Publication" is the distribution of copies or phonorecords of a work to the public by sale or other transfer of ownership, or by rental, lease, or lending.)
SPECIAL
LEARNING CASSETTES
Reference: 17 USC 101. See "PUBLICATION."
In this book, Page 43

STEP 5
Two copies of the best edition (which contain the copyright notice) are sent to the Copyright Office.
Enclosed are:
1. FILING FEE: $____
2. COPYRIGHT OFFICE FORM
3. TWO COPIES OF THE BEST EDITION
Yours Truly,
Copyright Claimant
Letter to: COPYRIGHT OFFICE, WASHINGTON, D.C.

SUBJECT MATTER OF COPYRIGHT
BOOKS
DRAMATIC WORKS
ONYX
A PLAY
by
DON RICO
PANTOMIME & CHOREOGRAPHIC WORKS
PICTORIAL, GRAPHIC & SCULPTURE WORKS
MOTION PICTURE AND OTHER AUDIO-VISUAL WORKS
SOUND RECORDINGS
Reference: 17 USC 102

TABLE OF CONTENTS

We have available cassette tape recordings on Copyright Law of contents contained in this book.

These cassettes are basically for the person who likes to listen more than he likes to read. There will be some changes from the text and some additional material.

PRICE FOR COPYRIGHT CASSETTE ALBUM
$49.50

You may also order cassette up-dated annual lectures on NEW COPYRIGHT DEVELOPMENTS.

PRICE FOR EACH ANNUAL LECTURE ON CASSETTE
$10.00

Send money with order to: SEVEN ARTS PRESS, INC.
Dept. #CC1
6605 Hollywood Blvd.
Hollywood, CA 90028

INTRODUCTION TO SCHOLARLY MATERIAL ON PAGES 1 through 37

A century ago, persons interested in copyright law were exploring the history of copyright law and were urging Congress to pass a new and better act.

For those of you who are scholarly minded, and those who pretend to be, and those lucky adults who have curiousity, we have legally pirated and reproduced two articles in the public domain.

The articles are:

THE NATURE AND ORIGIN OF COPYRIGHT, by R. R. Bowker.

THE EVOLUTION OF COPYRIGHT, by Brander Matthews.

They appeared in the book "THE QUESTION OF COPYRIGHT, by Geo. Haven Putman, which was published in 1891.

Initially, these articles were protected by copyright, thus benefiting the creator and the publisher. After the period of copyright expired, the work entered the public domain, thus benefiting you, the public.

THE QUESTION OF COPYRIGHT.

I.

THE NATURE AND ORIGIN OF COPYRIGHT.

By R. R. Bowker.

COPYRIGHT (from the Latin *copia*, plenty) means, in general, the right to copy, to make plenty. In its specific application it means the right to multiply copies of those products of the human brain known as literature and art.

There is another legal sense of the word "copyright" much emphasized by several English justices. Through the low Latin use of the word *copia*, our word "copy" has a secondary and reversed meaning, as the pattern to be copied or made plenty, in which sense the schoolboy copies from the "copy" set in his copy-book, and the modern printer calls for the author's "copy." Copyright, accordingly, may also mean the right in copy made (whether the original work or a duplication of it), as well as the right to make copies, which by no means goes with the work or any duplicate of it. Said Lord St. Leonards: "When we are talking of the right of an author we must distinguish between the mere right to his manuscript, and to any copy which he may choose to make of it, as his property, just like any other personal chattel, and the right to multiply copies to the exclusion of every other person. Nothing can be more distinct than these two things. The common law does give a man who has composed a work a right to it as composition, just as he has a right to any other part of his personal property; but the question of the right of excluding all the world from copying, and of himself claiming the exclusive right of forever copying his own composition after he has published it to the world, is a totally different thing." Baron Parks, in the same case, pointed out expressly these two different legal senses of the word copyright, the right *in* copy, a right of possession, always fully protected by the common law, and the right *to* copy, a right of multiplication, which alone has been the subject of special statutory protection.

There is nothing which may more properly be called property than the creation of the individual brain. For property means a man's very *own*, and there is nothing more his own than the thought, created, made out of no material thing (unless the nerve-food which the brain consumes in the act of thinking be so counted), which uses material things only for its record or manifestation. The best proof of *own*-ership is that, if this individual man or woman had not thought this individual thought, realized in writing or in music or in marble, it would not exist. Or if the individual, thinking it, had put it aside without such record, it would not, in any practical sense, exist. We cannot know what "might have beens" of untold value have been lost to the world where thinkers, such as inventors, have had no inducement or opportunity to so materialize their thoughts.

It is sometimes said, as a bar to this idea of property, that no thought is new—that every thinker is dependent upon the gifts of nature and the thoughts of other thinkers before him, as every tiller of the soil is dependent upon the land as given by nature and improved by the men who have toiled and tilled before him—a view of which Henry C. Carey has been the chief exponent in this country. But there is no real analogy—aside from the question whether the denial of individual property in land would not be setting back the hands of progress. If Farmer Jones does not raise potatoes from a piece of land, Farmer Smith can; but Shakespeare cannot write *Paradise Lost* nor Milton *Much Ado*, though before both Dante dreamed and Boccaccio told his tales. It was because of Milton and Shakespeare writing, not because of Dante and Boccaccio, who had written, that these immortal works are treasures of the English tongue. It was the very self of each, *in propria persona*, that gave these form and worth, though they used words that had come down from generations as the common heritage of English-speaking men. Property in a stream of water, as has been pointed out, is not in the atoms of the water but in the flow of the stream.

Property right in unpublished works has never been effectively questioned—a fact which in itself confirms the view that intellectual property is a natural inherent right. The author has "supreme control" over an unpublished work, and his manuscript cannot be utilized by creditors as assets without his consent. "If he lends a copy to another," says Baron Parkes, "his right is not gone; if he sends it to another under an implied undertaking that he is not to part with it or publish it he has a right to enforce that undertaking." The receiver of a letter, to whom the paper containing the writing has undoubtedly been given, has no right to publish or otherwise use the letter without the writer's consent. The theory that, by permitting copies to be made, an author dedicates his writing to the public, as an owner of land dedicates a road to the public by permitting public use of it for twenty-one years, overlooks the fact that in so doing the author only conveys to each holder of his book the right to individual use, and not the right to multiply copies; as though the landowner should not give, but sell, permission to individuals to pass over his road, without any permission to them to sell tickets for the same privilege to other people. The owner of a right does not forfeit a right by selling a privilege.

It is at the moment of publication that the undisputed possessory right passes over into the much-disputed right to multiply copies, and that the vexed question of the true theory of copyright property arises. The broad view of literary property holds that the one kind of copyright is involved in the other. The right to have is the right to use. An author cannot use—that is, get beneficial results from—his work, without offering copies for sale. He would be otherwise like the owner of a loaf of bread who was told that the bread was his until he wanted to eat it. That sale would seem to contain "an implied undertaking" that the buyer has liberty to use his copy but not to multiply it. Peculiarly in this kind of property the right of ownership consists in the right to prevent use of one's property by others without the owner's consent. The right of exclusion seems to be, indeed, a part of ownership. In the case of land the owner is entitled to prevent trespass to the extent of a shot-gun, and in the same way, the law recognizes the right to use violence, even to the extreme, in preventing others from possession of one's own property of any kind. The owner of a literary property has, however, no physical means of defence or redress; the very act of publication by which he gets a market for his productions opens him to the danger of wider multiplication and publication without his consent. There is, therefore, no kind of property which is so dependent on the help of the law for the protection of the real owner.

The inherent right of authors is a right at what is called common law—that is, natural or customary law. So far as concerns the undisputed rights before publication, the copyright laws are auxiliary merely to common law. Rights exist before remedies; remedies are merely invented to enforce rights. "The seeking for the law of the right of property in the law of procedure relating to the remedies," says Copinger, "is a mistake similar to supposing that the mark on the ear of an animal is the cause, instead of the consequence, of property therein." After the invention of printing it became evident that new methods of procedure must be devised to enforce common law rights. Copyright became, therefore, the subject of statute law, by the passage of laws imposing penalties for a theft which, without such laws, could not be punished.

These laws, covering, naturally enough, only the country of the author, and specifying a time during which the penalties could be enforced, and providing means of registration by which authors could register their property rights, as the title to a house is registered when it is sold, had an unexpected result. The statute of Anne, which is the foundation of present English copyright law, intended to protect authors' rights by providing penalties against their violation, had the effect of limiting those rights. It was doubtless the intention of those who framed the statute of Anne to establish, for the benefit of authors, specific means of redress. Overlooking, apparently, the fact that law and equity, as their principles were then established, enabled authors to use the same means of redress, so far as they held good, which persons suffering wrongs as to other property had, the law was so drawn that, in 1774, the English House of Lords (against, however, the weight of one half of English judicial opinion) decided that, instead of giving additional sanction to a formerly existing right, the statute of Anne had substituted a new and lesser right, to the exclusion of what the majority of English judges held to have been an old and greater right. Literary and like property to this extent lost the character of copy-*right*, and became the subject of copy-*privilege*, depending on legal enactment for the security of the private owner. American courts, wont to follow English precedent, have rather taken for granted this view of the law of literary property, and our Constitution, in authorizing Congress to secure "for limited terms to authors and inventors the exclusive right to their respective writings and discoveries," was evidently drawn from the same point of view, though it does not in itself deny or withdraw the natural rights of the author at common law.

II.

THE EVOLUTION OF COPYRIGHT.

By Brander Matthews.

(Reprinted from the *Political Science Quarterly*.)

"THE only thing that divides us on the question of copyright seems to be a question as to how much property there is in books," said James Russell Lowell, two or three years ago; and he continued,

"but that is a question we may be well content to waive till we have decided that there is any property at all in them. I think that, in order that the two sides should come together, nothing more is necessary than that both should understand clearly that property, whether in books or in land or in anything else, is artificial; that it is purely a creature of law; and, more than that, of local and municipal law. When we have come to an agreement of this sort, I think we shall not find it difficult to come to an agreement that it will be best for us to get whatever acknowledgment of property we can, in books, to start with."

"An author has no natural right to a property in his production," said the late Matthew Arnold, in his acute and suggestive essay on copyright,

"but then neither has he a natural right to anything whatever which he may produce or acquire. What is true is that a man has a strong instinct making him seek to possess what he has produced or acquired, to have it at his own disposal; that he finds pleasure in so having it, and finds profit. The instinct is natural and salutary, although it may be over-stimulated and indulged to excess. One of the first objects of men, in combining themselves in society, has been to afford to the individual, in his pursuit of this instinct, the sanction and assistance of the laws, so far as may be consistent with the general advantage of the community. The author, like other people, seeks the pleasure and the profit of having at his own disposal what he produces. Literary production, wherever it is sound, is its own exceeding great reward; but that does not destroy or diminish the author's desire and claim to be allowed to have at his disposal, like other people, that which he produces, and to be free to turn it to account. It happens that the thing which he produces is a thing hard for him to keep at his own disposal, easy for other people to appropriate; but then, on the other hand, he is an interesting producer, giving often a great deal of pleasure by what he produces, and not provoking Nemesis by any huge and immoderate profits on his production, even when it is suffered to be at his own disposal. So society has taken him under its protection, and has sanctioned his property in his work, and enabled him to have it at his own disposal."

Perhaps a consideration of the evolution of copyright in the past will conduce to a closer understanding of its condition at present, and to a clearer appreciation of its probable development in the future. It is instructive as well as entertaining to trace the steps by which men, combining themselves in society, in Arnold's phrase, have afforded to the individual author the sanction of the law in possessing what he has produced; and it is no less instructive to note the successive enlargements of jurisprudence by which property in books—which is, as Lowell says, the creature of local municipal law—has slowly developed until it demands and receives international recognition.

I.

The maxim that "there is no wrong without a remedy," indicates the line of legal development.

The instinct of possession is strong; and in the early communities, where most things were in common, it tended more and more to assert itself. When anything which a man claimed as his own was taken from him, he had a sense of wrong, and his first movement was to seek vengeance—much as a dog defends his bone, growling when it is taken from him, or even biting. If public opinion supported the claim of possession, the claimant would be sustained in his effort to get revenge. So, from the admission of a wrong, would grow up the recognition of a right. The moral right became a legal right as soon as it received the sanction of the State. The State first commuted the right of vengeance, and awarded damages, and the action of tort was born. For a long period property was protected only by the action for damages for disseizin; but this action steadily widened in scope until it became an action for recovery; and the idea of possession or seizin broadened into the idea of ownership. This development went on slowly, bit by bit and day by day, under the influence of individual self-assertion and the resulting pressure of public opinion, which, as Lowell once tersely put it, is like that of the atmosphere: "You can't see it, but it is fifteen pounds to the square inch all the same."

The individual sense of wrong stimulates the moral growth of society at large; and in due course of time, after a strenuous struggle with those who profit by the denial of justice, there comes a calm at last, and ethics crystallize into law. In more modern periods of development, the recognition of new forms of property generally passes through three stages. First, there is a mere moral right, asserted by the individual and admitted by most other individuals, but not acknowledged by society as a whole. Second, there is a desire on the part of those in authority to find some means of protection for this admitted moral right, and the action in equity is allowed—this being an effort to command the conscience of those whom the ordinary policeman is incompetent to deal with. And thirdly, in the fullness of time, there is declared a law setting forth clearly the privileges of the producer and the means whereby he can defend his property and recover damages for an attack on it. This process of legislative declaration of rights is still going on all about us and in all departments of law, as modern life develops and spreads out and becomes more and more complex; and we have come to a point where we can accept Jhering's definition of a legal right as "a legally protected interest."

As it happens, this growth of a self-asserted claim into a legally protected interest can be traced with unusual ease in the evolution of copyright, because copyright itself is comparatively a new thing. The idea of property was probably first recognized in the tools which early man made for himself, and in the animals or men whom he subdued; later, in the soil which he cultivated. In the beginning the idea attached only to tangible things—to actual physical possession—to that which a man might pass from hand to hand. Now, in the dawn of history nothing was less a physical possession than literature; it was not only intangible, it was invisible even. There was literature before there was any writing, before an author could set down his lines in black and white. Homer and the rhapsodists published their poems by word of mouth. *Litera scripta manet;* but the spoken poem flew away with the voice of the speaker and lingered only in the memory. Even after writing was invented, and after parchment and papyrus made it possible to preserve the labors of the poet and the historian, these authors had not, for many a century yet, any thought of making money by multiplying copies of their works.

The Greek dramatists, like the dramatists of to-day, relied for their pecuniary reward on the public performance of their plays. There is a tradition that Herodotus, when an old man, read his *History* to an Athenian audience at the Panathenaic festival, and so delighted them that they gave him as a recompense ten talents—more than twelve thousand dollars of our money. In Rome, where there were booksellers having scores of trained slaves to transcribe manuscripts for sale, perhaps the successful author was paid for a poem, but we find no trace of copyright or of anything like it. Horace (*Ars Poetica*, 345) speaks of a certain book as likely to make money for a certain firm of booksellers. In the other Latin poets, and even in the prose writers of Rome, we read more than one cry of suffering over the blunders of the copyists, and more than one protest in anger against the mangled manuscripts of the hurried, servile transcribers. But nowhere do we find any complaint that the author's rights have been infringed; and this, no doubt, was because the author did not yet know that he had any wrongs. Indeed, it was only after the invention of printing that an author had an awakened sense of the injury done him in depriving him of the profit of vending his own writings; because it was only after Gutenberg had set up as a printer that the possibility of definite profit from the sale of his works became visible to the author. Before then he had felt no sense of wrong; he had thought mainly of the honor of a wide circulation of his writings; and he had been solicitous chiefly about the exactness of the copies. With the invention of printing there was a chance of profit; and as soon as the author saw this profit diminished by an unauthorized reprint, he was conscious of injury, and he protested with all the strength that in him lay. He has continued to protest from that day to this; and public opinion has been aroused, until by slow steps the author is gaining the protection he claims.

It is after the invention of printing that we must seek the origin of copyright. Mr. De Vinne shows that Gutenberg printed a book with movable types, at Mentz, in 1451. Fourteen years later, in 1465, two Germans began to print in a monastery near Rome, and removed to Rome itself in 1467; and in 1469 John of Spira began printing in Venice. Louis XI. sent to Mentz Nicholas Jenson, who introduced the art into France in 1469. Caxton set up the first press in England in 1474.

In the beginning these printers were publishers also; most of their first books were Bibles, prayer-books, and the like; but in 1465, probably not more than fifteen years after the first use of movable types, Fust and Schoeffer put forth an edition of Cicero's *Offices*—"the first tribute of the new art to polite literature," Hallam calls it. The original editing of the works of a classic author, the comparison of manuscripts, the supplying of *lacunæ*, the revision of the text, called for scholarship of a high order; this scholarship was sometimes possessed by the printer-publisher himself; but more often than not he engaged learned men to prepare the work for him and to see it through the press. This first edition was a true pioneer's task; it was a blazing of the path and a clearing of the field. Once done, the labor of printing again that author's writings in a condition acceptable to students would be easy. Therefore the printer-publisher who had given time and money and hard work to the proper presentation of a Greek or Latin book was outraged when a rival press sent forth a copy of his edition, and sold the volume at a lower price, possibly, because there had been no need to pay for the scholarship which the first edition had demanded. That the earliest person to feel the need of copyright production should have been a printer-publisher is worthy of remark; obviously, in this case, the printer-publisher stood for the author and was exactly in his position. He was prompt to protest against this disseizin[1]

[1] If any lawyer objects to the use of the word "disseizin" in connection with other than real property, he is referred to Prof. J. B. Ames's articles on Disseizin of Chattels, in the *Harvard Law Review*, Jan.—March, 1890.

of the fruit of his labors; and the earliest legal recognition of his rights was granted less than a score of years after the invention of printing had made the injury possible. It is pleasant for us Americans to know that this first feeble acknowledgment of copyright was made by a republic. The Senate of Venice issued an order, in 1469, that John of Spira should have the exclusive right for five years to print the epistles of Cicero and of Pliny.[1]

This privilege was plainly an exceptional exercise of the power of the sovereign state to protect the exceptional merit of a worthy citizen; it gave but a limited protection; it guarded but two books, for a brief period only, and only within the narrow limits of one commonwealth. But, at least, it established a precedent—a precedent which has broadened down the centuries until now, four hundred years later, any book published in Venice is, by international conventions, protected from pillage for a period of at least fifty years, through a territory which includes almost every important country of continental Europe. If John of Spira were to issue to-day his edition of Tully's *Letters*, he need not fear an unauthorized reprint anywhere in the kingdom of which Venice now forms a part, or in his native land, Germany, or in France, Belgium, or Spain, or even in Tunis, Liberia, or Hayti.

The habit of asking for a special privilege from the authorities of the State wherein the book was printed spread rapidly. In 1491 Venice gave the pub-

[1] Sanuto, *Script. Rerum. Italic.*, t. xxii., p. 1189; cited by Hallam, *History of Middle Ages*, chap. ix., part ii.

licist, Peter of Ravenna, and the publisher of his choice the exclusive right to print and sell his *Phœnix*[1] —the first recorded instance of a copyright awarded directly to an author. Other Italian states "encouraged printing by granting to different printers exclusive rights for fourteen years, more or less, of printing specified classics," and thus the time of the protection accorded to John of Spira was doubled. In Germany the first privilege was issued at Nuremberg, in 1501. In France the privilege covered but one edition of a book; and if the work went to press again, the publisher had to seek a second patent.

In England, in 1518, Richard Pynson, the King's Printer, issued the first book *cum privilegio;* the title-page declaring that no one else should print or import in England any other copies for two years; and in 1530 a privilege for seven years was granted to John Palsgrave "in the consideration of the value of his work and the time spent on it; this being the first recognition of the nature of copyright as furnishing a reward to the author for his labor."[2] In 1533 Wynkyn de Worde obtained the king's privilege for his second edition of Witinton's *Grammar*. The first edition of this book had been issued ten years before, and during the decade it had been reprinted by Peter Trevers without leave—a despoilment against which Wynkyn de Worde protested vigorously in the preface to the later edition, and on account of which he applied for and secured pro-

[1] Bowker, *Copyright*, p. 5.
[2] T. E. Scrutton, *Laws of Copyright*, p. 72.

tection. Here again is evidence that a man does not think of his rights until he feels a wrong. Jhering bases the struggle for law on the instinct of ownership as something personal, and the feeling that the person is attacked whenever a man is deprived of his property; and, as Walter Savage Landor wrote: "No property is so entirely and purely and religiously a man's own as what comes to him immediately from God, without intervention or participation." The development of copyright, and especially its rapid growth within the past century, is due to the loud protests of authors deprived of the results of their labors, and therefore smarting as acutely as under a personal insult.[1]

The invention of printing was almost simultaneous with the Reformation, with the discovery of America, and with the first voyage around the Cape of Good Hope. There was in those days a ferment throughout Europe, and men's minds were making ready for a great outbreak. Of this movement, intellectual on one side and religious on the other, the governments of the time were afraid; they saw that the press was spreading broadcast new ideas which might take root in the most inconvenient places, and spring up at the most inopportune moments; so they sought at once to control the printing of books. In less than a century after Gutenberg had cast the first type, the privileges granted for the encouragement and reward of the printer-publisher and of the author were utilized to enable those in authority to prevent the sending forth of such works

[1] Jhering, *The Struggle for Law* (translated by J. J. Lalor).

2

as they might choose to consider treasonable or heretical. For a while, therefore, the history of the development of copyright is inextricably mixed with the story of press-censorship. In France, for example, the edict of Moulins, in 1566, forbade "any person whatsoever printing or causing to be printed any book or treatise without leave and permission of the king, and letters of privilege."[1] Of course, no privilege was granted to publisher or to author if the royal censors did not approve of the book.

In England the "declared purpose of the Stationers' Company, chartered by Philip and Mary in 1556, was to prevent the propagation of the Protestant Reformation."[2] The famous "Decree of Star Chamber concerning printing," issued in 1637, set forth,

> "that no person or persons whatsoever shall at any time print or cause to be imprinted any book or pamphlet whatsoever, unless the same book or pamphlet, and also all and every the titles, epistles, prefaces, proems, preambles, introductions, tables, dedications, and other matters and things whatsoever thereunto annexed, or therewith imprinted, shall be first lawfully licensed."

In his learned introduction to the beautiful edition of this decree, made by him for the Grolier Club, Mr. De Vinne remarks that at this time the people of England were boiling with discontent; and, "annoyed by a little hissing of steam," the ministers of Charles I. "closed all the valves and outlets, but did not draw or deaden the fires which made the steam;"

[1] Alcide Darras, *Du Droit des Auteurs*, p. 169.

[2] E. S. Drone, *A Treatise on the Law of Property in Intellectual Productions*, p. 56.

then "they sat down in peace, gratified with their work, just before the explosion which destroyed them." This decree was made the eleventh day of July, 1637; and in 1641 the Star Chamber was abolished; and eight years later the king was beheaded at Whitehall.

The slow growth of a protection, which was in the beginning only a privilege granted at the caprice of the officials, into a legal right, to be obtained by the author by observing the simple formalities of registration and deposit, is shown in a table given in the appendix (page 370) to the *Report of the Copyright Commission* (London, 1878). The salient dates in this table are these:

"1637.—Star Chamber Decree supporting copyright.

1643.—Ordinance of the Commonwealth concerning licensing. Copyright maintained, but subordinate to political objects.

1662.—13 and 14 Car. II., c. 33.—Licensing Act continued by successive Parliaments; gives copyright coupled with license.

1710.—8 Anne, c. 19.—First Copyright Act. Copyright to be for fourteen years, and if author then alive, for fourteen years more. Power to regulate price.

1814.—54 Geo. III., c. 156.—Copyright to be for twenty-eight years absolutely, and further for the life of the author, if then living.

1842.—5 and 6 Vict., c. 45.—Copyright to be for the life of the author and seven years longer; or for forty-two years, whichever term last expires."

From Mr. Bowker's chapter on the *History of Copyright in the United States*, it is easy to draw up a similar table showing the development in this country:

"1793.—Connecticut, in January, and Massachusetts, in March, passed acts granting copyrights for twenty-one years. In May

Congress recommended the States to pass acts granting copyright for fourteen years—seemingly a step backward from the Connecticut and Massachusetts statutes.

1785 and 1786.—Copyright Acts passed in Virginia, New York, and New Jersey.

1786.—Adoption of the Constitution of the United States, authorizing Congress 'to promote the progress of science and useful arts by securing for limited times, to authors and inventors, the exclusive right to their respective writings and discoveries.'

1790.—First United States Copyright Act. Copyright to citizens or residents for fourteen years, with a renewal for fourteen years more if the author were living at the expiration of the first term.

1831.—Copyright to be for twenty-eight years, with a renewal for fourteen years more, if the author, his widow, or his children are living at the expiration of the first term.

1856.—Act securing to dramatists stage-right; that is, the sole right to license the performance of a play.

1873–4.—The Copyright Laws were included in the Revised Statutes (sections 4948 to 4971)."

From the exhaustive and excellent work of M. Lyon-Caen and M. Paul Delalain on *Literary and Artistic Property*[1] we see that France, now, perhaps, the foremost of all nations in the protection it accords to literary property, lagged behind Great Britain and the United States in taking the second step in the evolution of copyright. It was in 1710 that the act of Anne gave the British author a legal right independent of the caprice of any official; and as soon as the United States came into being, the same right was promptly confirmed to our citizens; but it was not until the fall of the ancient *régime* that a Frenchman was enabled to take out a copy-

[1] *La Propriété Littéraire et Artistique : Lois Françaises et Étrangères* (Paris, Pichon, 1889, 2 vols.).

right at will. Up to the eve of the Revolution of 1789, French authors could do no more, say MM. Lyon-Caen and Delalain, "than ask for a privilege which might always be refused them" (page 8). As was becoming in a country where the drama has ever been the most important department of literature, the first step taken was a recognition of the stage-right of the dramatist, in a law passed in 1791. Before that, a printed play could have been acted in France by any one, but thereafter the exclusive right of performance was reserved to the playwright; and at one bound the French went far beyond the limit of time for which any copyright was then granted either in England or America, as the duration of stage-right was to be for the author's life and for five years more. It is to be noted, also, that stage-right was not acquired by British and American authors for many years after 1791.

Two years after the French law protecting stage-right, in the dark and bloody year of 1793, an act was passed in France granting copyright for the life of the author and for ten years after his death. It is worthy of remark that, as soon as the privileges and monopolies of the monarchy were abolished, the strong respect the French people have always felt for literature and art was shown by the extension of the term of copyright far beyond that then accorded in Great Britain and the United States; and although both the British and the American term of copyright has been prolonged since 1793, so also has the French, and it is now for life of the author and for fifty years after his death.

The rapid development of law within the past century and the effort it makes to keep pace with the moral sense of society—a sense that becomes finer as society becomes more complicated and as the perception of personal wrong is sharpened—can be seen in this brief summary of copyright development in France, where, but a hundred years ago, an author had only the power of asking for a privilege which might be refused him. The other countries of Europe, following the lead of France as they have been wont to do, have formulated copyright laws not unlike hers. In prolonging the duration of the term of copyright, one country has been even more liberal. Spain extends it for eighty years after the author's death. Hungary, Belgium, and Russia accept the French term of the author's life and half a century more. Germany, Austria, and Switzerland grant only thirty years after the author dies. Italy gives the author copyright for his life, with exclusive control to his heirs for forty years after his death; after that period the exclusive rights cease, but a royalty of five per cent. on the retail price of every copy of every edition, by whomsoever issued, must be paid to the author's heirs for a further term of forty years: thus a quasi-copyright is granted for a period extending to eighty years after the author's death, and the Italian term is approximated to the Spanish. Certain of the Spanish-American nations have exceeded the liberality of the mother-country: in Mexico, in

Guatemala, and in Venezuela the author's rights are not terminated by the lapse of time, and copyright is perpetual.[1]

To set down with precision what has been done in various countries will help us to see more clearly what remains to be done in our own. It is only by considering the trend of legal development that we can make sure of the direction in which efforts toward improvement can be guided most effectively. For example: the facts contained in the preceding paragraphs show that no one of the great nations of continental Europe grants copyright for a less term than the life of the author and a subsequent period varying from thirty to eighty years. A comparison also of the laws of the various countries, as contained in the invaluable volumes of MM. Lyon-Caen and Delalain, reveals to us the fact that there is a steady tendency to lengthen this term of years, and that the more recent the legislation the more likely is the term to be long. In Austria, for instance, where the term was fixed in 1846, it is for thirty years after the author's death; while in the twin-kingdom of Hungary, where the term was fixed in 1884, it is for fifty years.

On a contrast of the terms of copyright granted by the chief nations of continental Europe with those granted by Great Britain and the United

[1] Here again it may be noted that certain decisions in the United States courts, to the effect that the performance of a play is not publication, and that therefore an unpublished play is protected by the common law and not by the copyright acts, recognize the perpetual stage-right of any dramatist who will forego the doubtful profit of appearing in print.

States, it will be seen that the English-speaking race, which was first to make the change from privilege to copyright, and was thus the foremost in the protection of the author, now lags sadly behind. The British law declares that the term of copyright shall be for the life of the author and only seven years thereafter, or for forty-two years, whichever term last expires. The American law does not even give an author copyright for the whole of his life, if he should be so unlucky as to survive forty-two years after the publication of his earlier books; it grants copyright for twenty-eight years only, with a permission to the author himself, his widow, or his children to renew for fourteen years more. This is niggardly when set beside the liberality of France, to say nothing of that of Italy and Spain. Those who are unwilling to concede that the ethical development of France, Italy, and Spain is more advanced than that of Great Britain and the United States, at least as far as literary property is concerned, may find some comfort in recalling the fact that the British act was passed in 1842 and the American in 1831—and in threescore years the world moves.

There is no need to dwell on the disadvantages of the existing American law, and on the injustice which it works. It may take from an author the control of his book at the very moment when he is at the height of his fame and when the infirmities of age make the revenue from his copyrights most necessary. An example or two from contemporary American literature will serve to show the demerits of the existing law. The first part of Bancroft's

History of the United States, the history of the colonization, was published in three successive volumes in 1834, 1837, and 1840; and although the author, before his death, revised and amended this part of his work, it has been lawful, since 1882, for any man to take the unrevised and incorrect first edition and to reprint it, despite the protests of the author, and in competition with the improved version which contains the results of the author's increased knowledge and keener taste.

At this time of writing (1890) all books published in the United States prior to 1848 are open to any reprinter; and the reprinter has not been slow to avail himself of this permission. The children of Fenimore Cooper are alive, and so are the nieces of Washington Irving; but they derive no income from the rival reprints of the *Leatherstocking Tales* or of the *Sketch Book*, reproduced from the earliest editions without any of the authors' later emendations.[1] Though the family of Cooper and the family of Irving survive, Cooper and Irving are dead themselves, and cannot protest. But there are living American authors besides Bancroft who are despoiled in like manner. Half a dozen volumes were published by Mr. Whittier and by Dr. Holmes before 1848, and these early, immature, uncorrected verses are now reprinted and offered to the public as "*Whittier's Poems*" and "*Holmes's Poems*." Sometimes the tree of poesy flowers early and bears fruit late. So it is with Lowell, whose

[1] The emendations, having been made within forty-two years, are, of course, still guarded by copyright.

Heartsease and Rue we received with delight only a year or two ago, but whose *Legend of Brittany*, *Vision of Sir Launfal*, *Fable for Critics* and first series of *Biglow Papers* were all published forty-two years ago or more, and are therefore no longer the property of their author, but have passed from his control absolutely and forever.

Besides the broadening of a capricious privilege into a legal right, and besides the lengthening of the time during which this right is enforced, a steady progress of the idea that the literary laborer is worthy of his hire is to be seen in various newer and subsidiary developments. With the evolution of copyright, the author can now reserve certain secondary rights of abridgment, of adaptation, and of translation. In all the leading countries of the world the dramatist can now secure stage-right,[1] *i.e.*, the sole right to authorize the performance of a play on a stage. Copyright and stage-right are wholly different; and a dramatist is entitled to both. The author of a play has made something which may be capable of a double use, and it seems proper that he should derive profit from both uses. His play may be read only and not acted, like Lord Tennyson's *Harold* and Longfellow's *Spanish Student*, in which case the copyright is more valuable than the stage-right. Or the play may be acted only, like the imported British melodramas, and of so slight a literary merit that no one would care

[1] Mr. Drone uses the word "playright," but this is identical in sound with "playwright," and it seems better to adopt the word "stage-right," first employed by Charles Reade.

to read it, in which case the stage-right would be more valuable than the copyright. Or the drama may be both readable and actable, like Shakespeare's and Sheridan's plays, like Augier's and Labiche's, in which case the author derives a double profit, controlling the publication by copyright and controlling performance by stage-right. It was in 1791, as we have seen, that France granted stage-right. In England, "the first statute giving to dramatists the exclusive right of performing their plays was the 3 and 4 William IV., c. 15, passed in 1833," says Mr. Drone (page 601). In the United States, stage-right was granted in 1851 to dramatists who had copyrighted their plays here.

Closely akin to the stage-right accorded to the dramatist is the sole right of dramatization accorded to the novelist. Indeed, the latter is an obvious outgrowth of the former. Until the enormous increase of the reading public in this century, consequent upon the spread of education, the novel was an inferior form to the drama and far less profitable pecuniarily. It is only within the past hundred years—one might say, fairly enough, that it is only since the Waverley novels took the world by storm—that the romance has claimed equality with the play. Until it did so, no novelist felt wronged when his tale was turned to account on the stage, and no novelist ever thought of claiming a sole right to the theatrical use of his own story. Lodge, the author of *Rosalynde*, would have been greatly surprised if any one had told him that Shakespeare had made an improper use of his story in founding on it *As You*

Like It. On the contrary, in fact, literary history would furnish many an instance to prove that the writer of fiction felt that a pleasant compliment had been paid him when his material was made over by a writer for the stage. Scott, for example, aided Terry in adapting his novels for theatrical performance; and he did this without any thought of reward. But by the time that Dickens succeeded Scott as the most popular of English novelists the sentiment was changing. In *Nicholas Nickleby* the author protested with acerbity against the hack playwrights who made haste to put a story on the stage even before its serial publication was finished. His sense of injury was sharpened by the clumsy disfiguring of his work. Perhaps the injustice was never so apparent as when a British playwright, one Fitzball, captured Fenimore Cooper's *Pilot* in 1826 and turned Long Tom Coffin into a British sailor! —an act of piracy which a recent historian of the London theatres, Mr. H. B. Baker, records with hearty approval. The possibility of an outrage like this still exists in England. In France, of course, the novelist has long had the exclusive right to adapt his own story to the stage; and in the United States, also, he has it, if he gives notice formally on every copy of the book itself that he desires to reserve to himself the right of dramatization. But England has not as yet advanced thus far; and no English author can make sure that he may not see a play ill-made out of his disfigured novel. Charles Reade protested in vain against unauthorized dramatization of his novels, and then, with characteristic inconsistency, made plays out of novels by Anthony Trollope and Mrs. Hodgson Burnett without asking their consent. But the unauthorized British adapter may not lawfully print the play he has compounded from a copyright novel, as any multiplication of copies would be an infringement of the copyright; and Mrs. Hodgson Burnett succeeded in getting an injunction against an unauthorized dramatization of *Little Lord Fauntleroy* on proof that more than one copy of the unauthorized play had been made for use in the theatre. It is likely that one of the forthcoming modifications of the British law will be the extension to the novelist of the sole right to dramatize his own novel.

II.

From a consideration of the lengthening of the term of copyright and the development of certain subsidiary rights now acquired by an author, we come to a consideration of the next step in the process of evolution. This is the extension of an author's rights beyond the boundaries of the country of which he is a citizen, so that a book formally registered in one country shall by that single act and without further formality be protected from piracy[1] throughout the world. This great and needful improvement is now in course of accom-

[1] "Piracy" is a term available for popular appeal but perhaps lacking in scientific precision. The present writer used it in a little pamphlet on *American Authors and British Pirates* rather by way of retort to English taunts. Yet the inexact use of the word indicates the tendency of public opinion.

plishment; it is still far from complete, but year by year it advances farther and farther.

In the beginning the sovereign who granted a privilege, or at his caprice withheld it, could not, however strong his good-will, protect his subject's book beyond the borders of his realm; and even when privilege broadened into copyright, a book duly registered was protected only within the State wherein the certificate was taken out. Very soon after Venice accorded the first privilege to John of Spira, the extension of the protection to the limits of a single State only was found to be a great disadvantage. Printing was invented when central Europe was divided and subdivided into countless little states almost independent, but nominally bound together in the Holy Roman Empire. What is now the kingdom of Italy was cut up into more than a score of separate states, each with its own laws and its own executive. What is now the German Empire was then a disconnected medley of electorates, margravates, duchies, and grand-duchies, bishoprics and principalities, free towns and knight-fees, with no centre, no head, and no unity of thought or of feeling or of action. The printer-publisher made an obvious effort for wider protection when he begged and obtained a privilege not only from the authorities of the State in which he was working but also from other sovereigns. Thus, when the Florentine edition of the *Pandects* was issued in 1553, the publisher secured privileges in Florence first, and also in Spain, in the Two Sicilies, and in France. But privileges of this sort granted to non-residents were very infrequent, and no really efficacious protection for the books printed in another State was practically attainable in this way. Such protection, indeed, was wholly contrary to the spirit of the times, which held that an alien had no rights. In France, for example, a ship wrecked on the coasts was seized by the feudal lord and retained as his, subject only to the salvage claim.[1] In England a wreck belonged to the king unless a living being (man, dog, or cat) escaped alive from it; and this claim of the crown to all the property of the unfortunate foreign owner of the lost ship was raised as late as 1771, when Lord Mansfield decided against it. When aliens were thus rudely robbed of their tangible possessions, without public protest, there was not likely to be felt any keen sense of wrong at the appropriation of a possession so intangible as copyright.

What was needed was, first of all, an amelioration of the feeling toward aliens as such; and second, such a federation of the petty states as would make a single copyright effective throughout a nation, and as would also make possible an international agreement for the reciprocal protection of literary property. Only within the past hundred years or so, has this consolidation into compact and homogeneous nationalities taken place. In the last century, for example, Ireland had its own laws, and Irish pirates reprinted at will books covered by English copyright. In the preface to *Sir Charles Grandison*, published in 1753, Richardson, novelist and printer, inveighed against

[1] A. C. Bernheim, *History of the Law of Aliens* (N. Y., 1885), p. 58.

the piratical customs of the Hibernian publishers. In Italy, what was published in Rome had no protection in Naples or Florence. In Germany, where Luther in his day had protested in vain against the reprinters, Goethe and Schiller were able to make but little money from their writings, as these were constantly pirated in the other German states, and even imported into that in which they were protected, to compete with the author's edition. In 1826, Goethe announced a complete edition of his works, and, as a special honor to the poet in his old age, "the *Bundestag* undertook to secure him from piracy in German cities."[1] With the union of Ireland and Great Britain, with the accretion about the kingdom of Sardinia of the other provinces of Italy, with the compacting of Germany under the hegemony of Prussia, this inter-provincial piracy has wholly disappeared within the limits of these national states.

The suppression of international piracy passes through three phases. First, the nation whose citizens are most often despoiled—and this nation has nearly always been France—endeavors to negotiate reciprocity treaties, by which the writers of each of the contracting countries may be enabled to take out copyrights in the other. Thus France had, prior to 1852, special treaties with Holland, Sardinia, Portugal, Hanover, and Great Britain. Secondly, a certain number of nations join in an international convention, extending to the citizens of all the copyright advantages that the citizens of each

[1] G. H. Lewes, *Life and Works of Goethe*, p. 545.

enjoy at home. Third, a State modifies its own local copyright law so as to remove the disability of the alien. This last step was taken by France in 1852; and in 1886 Belgium followed her example.

The French, seeking equity, are willing to do equity; they ask no questions as to the nationality or residence of an author who offers a book for copyright; and they do not demand reciprocity as a condition precedent. Time was when the chief complaint of French authors was against the Belgian reprinters; but the Belgians, believing that the ship of state was ill-manned when she carried pirates in her crew, first made a treaty with France and then modified their local law into conformity with the French. These two nations, one of which was long the headquarters of piracy, now stand forward most honorably as the only two which really protect the full rights of an author.

Most of the states which had special copyright treaties one with another have adhered to the convention of Berne, finally ratified in 1887. Among them are France, Belgium, Germany, Spain, Italy, Great Britain, and Switzerland. The adhesion of Austro-Hungary, Holland, Norway, and Sweden is likely not long to be delayed. The result of this convention is substantially to abolish the distinction between the subjects of the adhering powers and to give to the authors of each country the same faculty of copyright and of stage-right that they enjoy at home, without any annoying and expensive formalities of registration or deposit in the foreign State.

The United States of America is now the only

3

one of the great powers of the world which absolutely refuses the protection of its laws to the books of a friendly alien.[1] From having been one of the foremost states of the world in the evolution of copyright, the United States has now become one of the most backward. Nothing could be more striking than a contrast of the liberality with which the American law treats the foreign inventor and the niggardliness with which it treats the foreign author. In his *Popular Government* (page 247) the late Sir Henry Sumner Maine declared that "the power to grant patents by federal authority has . . . made the American people the first in the world for the number and ingenuity of the inventions by which it has promoted the 'useful arts;' while, on the other hand, the neglect to exercise this power for the advantage of foreign writers has condemned the whole American community to a literary servitude unparalleled in the history of thought."

[1] If a foreign dramatist chooses to keep his play in manuscript, then the American courts will defend his stage-right; but the foreign dramatist is the only alien author whose literary property is assured to him by our courts.

November, 1890.

QUESTIONS AND ANSWERS ON THE NEW COPYRIGHT LAW

American Society of Composers, Authors and Publishers
One Lincoln Plaza, New York, N.Y. 10023
Area Code (212) 595-3050

Is the new law better than the old law for creators?

Yes. The new law grants longer protection and greater rights for creators.

What is the new term for copyrighted works?

Works copyrighted before January 1, 1978 will have a total copyright term of 75 years—an initial term of 28 years, and a renewal term of 47 years.

For works first created or copyrighted after January 1, 1978, the term of copyright will be the life of the author—the creator—plus 50 years. A work is "created" when it is "fixed in a copy or phonorecord for the first time." The term "author" includes composer and lyricist.

What's the term for a work created after January 1, 1978 by two or more people?

The life plus 50 year term applies to works of joint authorship, but the "life" is the life of the last surviving co-author. For example, a work jointly written in 1978 by two creators, one of whom dies in 1980, and the other in 1990, will be protected until 2040—50 years after the death of the last surviving co-author.

What about works made for hire?

Works created after January 1, 1978 which are made for hire are protected for 75 years from publication, or 100 years from creation—whichever period expires first.

What will be the term for an anonymous or pseudonymous work?

The copyright term applicable to works made for hire (75 years from publication or 100 years from creation) also applies to anonymous or pseudonymous works. But, if the identity of the author is revealed—by a statement filed with the Copyright Office—the life plus 50 year term applies.

Will there be a renewal term for new works?

No. The life plus 50 year term is not dependent on any renewal.

Must I renew a work copyrighted before January 1, 1978?

Yes. The renewal provisions still apply to works first copyrighted before January 1, 1978. For example, a work copyrighted in 1970 will have to be renewed within one year prior to the expiration of the initial 28 year term in 1998. The 47-year renewal will then extend the copyright term through the end of the year 2045.

What about copyrights already in their renewal term?

Works already in their renewal term on the date the law was signed—October 19, 1976—automatically and immediately had their renewal terms extended for 19 years, to a total of 75 years. The 47-year renewal term also applies to works which will be renewed before January 1, 1978, the effective date of the new law.

Does the new 75 year term also apply to works whose renewed copyrights have been extended since September 19, 1962?

Yes. While considering the copyright bill, Congress from time to time extended copyrights in their renewal term which otherwise would have expired on or after September 19, 1962. The extensions saved all renewed copyrights in works first copyrighted between September 19, 1906, and December 31, 1920. Those copyrights are automatically and immediately extended to a total of 75 years. For example, copyright in a work first copyrighted on September 30, 1906 will expire on December 31, 1981.

Can a writer terminate a grant of a transfer or license?

Yes. The new law permits termination of a grant of a transfer or license of copyright made after January 1, 1978 on certain conditions and on notice to be given in accordance with regulations to be prescribed by the Copyright Office.

Similarly, grants made prior to January 1, 1978 may be terminated as to the additional 19 years added to the renewal term on certain conditions and on notice to be given in accordance with regulations to be prescribed by the Copyright Office.

What should I do about my works "in the trunk"?

Under the old law, works which had been created but not published or copyrighted were protected perpetually, under state common law. The new law "pre-empts"—in effect, abolishes—the state common law. Works created but not published or copyrighted before January 1, 1978 will be protected under the new, federal, law for the life plus 50 year term. However, in no case will the copyright on such works expire before December 31, 2002, no matter how long the author has been dead. And, if the work is published before December 31, 2002, the copyright will in no case expire before December 31, 2027.

Older writers may want to copyright works "in the trunk" *before* December 31, 1977. If they do so, the works will, if renewed, be protected for 75 years; if not copyrighted before 1978, such works will have the life plus 50 year term of protection. Accordingly, if a writer's life expectancy is less than 25 years and he does not copyright an already-written work before 1978, the new term of life plus fifty years may add up to less than the 75 year term the work would enjoy if copyrighted before 1978.

Will my copyrights expire precisely on their anniversary dates?

No. The new law extends copyrights to the end of the year in which they would otherwise expire. For example, a work first copyrighted on July 1, 1950 and properly renewed at the end of the 28 year initial term will expire on December 31, 2025—not July 1, 2025.

Will the new law affect ASCAP's licensing of nondramatic musical performing rights?

Yes. The nondramatic performing right which ASCAP licenses has been expanded.

Is the nondramatic musical performing right still limited to public performances "for profit"?

No. The "for profit" limitation has been eliminated from the law. In its place, limited and specific exemptions are substituted for performances with certain educational and religious purposes. Generally, performances in the course of face-to-face teaching activities or religious services at a place of worship are exempt and don't require licenses. Performances without any purpose of direct or indirect commercial advantage—and where no performer, promoter, or organizer is paid—are also exempt in limited circumstances. Except for these (and some other) limited exemptions, all public performances of nondramatic musical works—whether "for profit" or not—must be licensed.

Under the old law, some user industries avoided paying for music. Does the new law correct this?

Yes. Certain user industries which had been exempt or had not paid license fees under the old law will now be required to pay for the music they use after the new law's effective date, January 1, 1978. The jukebox, cable television and public broadcasting industries will all pay under statutory compulsory licenses. For them, a new government agency—the Copyright Royalty Tribunal—will periodically review and adjust the statutory compulsory license fees.

Has the so-called "juke box exemption" been repealed?

Yes. Juke box operators will now pay an annual compulsory license fee of $8 per jukebox. These royalties will be divided among the several performing rights licensing organizations—or by the Copyright Royalty Tribunal if those organizations cannot agree on a division. The $8 fee will be subject to Tribunal review and adjustment every ten years, beginning 1980.

Will cable television now pay license fees?

Yes. Cable television will pay compulsory license fees for secondary transmissions under a complicated statutory formula. Again, the Tribunal will be able to adjust the fees in the future.

Will public broadcasting finally pay license fees?

Yes. The new law gives public broadcasting a compulsory license for nondramatic performance of music, but it does not fix any statutory fee. If voluntary licensing arrangements are not worked out, the compulsory license fee will be set by the Copyright Royalty Tribunal which will also review and adjust the fees in the future.

Has the mechanical royalty for phonograph records been increased?

Yes. The new law grants a modest increase in the statutory compulsory license for making sound recordings. Under the 1909 law, the fee was 2 cents per song per record. Under the new law, it will be 2¾ cents, or ½ cent per minute (or fraction thereof) of playing time, whichever is greater. Again, the rate will be subject to Copyright Royalty Tribunal review and adjustment.

Who will sit on the Copyright Royalty Tribunal?

The Tribunal is composed of five members, who sit for staggered seven year terms. The members will be appointed by the President, subject to approval by the Senate. The provisions establishing the Tribunal took effect when the law was signed, and the Tribunal is expected to be named by President Jimmy Carter next year.

Where can I get a copy of the new law and more information about it?

Copies may be obtained by writing to:

Copyright Office
Library of Congress
Washington, D. C. 20559

The Copyright Office will be preparing new regulations and Information Circulars. Questions about the effect of the new law on ASCAP or a member's relationship with ASCAP should be directed to the ASCAP Legal Department. Members having questions calling for legal advice not related to their ASCAP membership should consult their own counsel.

Public Law 94-553
94th Congress

An Act

For the general revision of the Copyright Law, title 17 of the United States Code, and for other purposes.

Oct. 19, 1976
[S. 22]

Be it enacted by the Senate and House of Representatives of the United States of America in Congress assembled,

Title 17, USC, Copyrights.

TITLE I—GENERAL REVISION OF COPYRIGHT LAW

Sec. 101. Title 17 of the United States Code, entitled "Copyrights", is hereby amended in its entirety to read as follows:

TITLE 17—COPYRIGHTS

Chapter 1.—SUBJECT MATTER AND SCOPE OF COPYRIGHT

§ 101. Definitions

17 USC 101.

As used in this title, the following terms and their variant forms mean the following:

An "anonymous work" is a work on the copies or phonorecords of which no natural person is identified as author.

"Audiovisual works" are works that consist of a series of related images which are intrinsically intended to be shown by the use of machines or devices such as projectors, viewers, or electronic equipment, together with accompanying sounds, if any, regardless of the nature of the material objects, such as films or tapes, in which the works are embodied.

The "best edition" of a work is the edition, published in the United States at any time before the date of deposit, that the Library of Congress determines to be most suitable for its purposes.

A person's "children" are that person's immediate offspring, whether legitimate or not, and any children legally adopted by that person.

A "collective work" is a work, such as a periodical issue, anthology, or encyclopedia, in which a number of contributions, constituting separate and independent works in themselves, are assembled into a collective whole.

A "compilation" is a work formed by the collection and assembling of preexisting materials or of data that are selected, coordinated, or arranged in such a way that the resulting work as a whole constitutes an original work of authorship. The term "compilation" includes collective works.

"Copies" are material objects, other than phonorecords, in which a work is fixed by any method now known or later developed, and from which the work can be perceived, reproduced, or otherwise communicated, either directly or with the aid of a machine or device. The term "copies" includes the material object, other than a phonorecord, in which the work is first fixed.

"Copyright owner", with respect to any one of the exclusive rights comprised in a copyright, refers to the owner of that particular right.

A work is "created" when it is fixed in a copy or phonorecord for the first time; where a work is prepared over a period of time, the portion of it that has been fixed at any particular time constitutes the work as of that time, and where the work has been prepared in different versions, each version constitutes a separate work.

A "derivative work" is a work based upon one or more preexisting works, such as a translation, musical arrangement, dramatization, fictionalization, motion picture version, sound recording, art reproduction, abridgment, condensation, or any other form in which a work may be recast, transformed, or adapted. A work consisting of editorial revisions, annotations, elaborations, or other modifications which, as a whole, represent an original work of authorship, is a "derivative work".

A "device", "machine", or "process" is one now known or later developed.

To "display" a work means to show a copy of it, either directly or by means of a film, slide, television image, or any other device or process or, in the case of a motion picture or other audiovisual work, to show individual images nonsequentially.

A work is "fixed" in a tangible medium of expression when its embodiment in a copy or phonorecord, by or under the authority of the author, is sufficiently permanent or stable to permit it to be perceived, reproduced, or otherwise communicated for a period of more than transitory duration. A work consisting of sounds, images, or both, that are being transmitted, is "fixed" for purposes of this title if a fixation of the work is being made simultaneously with its transmission.

The terms "including" and "such as" are illustrative and not limitative.

A "joint work" is a work prepared by two or more authors with the intention that their contributions be merged into inseparable or interdependent parts of a unitary whole.

"Literary works" are works, other than audiovisual works, expressed in words, numbers, or other verbal or numerical symbols or indicia, regardless of the nature of the material objects, such as books, periodicals, manuscripts, phonorecords, film, tapes, disks, or cards, in which they are embodied.

"Motion pictures" are audiovisual works consisting of a series of related images which, when shown in succession, impart an impression of motion, together with accompanying sounds, if any.

To "perform" a work means to recite, render, play, dance, or act it, either directly or by means of any device or process or, in the case of a motion picture or other audiovisual work, to show its images in any sequence or to make the sounds accompanying it audible.

"Phonorecords" are material objects in which sounds, other than those accompanying a motion picture or other audiovisual work, are fixed by any method now known or later developed, and from which the sounds can be perceived, reproduced, or otherwise communicated, either directly or with the aid of a machine or device. The term "phonorecords" includes the material object in which the sounds are first fixed.

"Pictorial, graphic, and sculptural works" include two-dimensional and three-dimensional works of fine, graphic, and applied art, photographs, prints and art reproductions, maps, globes, charts, technical drawings, diagrams, and models. Such works shall include works of artistic craftsmanship insofar as their form but not their mechanical or utilitarian aspects are concerned; the design of a useful article, as defined in this section, shall be considered a pictorial, graphic, or sculptural work only if, and only to the extent that, such design incorporates pictorial, graphic, or sculptural features that can be identified separately from, and are capable of existing independently of, the utilitarian aspects of the article.

A "pseudonymous work" is a work on the copies or phonorecords of which the author is identified under a fictitious name.

"Publication" is the distribution of copies or phonorecords of a work to the public by sale or other transfer of ownership, or by rental, lease, or lending. The offering to distribute copies or phonorecords to a group of persons for purposes of further distribution, public performance, or public display, constitutes publication. A public performance or display of a work does not of itself constitute publication.

To perform or display a work "publicly" means—

(1) to perform or display it at a place open to the public or at any place where a substantial number of persons outside of a normal circle of a family and its social acquaintances is gathered; or

(2) to transmit or otherwise communicate a performance or display of the work to a place specified by clause (1) or to the public, by means of any device or processs, whether the members of the public capable of receiving the performance or display receive it in the same place or in separate places and at the same time or at different times.

"Sound recordings" are works that result from the fixation of a series of musical, spoken, or other sounds, but not including the sounds accompanying a motion picture or other audiovisual work, regardless of the nature of the material objects, such as disks, tapes, or other phonorecords, in which they are embodied.

"State" includes the District of Columbia and the Commonwealth of Puerto Rico, and any territories to which this title is made applicable by an Act of Congress.

A "transfer of copyright ownership" is an assignment, mortgage, exclusive license, or any other conveyance, alienation, or hypothecation of a copyright or of any of the exclusive rights comprised in a copyright, whether or not it is limited in time or place of effect, but not including a nonexclusive license.

A "transmission program" is a body of material that, as an aggregate, has been produced for the sole purpose of transmission to the public in sequence and as a unit.

To "transmit" a performance or display is to communicate it by any device or process whereby images or sounds are received beyond the place from which they are sent.

The "United States", when used in a geographical sense, comprises the several States, the District of Columbia and the Commonwealth of Puerto Rico, and the organized territories under the jurisdiction of the United States Government.

A "useful article" is an article having an intrinsic utilitarian function that is not merely to portray the appearance of the article or to convey information. An article that is normally a part of a useful article is considered a "useful article".

The author's "widow" or "widower" is the author's surviving spouse under the law of the author's domicile at the time of his or her death, whether or not the spouse has later remarried.

A "work of the United States Government" is a work prepared by an officer or employee of the United States Government as part of that person's official duties.

A "work made for hire" is—

(1) a work prepared by an employee within the scope of his or her employment; or

(2) a work specially ordered or commissioned for use as a contribution to a collective work, as a part of a motion picture or other audiovisual work, as a translation, as a supplementary work, as a compilation, as an instructional text, as a test, as answer material for a test, or as an atlas, if the parties expressly agree in a written instrument signed by them that the work shall be considered a work made for hire. For the purpose of the foregoing sentence, a "supplementary work" is a work prepared for publication as a secondary adjunct to a work by another author for the purpose of introducing, concluding, illustrating, explaining, revising, commenting upon, or assisting in the use of the other work, such as forewords, afterwords, pictorial illustrations, maps, charts, tables, editorial notes, musical arrangements, answer material for tests, bibliographies, appendixes, and indexes, and an "instructional text" is a literary, pictorial, or graphic work prepared for publication and with the purpose of use in systematic instructional activities.

17 USC 102.

§ 102. Subject matter of copyright: In general

(a) Copyright protection subsists, in accordance with this title, in original works of authorship fixed in any tangible medium of expression, now known or later developed, from which they can be perceived, reproduced, or otherwise communicated, either directly or with the aid of a machine or device. Works of authorship include the following categories: Works of authorship.

(1) literary works;
(2) musical works, including any accompanying words;
(3) dramatic works, including any accompanying music;
(4) pantomimes and choreographic works;
(5) pictorial, graphic, and sculptural works;
(6) motion pictures and other audiovisual works; and
(7) sound recordings.

(b) In no case does copyright protection for an original work of authorship extend to any idea, procedure, process, system, method of operation, concept, principle, or discovery, regardless of the form in which it is described, explained, illustrated, or embodied in such work.

§ 103. Subject matter of copyright: Compilations and derivative works

17 USC 103.

(a) The subject matter of copyright as specified by section 102 includes compilations and derivative works, but protection for a work employing preexisting material in which copyright subsists does not extend to any part of the work in which such material has been used unlawfully.

(b) The copyright in a compilation or derivative work extends only to the material contributed by the author of such work, as distinguished from the preexisting material employed in the work, and does not imply any exclusive right in the preexisting material. The copyright in such work is independent of, and does not affect or enlarge the scope, duration, ownership, or subsistence of, any copyright protection in the preexisting material.

§ 104. Subject matter of copyright: National origin

17 USC 104.

(a) UNPUBLISHED WORKS.—The works specified by sections 102 and 103, while unpublished, are subject to protection under this title without regard to the nationality or domicile of the author.

(b) PUBLISHED WORKS.—The works specified by sections 102 and 103, when published, are subject to protection under this title if—

(1) on the date of first publication, one or more of the authors is a national or domiciliary of the United States, or is a national, domiciliary, or sovereign authority of a foreign nation that is a party to a copyright treaty to which the United States is also a party, or is a stateless person, wherever that person may be domiciled; or

(2) the work is first published in the United States or in a foreign nation that, on the date of first publication, is a party to the Universal Copyright Convention; or

(3) the work is first published by the United Nations or any of its specialized agencies, or by the Organization of American States; or

(4) the work comes within the scope of a Presidential proclamation. Whenever the President finds that a particular foreign nation extends, to works by authors who are nationals or domiciliaries of the United States or to works that are first published in the United States, copyright protection on substantially the same basis as that on which the foreign nation extends protection to works of its own nationals and domiciliaries and works first published in that nation, the President may by proclamation extend protection under this title to works of which one or more

of the authors is, on the date of first publication, a national, domiciliary, or sovereign authority of that nation, or which was first published in that nation. The President may revise, suspend, or revoke any such proclamation or impose any conditions or limitations on protection under a proclamation.

17 USC 105.

§ 105. Subject matter of copyright: United States Government works

Copyright protection under this title is not available for any work of the United States Government, but the United States Government is not precluded from receiving and holding copyrights transferred to it by assignment, bequest, or otherwise.

17 USC 106.

§ 106. Exclusive rights in copyrighted works

Subject to sections 107 through 118, the owner of copyright under this title has the exclusive rights to do and to authorize any of the following:

(1) to reproduce the copyrighted work in copies or phonorecords;

(2) to prepare derivative works based upon the copyrighted work;

(3) to distribute copies or phonorecords of the copyrighted work to the public by sale or other transfer of ownership, or by rental, lease, or lending;

(4) in the case of literary, musical, dramatic, and choreographic works, pantomimes, and motion pictures and other audiovisual works, to perform the copyrighted work publicly; and

(5) in the case of literary, musical, dramatic, and choreographic works, pantomimes, and pictorial, graphic, or sculptural works, including the individual images of a motion picture or other audiovisual work, to display the copyrighted work publicly.

17 USC 107.

§ 107. Limitations on exclusive rights: Fair use

Notwithstanding the provisions of section 106, the fair use of a copyrighted work, including such use by reproduction in copies or phonorecords or by any other means specified by that section, for purposes such as criticism, comment, news reporting, teaching (including multiple copies for classroom use), scholarship, or research, is not an infringement of copyright. In determining whether the use made of a work in any particular case is a fair use the factors to be considered shall include—

(1) the purpose and character of the use, including whether such use is of a commercial nature or is for nonprofit educational purposes;

(2) the nature of the copyrighted work;

(3) the amount and substantiality of the portion used in relation to the copyrighted work as a whole; and

(4) the effect of the use upon the potential market for or value of the copyrighted work.

17 USC 108.

§ 108. Limitations on exclusive rights: Reproduction by libraries and archives

(a) Notwithstanding the provisions of section 106, it is not an infringement of copyright for a library or archives, or any of its employees acting within the scope of their employment, to reproduce no more than one copy or phonorecord of a work, or to distribute such copy or phonorecord, under the conditions specified by this section, if—

(1) the reproduction or distribution is made without any purpose of direct or indirect commercial advantage;

(2) the collections of the library or archives are (i) open to the public, or (ii) available not only to researchers affiliated with the library or archives or with the institution of which it is a part, but also to other persons doing research in a specialized field; and

(3) the reproduction or distribution of the work includes a notice of copyright.

(b) The rights of reproduction and distribution under this section apply to a copy or phonorecord of an unpublished work duplicated in facsimile form solely for purposes of preservation and security or for deposit for research use in another library or archives of the type described by clause (2) of subsection (a), if the copy or phonorecord reproduced is currently in the collections of the library or archives.

(c) The right of reproduction under this section applies to a copy or phonorecord of a published work duplicated in facsimile form solely for the purpose of replacement of a copy or phonorecord that is damaged, deteriorating, lost, or stolen, if the library or archives has, after a reasonable effort, determined that an unused replacement cannot be obtained at a fair price.

(d) The rights of reproduction and distribution under this section apply to a copy, made from the collection of a library or archives where the user makes his or her request or from that of another library or archives, of no more than one article or other contribution to a copyrighted collection or periodical issue, or to a copy or phonorecord of a small part of any other copyrighted work, if—

(1) the copy or phonorecord becomes the property of the user, and the library or archives has had no notice that the copy or phonorecord would be used for any purpose other than private study, scholarship, or research; and

(2) the library or archives displays prominently, at the place where orders are accepted, and includes on its order form, a warning of copyright in accordance with requirements that the Register of Copyrights shall prescribe by regulation.

(e) The rights of reproduction and distribution under this section apply to the entire work, or to a substantial part of it, made from the collection of a library or archives where the user makes his or her request or from that of another library or archives, if the library or archives has first determined, on the basis of a reasonable investigation, that a copy or phonorecord of the copyrighted work cannot be obtained at a pair price, if—

(1) the copy or phonorecord becomes the property of the user, and the library or archives has had no notice that the copy or phonorecord would be used for any purpose other than private study, scholarship, or research; and

(2) the library or archives displays prominently, at the place where orders are accepted, and includes on its order form, a warning of copyright in accordance with requirements that the Register of Copyrights shall prescribe by regulation.

(f) Nothing in this section—

(1) shall be construed to impose liability for copyright infringement upon a library or archives or its employees for the unsupervised use of reproducing equipment located on its premises: *Provided*, That such equipment displays a notice that the making of a copy may be subject to the copyright law;

(2) excuses a person who uses such reproducing equipment or who requests a copy or phonorecord under subsection (d) from liability for copyright infringement for any such act, or for any later use of such copy or phonorecord, if it exceeds fair use as provided by section 107;

(3) shall be construed to limit the reproduction and distribution by lending of a limited number of copies and excerpts by a library or archives of an audiovisual news program, subject to clauses (1), (2), and (3) of subsection (a); or

(4) in any way affects the right of fair use as provided by section 107, or any contractual obligations assumed at any time by the library or archives when it obtained a copy or phonorecord of a work in its collections.

(g) The rights of reproduction and distribution under this section extend to the isolated and unrelated reproduction or distribution of a single copy or phonorecord of the same material on separate occasions, but do not extend to cases where the library or archives, or its employee—

(1) is aware or has substantial reason to believe that it is engaging in the related or concerted reproduction or distribution of multiple copies or phonorecords of the same material, whether made on one occasion or over a period of time, and whether intended for aggregate use by one or more individuals or for separate use by the individual members of a group; or

(2) engages in the systematic reproduction or distribution of single or multiple copies or phonorecords of material described in subsection (d): *Provided*, That nothing in this clause prevents a library or archives from participating in interlibrary arrangements that do not have, as their purpose or effect, that the library or archives receiving such copies or phonorecords for distribution does so in such aggregate quantities as to substitute for a subscription to or purchase of such work.

(h) The rights of reproduction and distribution under this section do not apply to a musical work, a pictorial, graphic or sculptural work, or a motion picture or other audiovisual work other than an audiovisual work dealing with news, except that no such limitation shall apply with respect to rights granted by subsections (b) and(c), or with respect to pictorial or graphic works published as illustrations, diagrams, or similar adjuncts to works of which copies are reproduced or distributed in accordance with subsections (d) and (e).

Report to Congress.

(i) Five years from the effective date of this Act, and at five-year intervals thereafter, the Register of Copyrights, after consulting with representatives of authors, book and periodical publishers, and other owners of copyrighted materials, and with representatives of library users and librarians, shall submit to the Congress a report setting forth the extent to which this section has achieved the intended statutory balancing of the rights of creators, and the needs of users. The report should also describe any problems that may have arisen, and present legislative or other recommendations, if warranted.

17 USC 109.

§ 109. Limitations on exclusive rights: Effect of transfer of particular copy or phonorecord

Disposal.

(a) Notwithstanding the provisions of section 106(3), the owner of a particular copy or phonorecord lawfully made under this title, or any person authorized by such owner, is entitled, without the authority of the copyright owner, to sell or otherwise dispose of the possession of that copy or phonorecord.

Public display.

(b) Notwithstanding the provisions of section 106(5), the owner of a particular copy lawfully made under this title, or any person authorized by such owner, is entitled, without the authority of the copyright owner, to display that copy publicly, either directly or by the projection of no more than one image at a time, to viewers present at the place where the copy is located.

(c) The privileges prescribed by subsections (a) and (b) do not, unless authorized by the coyright owner, extend to any person who has acquired possession of the copy or phonorecord from the copyright owner, by rental, lease, loan, or otherwise, without acquiring ownership of it.

§ 110. Limitations on exclusive rights: Exemption of certain performances and displays 17 USC 110.

Notwithstanding the provisions of section 106, the following are not infringements of copyright:

(1) performance or display of a work by instructors or pupils in the course of face-to-face teaching activities of a nonprofit educational institution, in a classroom or similar place devoted to instruction, unless, in the case of a motion picture or other audiovisual work, the performance, or the display of individual images, is given by means of a copy that was not lawfully made under this title, and that the person responsible for the performance knew or had reason to believe was not lawfully made;

(2) performance of a nondramatic literary or musical work or display of a work, by or in the course of a transmission, if—

(A) the performance or display is a regular part of the systematic instructional activities of a governmental body or a nonprofit educational institution; and

(B) the performance or display is directly related and of material assistance to the teaching content of the transmission; and

(C) the transmission is made primarily for—

(i) reception in classrooms or similar places normally devoted to instruction, or

(ii) reception by persons to whom the transmission is directed because their disabilities or other special circumstances prevent their attendance in classrooms or similar places normally devoted to instruction, or

(iii) reception by officers or employees of governmental bodies as a part of their official duties or employment;

(3) performance of a nondramatic literary or musical work or of a dramatico-musical work of a religious nature, or display of a work, in the course of services at a place of worship or other religious assembly;

(4) performance of a nondramatic literary or musical work otherwise than in a transmission to the public, without any purpose of direct or indirect commercial advantage and without payment of any fee or other compensation for the performance to any of its performers, promoters, or organizers, if—

(A) there is no direct or indirect admission charge; or

(B) the proceeds, after deducting the reasonable costs of producing the performance, are used exclusively for educational, religious, or charitable purposes and not for private financial gain, except where the copyright owner has served notice of objection to the performance under the following conditions; Notice of objection to performance.

(i) the notice shall be in writing and signed by the copyright owner or such owner's duly authorized agent; and

(ii) the notice shall be served on the person responsible for the performance at least seven days before the date of the performance, and shall state the reasons for the objection; and

229-769 O - 77 - 2

Regulation.

(iii) the notice shall comply, in form, content, and manner of service, with requirements that the Register of Copyrights shall prescribe by regulation;

(5) communication of a transmission embodying a performance or display of a work by the public reception of the transmission on a single receiving apparatus of a kind commonly used in private homes, unless—

(A) a direct charge is made to see or hear the transmission; or

(B) the transmission thus received is further transmitted to the public;

(6) performance of a nondramatic musical work by a governmental body or a nonprofit agricultural or horticultural organization, in the course of an annual agricultural or horticultural fair or exhibition conducted by such body or organization; the exemption provided by this clause shall extend to any liability for copyright infringement that would otherwise be imposed on such body or organization, under doctrines of vicarious liability or related infringement, for a performance by a concessionnaire, business establishment, or other person at such fair or exhibition, but shall not excuse any such person from liability for the performance;

(7) performance of a nondramatic musical work by a vending establishment open to the public at large without any direct or indirect admission charge, where the sole purpose of the performance is to promote the retail sale of copies or phonorecords of the work, and the performance is not transmitted beyond the place where the establishment is located and is within the immediate area where the sale is occurring;

(8) performance of a nondramatic literary work, by or in the course of a transmission specifically designed for and primarily directed to blind or other handicapped persons who are unable to read normal printed material as a result of their handicap, or deaf or other handicapped persons who are unable to hear the aural signals accompanying a transmission of visual signals, if the performance is made without any purpose of direct or indirect commercial advantage and its transmission is made through the facilities of: (i) a governmental body; or (ii) a noncommercial educational broadcast station (as defined in section 397 of title 47); or (iii) a radio subcarrier authorization (as defined in 47 CFR 73.293–73.295 and 73.593–73.595); or (iv) a cable system (as defined in section 111(f)).

(9) performance on a single occasion of a dramatic literary work published at least ten years before the date of the performance, by or in the course of a transmission specifically designed for and primarily directed to blind or other handicapped persons who are unable to read normal printed material as a result of their handicap, if the performance is made without any purpose of direct or indirect commercial advantage and its transmission is made through the facilities of a radio subcarrier authorization referred to in clause (8)(iii), *Provided*, That the provisions of this clause shall not be applicable to more than one performance of the same work by the same performers or under the auspices of the same organization.

17 USC 111.

§ 111. Limitations on exclusive rights: Secondary transmissions

(a) Certain Secondary Transmissions Exempted.—The secondary transmission of a primary transmission embodying a performance or display of a work is not an infringement of copyright if—

(1) the secondary transmission is not made by a cable system, and consists entirely of the relaying, by the management of a hotel, apartment house, or similar establishment, of signals transmitted by a broadcast station licensed by the Federal Communications Commission, within the local service area of such station, to the private lodgings of guests or residents of such establishment, and no direct charge is made to see or hear the secondary transmission; or

(2) the secondary transmission is made solely for the purpose and under the conditions specified by clause (2) of section 110; or

(3) the secondary transmission is made by any carrier who has no direct or indirect control over the content or selection of the primary transmission or over the particular recipients of the secondary transmission, and whose activities with respect to the secondary transmission consist solely of providing wires, cables, or other communications channels for the use of others: *Provided*, That the provisions of this clause extend only to the activities of said carrier with respect to secondary transmissions and do not exempt from liability the activities of others with respect to their own primary or secondary transmissions; or

(4) the secondary transmission is not made by a cable system but is made by a governmental body, or other nonprofit organization, without any purpose of direct or indirect commercial advantage, and without charge to the recipients of the secondary transmission other than assessments necessary to defray the actual and reasonable costs of maintaining and operating the secondary transmission service.

(b) SECONDARY TRANSMISSION OF PRIMARY TRANSMISSION TO CONTROLLED GROUP.—Notwithstanding the provisions of subsections (a) and (c), the secondary transmission to the public of a primary transmission embodying a performance or display of a work is actionable as an act of infringement under section 501, and is fully subject to the remedies provided by sections 502 through 506 and 509, if the primary transmission is not made for reception by the public at large but is controlled and limited to reception by particular members of the public: *Provided*, however, That such secondary transmission is not actionable as an act of infringement if—

(1) the primary transmission is made by a broadcast station licensed by the Federal Communications Commission; and

(2) the carriage of the signals comprising the secondary transmission is required under the rules, regulations, or authorizations of the Federal Communications Commission; and

(3) the signal of the primary transmitter is not altered or changed in any way by the secondary transmitter.

(c) SECONDARY TRANSMISSIONS BY CABLE SYSTEMS.—

(1) Subject to the provisions of clauses (2), (3), and (4) of this subsection, secondary transmissions to the public by a cable system of a primary transmission made by a broadcast station licensed by the Federal Communications Commission or by an appropriate governmental authority of Canada or Mexico and embodying a performance or display of a work shall be subject to compulsory licensing upon compliance with the requirements of subsection (d) where the carriage of the signals comprising the secondary transmission is permissible under the rules, regulations, or authorizations of the Federal Communications Commission.

(2) Notwithstanding the provisions of clause (1) of this subsection, the willful or repeated secondary transmission to the public by a cable system of a primary transmission made by a

broadcast station licensed by the Federal Communications Commission or by an appropriate governmental authority of Canada or Mexico and embodying a performance or display of a work is actionable as an act of infringement under section 501, and is fully subject to the remedies provided by sections 502 through 506 and 509, in the following cases:

(A) where the carriage of the signals comprising the secondary transmission is not permissible under the rules, regulations, or authorizations of the Federal Communications Commission; or

(B) where the cable system has not recorded the notice specified by subsection (d) and deposited the statement of account and royalty fee required by subsection (d).

Alteration, deletion, or substitution.

(3) Notwithstanding the provisions of clause (1) of this subsection and subject to the provisions of subsection (e) of this section, the secondary transmission to the public by a cable system of a primary transmission made by a broadcast station licensed by the Federal Communications Commission or by an appropriate governmental authority of Canada or Mexico and embodying a performance or display of a work is actionable as an act of infringement under section 501, and is fully subject to the remedies provided by sections 502 through 506 and sections 509 and 510, if the content of the particular program in which the performance or display is embodied, or any commercial advertising or station announcements transmitted by the primary transmitter during, or immediately before or after, the transmission of such program, is in any way willfully altered by the cable system through changes, deletions, or additions, except for the alteration, deletion, or substitution of commercial advertisements performed by those engaged in television commercial advertising market research: *Provided*, That the research company has obtained the prior consent of the advertiser who has purchased the original commercial advertisement, the television station broadcasting that commercial advertisement, and the cable system performing the secondary transmission: *And provided further*, That such commercial alteration, deletion, or substitution is not performed for the purpose of deriving income from the sale of that commercial time.

Prior consent of advertiser.

(4) Notwithstanding the provisions of clause (1) of this subsection, the secondary transmission to the public by a cable system of a primary transmission made by a broadcast station licensed by an appropriate governmental authority of Canada or Mexico and embodying a performance or display of a work is actionable as an act of infringement under section 501, and is fully subject to the remedies provided by sections 502 through 506 and section 509, if (A) with respect to Canadian signals, the community of the cable system is located more than 150 miles from the United States-Canadian border and is also located south of the forty-second parallel of latitude, or (B) with respect to Mexican signals, the secondary transmission is made by a cable system which received the primary transmission by means other than direct interception of a free space radio wave emitted by such broadcast television station, unless prior to April 15, 1976, such cable system was actually carrying, or was specifically authorized to carry, the signal of such foreign station on the system pursuant to the rules, regulations, or authorizations of the Federal Communications Commission.

(d) COMPULSORY LICENSE FOR SECONDARY TRANSMISSIONS BY CABLE SYSTEMS.—

(1) For any secondary transmission to be subject to compulsory licensing under subsection (c), the cable system shall, at least one month before the date of the commencement of operations of the cable system or within one hundred and eighty days after the enactment of this Act, whichever is later, and thereafter within thirty days after each occasion on which the ownership or control or the signal carriage complement of the cable system changes, record in the Copyright Office a notice including a statement of the identity and address of the person who owns or operates the secondary transmission service or has power to exercise primary control over it, together with the name and location of the primary transmitter or primary transmitters whose signals are regularly carried by the cable system, and thereafter, from time to time, such further information as the Register of Copyrights, after consultation with the Copyright Royalty Tribunal (if and when the Tribunal has been constituted), shall prescribe by regulation to carry out the purpose of this clause. Notice.

(2) A cable system whose secondary transmissions have been subject to compulsory licensing under subsection (c) shall, on a semiannual basis, deposit with the Register of Copyrights, in accordance with requirements that the Register shall, after consultation with the Copyright Royalty Tribunal (if and when the Tribunal has been constituted), prescribe by regulation—

(A) a statement of account, covering the six months next preceding, specifying the number of channels on which the cable system made secondary transmissions to its subscribers, the names and locations of all primary transmitters whose transmissions were further transmitted by the cable system, the total number of subscribers, the gross amounts paid to the cable system for the basic service of providing secondary transmissions of primary broadcast transmitters, and such other data as the Register of Copyrights may, after consultation with the Copyright Royalty Tribunal (if and when the Tribunal has been constituted), from time to time prescribe by regulation. Such statement shall also include a special statement of account covering any nonnetwork television programming that was carried by the cable system in whole or in part beyond the local service area of the primary transmitter, under rules, regulations, or authorizations of the Federal Communications Commission permitting the substitution or addition of signals under certain circumstances, together with logs showing the times, dates, stations, and programs involved in such substituted or added carriage; and Statement of account. Nonnetwork television programming.

(B) except in the case of a cable system whose royalty is specified in subclause (C) or (D), a total royalty fee for the period covered by the statement, computed on the basis of specified percentages of the gross receipts from subscribers to the cable service during said period for the basic service of providing secondary transmissions of primary broadcast transmitters, as follows: Total royalty fee.

(i) 0.675 of 1 per centum of such gross receipts for the privilege of further transmitting any nonnetwork programing of a primary transmitter in whole or in part beyond the local service area of such primary transmitter, such amount to be applied against the fee, if any, payable pursuant to paragraphs (ii) through (iv);

(ii) 0.675 of 1 per centum of such gross receipts for the first distant signal equivalent;

(iii) 0.425 of 1 per centum of such gross receipts for each of the second, third, and fourth distant signal equivalents;

(iv) 0.2 of 1 per centum of such gross receipts for the fifth distant signal equivalent and each additional distant signal equivalent thereafter; and

in computing the amounts payable under paragraph (ii) through (iv), above, any fraction of a distant signal equivalent shall be computed at its fractional value and, in the case of any cable system located partly within and partly without the local service area of a primary transmitter, gross receipts shall be limited to those gross receipts derived from subscribers located without the local service area of such primary transmitter; and

(C) if the actual gross receipts paid by subscribers to a cable system for the period covered by the statement for the basic service of providing secondary transmissions of primary broadcast transmitters total $80,000 or less, gross receipts of the cable system for the purpose of this subclause shall be computed by subtracting from such actual gross receipts the amount by which $80,000 exceeds such actual gross receipts, except that in no case shall a cable system's gross receipts be reduced to less than $3,000. The royalty fee payable under this subclause shall be 0.5 of 1 per centum, regardless of the number of distant signal equivalents, if any; and

(D) if the actual gross receipts paid by subscribers to a cable system for the period covered by the statement, for the basic service of providing secondary transmissions of primary broadcast transmitters, are more than $80,000 but less than $160,000, the royalty fee payable under this subclause shall be (i) 0.5 of 1 per centum of any gross receipts up to $80,000; and (ii) 1 per centum of any gross receipts in excess of $80,000 but less than $160,000, regardless of the number of distant signal equivalents, if any.

(3) The Register of Copyrights shall receive all fees deposited under this section and, after deducting the reasonable costs incurred by the Copyright Office under this section, shall deposit the balance in the Treasury of the United States, in such manner as the Secretary of the Treasury directs. All funds held by the Secretary of the Treasury shall be invested in interest-bearing United States securities for later distribution with interest by the Copyright Royalty Tribunal as provided by this title. The Register shall submit to the Copyright Royalty Tribunal, on a semiannual basis, a compilation of all statements of account covering the relevant six-month period provided by clause (2) of this subsection.

Statements of account, submittal to Copyright Royalty Tribunal.

Royalty fees, distribution.

(4) The royalty fees thus deposited shall, in accordance with the procedures provided by clause (5), be distributed to those among the following copyright owners who claim that their works were the subject of secondary transmissions by cable systems during the relevant semiannual period:

(A) any such owner whose work was included in a secondary transmission made by a cable system of a nonnetwork television program in whole or in part beyond the local service area of the primary transmitter; and

(B) any such owner whose work was included in a secondary transmission identified in a special statement of account deposited under clause (2)(A); and

(C) any such owner whose work was included in nonnetwork programing consisting exclusively of aural signals carried by a cable system in whole or in part beyond the local service area of the primary transmitter of such programs.

(5) The royalty fees thus deposited shall be distributed in accordance with the following procedures:

Distribution procedures.

(A) During the month of July in each year, every person claiming to be entitled to compulsory license fees for secondary transmissions shall file a claim with the Copyright Royalty Tribunal, in accordance with requirements that the Tribunal shall prescribe by regulation. Notwithstanding any provisions of the antitrust laws, for purposes of this clause any claimants may agree among themselves as to the proportionate division of compulsory licensing fees among them, may lump their claims together and file them jointly or as a single claim, or may designate a common agent to receive payment on their behalf.

(B) After the first day of August of each year, the Copyright Royalty Tribunal shall determine whether there exists a controversy concerning the distribution of royalty fees. If the Tribunal determines that no such controversy exists, it shall, after deducting its reasonable administrative costs under this section, distribute such fees to the copyright owners entitled, or to their designated agents. If the Tribunal finds the existence of a controversy, it shall, pursuant to chapter 8 of this title, conduct a proceeding to determine the distribution of royalty fees.

(C) During the pendency of any proceeding under this subsection, the Copyright Royalty Tribunal shall withhold from distribution an amount sufficient to satisfy all claims with respect to which a controversy exists, but shall have discretion to proceed to distribute any amounts that are not in controversy.

(e) NONSIMULTANEOUS SECONDARY TRANSMISSIONS BY CABLE SYSTEMS.—

(1) Notwithstanding those provisions of the second paragraph of subsection (f) relating to nonsimultaneous secondary transmissions by a cable system, any such transmissions are actionable as an act of infringement under section 501, and are fully subject to the remedies provided by sections 502 through 506 and sections 509 and 510, unless—

(A) the program on the videotape is transmitted no more than one time to the cable system's subscribers; and

(B) the copyrighted program, episode, or motion picture videotape, including the commercials contained within such program, episode, or picture, is transmitted without deletion or editing; and

(C) an owner or officer of the cable system (i) prevents the duplication of the videotape while in the possession of the system, (ii) prevents unauthorized duplication while in the possession of the facility making the videotape for the system if the system owns or controls the facility, or takes reasonable precautions to prevent such duplication if it does not own or control the facility, (iii) takes adequate precautions to prevent duplication while the tape is being transported, and (iv) subject to clause (2), erases or destroys, or causes the erasure or destruction of, the videotape; and

(D) within forty-five days after the end of each calendar quarter, an owner or officer of the cable system executes an affidavit attesting (i) to the steps and precautions taken to prevent duplication of the videotape, and (ii) subject to clause (2), to the erasure or destruction of all videotapes made or used during such quarter; and

(E) such owner or officer places or causes each such affidavit, and affidavits received pursuant to clause (2)(C), to be placed in a file, open to public inspection, at such system's main office in the community where the transmission is made or in the nearest community where such system maintains an office; and

(F) the nonsimultaneous transmission is one that the cable system would be authorized to transmit under the rules, regulations, and authorizations of the Federal Communications Commission in effect at the time of the nonsimultaneous transmission if the transmission had been made simultaneously, except that this subclause shall not apply to inadvertent or accidental transmissions.

(2) If a cable system transfers to any person a videotape of a program nonsimultaneously transmitted by it, such transfer is actionable as an act of infringement under section 501, and is fully subject to the remedies provided by sections 502 through 506 and 509, except that, pursuant to a written, nonprofit contract providing for the equitable sharing of the costs of such videotape and its transfer, a videotape nonsimultaneously transmitted by it, in accordance with clause (1), may be transferred by one cable system in Alaska to another system in Alaska, by one cable system in Hawaii permitted to make such nonsimultaneous transmissions to another such cable system in Hawaii, or by one cable system in Guam, the Northern Mariana Islands, or the Trust Territory of the Pacific Islands, to another cable system in any of those three territories, if—

(A) each such contract is available for public inspection in the offices of the cable systems involved, and a copy of such contract is filed, within thirty days after such contract is entered into, with the Copyright Office (which Office shall make each such contract available for public inspection); and

(B) the cable system to which the videotape is transferred complies with clause (1)(A), (B), (C)(i), (iii), and (iv), and (D) through (F); and

(C) such system provides a copy of the affidavit required to be made in accordance with clause (1)(D) to each cable system making a previous nonsimultaneous transmission of the same videotape.

(3) This subsection shall not be construed to supersede the exclusivity protection provisions of any existing agreement, or any such agreement hereafter entered into, between a cable system and a television broadcast station in the area in which the cable system is located, or a network with which such station is affiliated.

"Videotape."

(4) As used in this subsection, the term "videotape", and each of its variant forms, means the reproduction of the images and

sounds of a program or programs broadcast by a television broadcast station licensed by the Federal Communications Commission, regardless of the nature of the material objects, such as tapes or films, in which the reproduction is embodied.

(f) DEFINITIONS.—As used in this section, the following terms and their variant forms mean the following:

A "primary transmission" is a transmission made to the public by the transmitting facility whose signals are being received and further transmitted by the secondary transmission service, regardless of where or when the performance or display was first transmitted.

A "secondary transmission" is the further transmitting of a primary transmission simultaneously with the primary transmission, or nonsimultaneously with the primary transmission if by a "cable system" not located in whole or in part within the boundary of the forty-eight contiguous States, Hawaii, or Puerto Rico: *Provided, however*, That a nonsimultaneous further transmission by a cable system located in Hawaii of a primary transmission shall be deemed to be a secondary transmission if the carriage of the television broadcast signal comprising such further transmission is permissible under the rules, regulations, or authorizations of the Federal Communications Commission.

A "cable system" is a facility, located in any State, Territory, Trust Territory, or Possession, that in whole or in part receives signals transmitted or programs broadcast by one or more television broadcast stations licensed by the Federal Communications Commission, and makes secondary transmissions of such signals or programs by wires, cables, or other communications channels to subscribing members of the public who pay for such service. For purposes of determining the royalty fee under subsection (d)(2), two or more cable systems in contiguous communities under common ownership or control or operating from one headend shall be considered as one system.

The "local service area of a primary transmitter", in the case of a television broadcast station, comprises the area in which such station is entitled to insist upon its signal being retransmitted by a cable system pursuant to the rules, regulations, and authorizations of the Federal Communications Commission in effect on April 15, 1976, or in the case of a television broadcast station licensed by an appropriate governmental authority of Canada or Mexico, the area in which it would be entitled to insist upon its signal being retransmitted if it were a television broadcast station subject to such rules, regulations, and authorizations. The "local service area of a primary transmitter", in the case of a radio broadcast station, comprises the primary service area of such station, pursuant to the rules and regulations of the Federal Communications Commission.

A "distant signal equivalent" is the value assigned to the secondary transmission of any nonnetwork television programing carried by a cable system in whole or in part beyond the local service area of the primary transmitter of such programing. It is computed by assigning a value of one to each independent station and a value of one-quarter to each network station and noncommercial educational station for the nonnetwork programing so carried pursuant to the rules, regulations, and authorizations of the Federal Communications Commission. The foregoing values for independent, network, and noncommercial educational stations are subject, however, to the following exceptions and limitations. Where the rules and regulations of the Federal Communications Commission require a cable system to omit the further transmission of a particular program and such rules and regulations also permit the substitution of another program embodying a performance or display of a work in place of the omitted transmission, or where such rules and regulations in effect on the date of enactment of this Act permit a cable system, at its election, to effect such deletion and substitution of a nonlive program or to carry additional programs not transmitted by primary transmitters within whose local service area the cable system is located, no value shall be assigned for the substituted or additional program; where the rules, regulations, or authorizations of the Federal Communications Commission in effect on the date of enactment of this Act permit a cable system, at its election, to omit the further transmission of a particular program and such rules, regulations, or authorizations also permit the substitution of another program embodying a performance or display of a work in place of the omitted transmission, the value assigned for the substituted or additional program shall be, in the case of a live program, the value of one full distant signal equivalent multiplied by a fraction that has as its numerator the number of days in the year in which such substitution occurs and as its denominator the number of days in the year. In the case of a station carried pursuant to the late-night or specialty programing rules of the Federal Communications Commission, or a station carried on a part-time basis where full-time carriage is not possible because the cable system lacks the activated channel capacity to retransmit on a full-time basis all signals which it is authorized to carry, the values for independent, network, and noncommercial educational stations set forth above, as the case may be, shall be multiplied by a fraction which is equal to the ratio of the broadcast hours of such station carried by the cable system to the total broadcast hours of the station.

A "network station" is a television broadcast station that is owned or operated by, or affiliated with, one or more of the television networks in the United States providing nationwide transmissons, and that transmits a substantial part of the programing supplied by such networks for a substantial part of that station's typical broadcast day.

An "independent station" is a commercial television broadcast station other than a network station.

A "noncommercial educational station" is a television station that is a noncommercial educational broadcast station as defined in section 397 of title 47.

47 USC 397.

17 USC 112.

§ 112. Limitations on exclusive rights: Ephemeral recordings

(a) Notwithstanding the provisions of section 106, and except in the case of a motion picture or other audiovisual work, it is not an infringement of copyright for a transmitting organization entitled to transmit to the public a performance or display of a work, under a license or transfer of the copyright or under the limitations on exclusive rights in sound recordings specified by section 114(a), to make no more than one copy or phonorecord of a particular transmission program embodying the performance or display, if—

(1) the copy or phonorecord is retained and used solely by the transmitting organization that made it, and no further copies or phonorecords are reproduced from it; and

(2) the copy or phonorecord is used solely for the transmitting organization's own transmissions within its local service area, or for purposes of archival preservation or security; and

(3) unless preserved exclusively for archival purposes, the copy or phonorecord is destroyed within six months from the date the transmission program was first transmitted to the public.

(b) Notwithstanding the provisions of section 106, it is not an infringement of copyright for a governmental body or other nonprofit organization entitled to transmit a performance or display of a work, under section 110(2) or under the limitations on exclusive rights in sound recordings specified by section 114(a), to make no more than thirty copies or phonorecords of a particular transmission program embodying the performance or display, if—

(1) no further copies or phonorecords are reproduced from the copies or phonorecords made under this clause; and

(2) except for one copy or phonorecord that may be preserved exclusively for archival purposes, the copies or phonorecords are destroyed within seven years from the date the transmission program was first transmitted to the public.

(c) Notwithstanding the provisions of section 106, it is not an infringment of copyright for a governmental body or other nonprofit organization to make for distribution no more than one copy or phonorecord, for each transmitting organization specified in clause (2) of this subsection, of a particular transmission program embodying a performance of a nondramatic musical work of a religious nature, or of a sound recording of such a musical work, if—

(1) there is no direct or indirect charge for making or distributing any such copies or phonorecords; and

(2) none of such copies or phonorecords is used for any performance other than a single transmission to the public by a transmitting organization entitled to transmit to the public a performance of the work under a license or transfer of the copyright; and

(3) except for one copy or phonorecord that may be preserved exclusively for archival purposes, the copies or phonorecords are all destroyed within one year from the date the transmission program was first transmitted to the public.

(d) Notwithstanding the provisions of section 106, it is not an infringement of copyright for a governmental body or other nonprofit organization entitled to transmit a performance of a work under section 110(8) to make no more than ten copies or phonorecords embodying the performance, or to permit the use of any such copy or phonorecord by any governmental body or nonprofit organization entitled to transmit a performance of a work under section 110(8), if—

(1) any such copy or phonorecord is retained and used solely by the organization that made it, or by a governmental body or nonprofit organization entitled to transmit a performance of a work under section 110(8), and no further copies or phonorecords are reproduced from it; and

(2) any such copy or phonorecord is used solely for transmissions authorized under section 110(8), or for purposes of archival preservation or security; and

(3) the governmental body or nonprofit organization permitting any use of any such copy or phonorecord by any governmental body or nonprofit organization under this subsection does not make any charge for such use.

(e) The transmission program embodied in a copy or phonorecord made under this section is not subject to protection as a derivative work under this title except with the express consent of the owners of copyright in the preexisting works employed in the program.

17 USC 113.

§ 113. Scope of exclusive rights in pictorial, graphic, and sculptural works

(a) Subject to the provisions of subsections (b) and (c) of this section, the exclusive right to reproduce a copyrighted pictorial, graphic, or sculptural work in copies under section 106 includes the right to reproduce the work in or on any kind of article, whether useful or otherwise.

(b) This title does not afford, to the owner of copyright in a work that portrays a useful article as such, any greater or lesser rights with respect to the making, distribution, or display of the useful article so portrayed than those afforded to such works under the law, whether title 17 or the common law or statutes of a State, in effect on December 31, 1977, as held applicable and construed by a court in an action brought under this title.

17 USC 1 *et seq.*

(c) In the case of a work lawfully reproduced in useful articles that have been offered for sale or other distribution to the public, copyright does not include any right to prevent the making, distribution, or display of pictures or photographs of such articles in connection with advertisements or commentaries related to the distribution or display of such articles, or in connection with news reports.

17 USC 114.

§ 114. Scope of exclusive rights in sound recordings

(a) The exclusive rights of the owner of copyright in a sound recording are limited to the rights specified by clauses (1), (2), and (3) of section 106, and do not include any right of performance under section 106(4).

(b) The exclusive right of the owner of copyright in a sound recording under clause (1) of section 106 is limited to the right to duplicate the sound recording in the form of phonorecords, or of copies of motion pictures and other audiovisual works, that directly or indirectly recapture the actual sounds fixed in the recording. The exclusive right of the owner of copyright in a sound recording under clause (2) of section 106 is limited to the right to prepare a derivative work in which the actual sounds fixed in the sound recording are rearranged, remixed, or otherwise altered in sequence or quality. The exclusive rights of the owner of copyright in a sound recording under clauses (1) and (2) of section 106 do not extend to the making or duplication of another sound recording that consists entirely of an independent fixation of other sounds, even though such sounds imitate or simulate those in the copyrighted sound recording. The exclusive rights of the owner of copyright in a sound recording under clauses (1), (2), and (3) of section 106 do not apply to sound recordings included in educational television and radio programs (as defined in section 397 of title 47) distributed or transmitted by or through public broadcasting entities (as defined by section 118(g)): *Provided*, That copies or phonorecords of said programs are not commercially distributed by or through public broadcasting entities to the general public.

47 USC 397.

(c) This section does not limit or impair the exclusive right to perform publicly, by means of a phonorecord, any of the works specified by section 106(4).

Report to Congress.

(d) On January 3, 1978, the Register of Copyrights, after consulting with representatives of owners of copyrighted materials, representatives of the broadcasting, recording, motion picture, entertainment industries, and arts organizations, representatives of organized labor and performers of copyrighted materials, shall submit to the Congress a report setting forth recommendations as to whether this section should be amended to provide for performers and copyright owners of copyrighted material any performance rights in such material. The report should describe the status of such rights in foreign countries, the views of major interested parties, and specific legislative or other recommendations, if any.

§ 115. Scope of exclusive rights in nondramatic musical works: Compulsory license for making and distributing phonorecords

17 USC 115.

In the case of nondramatic musical works, the exclusive rights provided by clauses (1) and (3) of section 106, to make and to distribute phonorecords of such works, are subject to compulsory licensing under the conditions specified by this section.

(a) Availability and Scope of Compulsory License.—

(1) When phonorecords of a nondramatic musical work have been distributed to the public in the United States under the authority of the copyright owner, any other person may, by complying with the provisions of this section, obtain a compulsory license to make and distribute phonorecords of the work. A person may obtain a compulsory license only if his or her primary purpose in making phonorecords is to distribute them to the public for private use. A person may not obtain a compulsory license for use of the work in the making of phonorecords duplicating a sound recording fixed by another, unless: (i) such sound recording was fixed lawfully; and (ii) the making of the phonorecords was authorized by the owner of copyright in the sound recording or, if the sound recording was fixed before February 15, 1972, by any person who fixed the sound recording pursuant to an express license from the owner of the copyright in the musical work or pursuant to a valid compulsory license for use of such work in a sound recording.

(2) A compulsory license includes the privilege of making a musical arrangement of the work to the extent necessary to conform it to the style or manner of interpretation of the performance involved, but the arrangement shall not change the basic melody or fundamental character of the work, and shall not be subject to protection as a derivative work under this title, except with the express consent of the copyright owner.

(b) Notice of Intention To Obtain Compulsory License.—

(1) Any person who wishes to obtain a compulsory license under this section shall, before or within thirty days after making, and before distributing any phonorecords of the work, serve notice of intention to do so on the copyright owner. If the registration or other public records of the Copyright Office do not identify the copyright owner and include an address at which notice can be served, it shall be sufficient to file the notice of intention in the Copyright Office. The notice shall comply, in form, content, and manner of service, with requirements that the Register of Copyrights shall prescribe by regulation.

(2) Failure to serve or file the notice required by clause (1) forecloses the possibility of a compulsory license and, in the absence of a negotiated license, renders the making and distribution of phonorecords actionable as acts of infringement under section 501 and fully subject to the remedies provided by sections 502 through 506 and 509.

Failure to serve or file notice, penalty.

(c) Royalty Payable Under Compulsory License.—

(1) To be entitled to receive royalties under a compulsory license, the copyright owner must be identified in the registration or other public records of the Copyright Office. The owner is entitled to royalties for phonorecords made and distributed after

being so identified, but is not entitled to recover for any phonorecords previously made and distributed.

(2) Except as provided by clause (1), the royalty under a compulsory license shall be payable for every phonorecord made and distributed in accordance with the license. For this purpose, a phonorecord is considered "distributed" if the person exercising the compulsory license has voluntarily and permanently parted with its possession. With respect to each work embodied in the phonorecord, the royalty shall be either two and three-fourths cents, or one-half of one cent per minute of playing time or fraction thereof, whichever amount is larger.

Royalty payments. Regulations.

(3) Royalty payments shall be made on or before the twentieth day of each month and shall include all royalties for the month next preceding. Each monthly payment shall be made under oath and shall comply with requirements that the Register of Copyrights shall prescribe by regulation. The Register shall also prescribe regulations under which detailed cumulative annual statements of account, certified by a certified public accountant, shall be filed for every compulsory license under this section. The regulations covering both the monthly and the annual statements of account shall prescribe the form, content, and manner of certification with respect to the number of records made and the number of records distributed.

(4) If the copyright owner does not receive the monthly payment and the monthly and annual statements of account when due, the owner may give written notice to the licensee that, unless the default is remedied within thirty days from the date of the notice, the compulsory license will be automatically terminated. Such termination renders either the making or the distribution, or both, of all phonorecords for which the royalty has not been paid, actionable as acts of infringement under section 501 and fully subject to the remedies provided by sections 502 through 506 and 509.

17 USC 116.

§ 116. Scope of exclusive rights in nondramatic musical works: Public performances by means of coin-operated phonorecord players

(a) Limitation on Exclusive Right.—In the case of a nondramatic musical work embodied in a phonorecord, the exclusive right under clause (4) of section 106 to perform the work publicly by means of a coin-operated phonorecord player is limited as follows:

(1) The proprietor of the establishment in which the public performance takes place is not liable for infringement with respect to such public performance unless—

(A) such proprietor is the operator of the phonorecord player; or

(B) such proprietor refuses or fails, within one month after receipt by registered or certified mail of a request, at a time during which the certificate required by clause (1)(C) of subsection (b) is not affixed to the phonorecord player, by the copyright owner, to make full disclosure, by registered or certified mail, of the identity of the operator of the phonorecord player.

(2) The operator of the coin-operated phonorecord player may obtain a compulsory license to perform the work publicly on that phonorecord player by filing the application, affixing the certificate, and paying the royalties provided by subsection (b).

(b) Recordation of Coin-Operated Phonorecord Player, Affixation of Certificate, and Royalty Payable Under Compulsory License.—

(1) Any operator who wishes to obtain a compulsory license for the public performance of works on a coin-operated phonorecord player shall fulfill the following requirements:

(A) Before or within one month after such performances are made available on a particular phonorecord player, and during the month of January in each succeeding year that such performances are made available on that particular phonorecord player, the operator shall file in the Copyright Office, in accordance with requirements that the Register of Copyrights, after consultation with the Copyright Royalty Tribunal (if and when the Tribunal has been constituted), shall prescribe by regulation, an application containing the name and address of the operator of the phonorecord player and the manufacturer and serial number or other explicit identification of the phonorecord player, and deposit with the Register of Copyrights a royalty fee for the current calendar year of $8 for that particular phonorecord player. If such performances are made available on a particular phonorecord player for the first time after July 1 of any year, the royalty fee to be deposited for the remainder of that year shall be $4.

(B) Within twenty days of receipt of an application and a royalty fee pursuant to subclause (A), the Register of Copyrights shall issue to the applicant a certificate for the phonorecord player.

(C) On or before March 1 of the year in which the certificate prescribed by subclause (B) of this clause is issued, or within ten days after the date of issue of the certificate, the operator shall affix to the particular phonorecord player, in a position where it can be readily examined by the public, the certificate, issued by the Register of Copyrights under subclause (B), of the latest application made by such operator under subclause (A) of this clause with respect to that phonorecord player.

(2) Failure to file the application, to affix the certificate, or to pay the royalty required by clause (1) of this subsection renders the public performance actionable as an act of infringement under section 501 and fully subject to the remedies provided by sections 502 through 506 and 509.

(c) Distribution of Royalties.—

(1) The Register of Copyrights shall receive all fees deposited under this section and, after deducting the reasonable costs incurred by the Copyright Office under this section, shall deposit the balance in the Treasury of the United States, in such manner as the Secretary of the Treasury directs. All funds held by the Secretary of the Treasury shall be invested in interest-bearing United States securities for later distribution with interest by the Copyright Royalty Tribunal as provided by this title. The Register shall submit to the Copyright Royalty Tribunal, on an annual basis, a detailed statement of account covering all fees received for the relevant period provided by subsection (b).

Statements of account, submittal to Copyright Royalty Tribunal.

Claims.

(2) During the month of January in each year, every person claiming to be entitled to compulsory license fees under this section for performances during the preceding twelve-month period shall file a claim with the Copyright Royalty Tribunal, in accordance with requirements that the Tribunal shall prescribe by regulation. Such claim shall include an agreement to accept as final,

except as provided in section 810 of this title, the determination of the Copyright Royalty Tribunal in any controversy concerning the distribution of royalty fees deposited under subclause (A) of subsection (b)(1) of this section to which the claimant is a party. Notwithstanding any provisions of the antitrust laws, for purposes of this subsection any claimants may agree among themselves as to the proportionate division of compulsory licensing fees among them, may lump their claims together and file them jointly or as a single claim, or may designate a common agent to receive payment on their behalf.

(3) After the first day of October of each year, the Copyright Royalty Tribunal shall determine whether there exists a controversy concerning the distribution of royalty fees deposited under subclause (A) of subsection (b)(1). If the Tribunal determines that no such controversy exists, it shall, after deducting its reasonable administrative costs under this section, distribute such fees to the copyright owners entitled, or to their designated agents. If it finds that such a controversy exists, it shall, pursuant to chapter 8 of this title, conduct a proceeding to determine the distribution of royalty fees.

Distribution procedures.

(4) The fees to be distributed shall be divided as follows:

(A) to every copyright owner not affiliated with a performing rights society, the pro rata share of the fees to be distributed to which such copyright owner proves entitlement.

(B) to the performing rights societies, the remainder of the fees to be distributed in such pro rata shares as they shall by agreement stipulate among themselves, or, if they fail to agree, the pro rata share to which such performing rights societies prove entitlement.

(C) during the pendency of any proceeding under this section, the Copyright Royalty Tribunal shall withhold from distribution an amount sufficient to satisfy all claims with respect to which a controversy exists, but shall have discretion to proceed to distribute any amounts that are not in controversy.

Regulations.

(5) The Copyright Royalty Tribunal shall promulgate regulations under which persons who can reasonably be expected to have claims may, during the year in which performances take place, without expense to or harassment of operators or proprietors of establishments in which phonorecord players are located, have such access to such establishments and to the phonorecord players located therein and such opportunity to obtain information with respect thereto as may be reasonably necessary to determine, by sampling procedures or otherwise, the proportion of contribution of the musical works of each such person to the earnings of the phonorecord players for which fees shall have been deposited.

Civil action.

Any person who alleges that he or she has been denied the access permitted under the regulations prescribed by the Copyright Royalty Tribunal may bring an action in the United States District Court for the District of Columbia for the cancellation of the compulsory license of the phonorecord player to which such access has been denied, and the court shall have the power to declare the compulsory license thereof invalid from the date of issue thereof.

(d) CRIMINAL PENALTIES.—Any person who knowingly makes a false representation of a material fact in an application filed under clause (1)(A) of subsection (b), or who knowingly alters a certificate issued under clause (1)(B) of subsection (b) or knowingly affixes such a certificate to a phonorecord player other than the one it covers, shall be fined not more than $2,500.

(e) DEFINITIONS.—As used in this section, the following terms and their variant forms mean the following:

(1) A "coin-operated phonorecord player" is a machine or device that—

(A) is employed solely for the performance of nondramatic musical works by means of phonorecords upon being activated by insertion of coins, currency, tokens, or other monetary units or their equivalent;

(B) is located in an establishment making no direct or indirect charge for admission;

(C) is accompanied by a list of the titles of all the musical works available for performance on it, which list is affixed to the phonorecord player or posted in the establishment in a prominent position where it can be readily examined by the public; and

(D) affords a choice of works available for performance and permits the choice to be made by the patrons of the establishment in which it is located.

(2) An "operator" is any person who, alone or jointly with others:

(A) owns a coin-operated phonorecord player; or

(B) has the power to make a coin-operated phonorecord player available for placement in an establishment for purposes of public performance; or

(C) has the power to exercise primary control over the selection of the musical works made available for public performance on a coin-operated phonorecord player.

(3) A "performing rights society" is an association or corporation that licenses the public performance of nondramatic musical works on behalf of the copyright owners, such as the American Society of Composers, Authors and Publishers, Broadcast Music, Inc., and SESAC, Inc.

§ 117. Scope of exclusive rights: Use in conjunction with computers and similar information systems

17 USC 117.

Notwithstanding the provisions of sections 106 through 116 and 118, this title does not afford to the owner of copyright in a work any greater or lesser rights with respect to the use of the work in conjunction with automatic systems capable of storing, processing, retrieving, or transferring information, or in conjunction with any similar device, machine, or process, than those afforded to works under the law, whether title 17 or the common law or statutes of a State, in effect on December 31, 1977, as held applicable and construed by a court in an action brought under this title.

§ 118. Scope of exclusive rights: Use of certain works in connection with noncommercial broadcasting

17 USC 118.

(a) The exclusive rights provided by section 106 shall, with respect to the works specified by subsection (b) and the activities specified by subsection (d), be subject to the conditions and limitations prescribed by this section.

Notice, publication in Federal Register.

(b) Not later than thirty days after the Copyright Royalty Tribunal has been constituted in accordance with section 802, the Chairman of the Tribunal shall cause notice to be published in the Federal Register of the initiation of proceedings for the purpose of determining reasonable terms and rates of royalty payments for the activities specified by subsection (d) with respect to published nondramatic musical works and published pictorial, graphic, and sculptural works during a period beginning as provided in clause (3) of this subsection and ending on December 31, 1982. Copyright owners and public broadcasting entities shall negotiate in good faith and cooperate fully with the Tribunal in an effort to reach reasonable and expeditious results. Notwithstanding any provision of the antitrust laws, any owners of copyright in works specified by this subsection and any public broadcasting entities, respectively, may negotiate and agree upon the terms and rates of royalty payments and the proportionate division of fees paid among various copyright owners, and may designate common agents to negotiate, agree to, pay, or receive payments.

(1) Any owner of copyright in a work specified in this subsection or any public broadcasting entity may, within one hundred and twenty days after publication of the notice specified in this subsection, submit to the Copyright Royalty Tribunal proposed licenses covering such activities with respect to such works. The Copyright Royalty Tribunal shall proceed on the basis of the proposals submitted to it as well as any other relevant information. The Copyright Royalty Tribunal shall permit any interested party to submit information relevant to such proceedings.

(2) License agreements voluntarily negotiated at any time between one or more copyright owners and one or more public broadcasting entities shall be given effect in lieu of any determination by the Tribunal: *Provided*, That copies of such agreements are filed in the Copyright Office within thirty days of execution in accordance with regulations that the Register of Copyrights shall prescribe.

Rates and terms, publication in Federal Register.

(3) Within six months, but not earlier than one hundred and twenty days, from the date of publication of the notice specified in this subsection the Copyright Royalty Tribunal shall make a determination and publish in the Federal Register a schedule of rates and terms which, subject to clause (2) of this subsection, shall be binding on all owners of copyright in works specified by this subsection and public broadcasting entities, regardless of whether or not such copyright owners and public broadcasting entities have submitted proposals to the Tribunal. In establishing such rates and terms the Copyright Royalty Tribunal may consider the rates for comparable circumstances under voluntary license agreements negotiated as provided in clause (2) of this subsection. The Copyright Royalty Tribunal shall also establish requirements by which copyright owners may receive reasonable notice of the use of their works under this section, and under which records of such use shall be kept by public broadcasting entities.

(4) With respect to the period beginning on the effective date of this title and ending on the date of publication of such rates and terms, this title shall not afford to owners of copyright or public broadcasting entities any greater or lesser rights with respect to the activities specified in subsection (d) as applied to works specified in this subsection than those afforded under the law in effect on December 31, 1977, as held applicable and construed by a court in an action brought under this title.

(c) The initial procedure specified in subsection (b) shall be repeated and concluded between June 30 and December 31, 1982, and at five-year intervals thereafter, in accordance with regulations that the Copyright Royalty Tribunal shall prescribe.

(d) Subject to the transitional provisions of subsection (b) (4), and to the terms of any voluntary license agreements that have been negotiated as provided by subsection (b) (2), a public broadcasting entity may, upon compliance with the provisions of this section, including the rates and terms established by the Copyright Royalty Tribunal under subsection (b) (3), engage in the following activities with respect to published nondramatic musical works and published pictorial, graphic, and sculptural works:

(1) performance or display of a work by or in the course of a transmission made by a noncommercial educational broadcast station referred to in subsection (g); and

(2) production of a transmission program, reproduction of copies or phonorecords of such a transmission program, and distribution of such copies or phonorecords, where such production, reproduction, or distribution is made by a nonprofit institution or organization solely for the purpose of transmissions specified in clause (1); and

(3) the making of reproductions by a governmental body or a nonprofit institution of a transmission program simultaneously with its transmission as specified in clause (1), and the performance or display of the contents of such program under the conditions specified by clause (1) of section 110, but only if the reproductions are used for performances or displays for a period of no more than seven days from the date of the transmission specified in clause (1), and are destroyed before or at the end of such period. No person supplying, in accordance with clause (2), a reproduction of a transmission program to governmental bodies or nonprofit institutions under this clause shall have any liability as a result of failure of such body or institution to destroy such reproduction: *Provided*, That it shall have notified such body or institution of the requirement for such destruction pursuant to this clause: *And provided further*, That if such body or institution itself fails to destroy such reproduction it shall be deemed to have infringed.

(e) Except as expressly provided in this subsection, this section shall have no applicability to works other than those specified in subsection (b).

(1) Owners of copyright in nondramatic literary works and public broadcasting entities may, during the course of voluntary negotiations, agree among themselves, respectively, as to the terms and rates of royalty payments without liability under the antitrust laws. Any such terms and rates of royalty payments shall be effective upon filing in the Copyright Office, in accordance with regulations that the Register of Copyrights shall prescribe.

Report to Congress.

(2) On January 3, 1980, the Register of Copyrights, after consulting with authors and other owners of copyright in nondramatic literary works and their representatives, and with public broadcasting entities and their representatives, shall submit to the Congress a report setting forth the extent to which voluntary licensing arrangements have been reached with respect to the use of nondramatic literary works by such broadcast stations. The report should also describe any problems that may have arisen, and present legislative or other recommendations, if warranted.

(f) Nothing in this section shall be construed to permit, beyond the limits of fair use as provided by section 107, the unauthorized dramatization of a nondramatic musical work, the production of a transmission program drawn to any substantial extent from a published compilation of pictorial, graphic, or sculptural works, or the unauthorized use of any portion of an audiovisual work.

"Public broadcasting entity." 47 USC 397.

(g) As used in this section, the term "public broadcasting entity" means a noncommercial educational broadcast station as defined in section 397 of title 47 and any nonprofit institution or organization engaged in the activities described in clause (2) of subsection (d).

Chapter 2.—COPYRIGHT OWNERSHIP AND TRANSFER

17 USC 201.

§ 201. Ownership of copyright

(a) Initial Ownership.—Copyright in a work protected under this title vests initially in the author or authors of the work. The authors of a joint work are coowners of copyright in the work.

(b) Works Made for Hire.—In the case of a work made for hire, the employer or other person for whom the work was prepared is considered the author for purposes of this title, and, unless the parties have expressly agreed otherwise in a written instrument signed by them, owns all of the rights comprised in the copyright.

(c) Contributions to Collective Works.—Copyright in each separate contribution to a collective work is distinct from copyright in the collective work as a whole, and vests initially in the author of the contribution. In the absence of an express transfer of the copyright or of any rights under it, the owner of copyright in the collective work is presumed to have acquired only the privilege of reproducing and distributing the contribution as part of that particular collective work, any revision of that collective work, and any later collective work in the same series.

(d) Transfer of Ownership.—

(1) The ownership of a copyright may be transferred in whole or in part by any means of conveyance or by operation of law, and may be bequeathed by will or pass as personal property by the applicable laws of intestate succession.

(2) Any of the exclusive rights comprised in a copyright, including any subdivision of any of the rights specified by section 106, may be transferred as provided by clause (1) and owned separately. The owner of any particular exclusive right is entitled, to the extent of that right, to all of the protection and remedies accorded to the copyright owner by this title.

(e) Involuntary Transfer.—When an individual author's ownership of a copyright, or of any of the exclusive rights under a copyright, has not previously been transferred voluntarily by that individual author, no action by any governmental body or other official or organization purporting to seize, expropriate, transfer, or exercise rights of ownership with respect to the copyright, or any of the exclusive rights under a copyright, shall be given effect under this title.

17 USC 202.

§ 202. Ownership of copyright as distinct from ownership of material object

Ownership of a copyright, or of any of the exclusive rights under a copyright, is distinct from ownership of any material object in which the work is embodied. Transfer of ownership of any material object, including the copy or phonorecord in which the work is first fixed, does not of itself convey any rights in the copyrighted work embodied in the object; nor, in the absence of an agreement, does transfer of ownership of a copyright or of any exclusive rights under a copyright convey property rights in any material object.

§ 203. Termination of transfers and licenses granted by the author

17 USC 203.

(a) CONDITIONS FOR TERMINATION.—In the case of any work other than a work made for hire, the exclusive or nonexclusive grant of a transfer or license of copyright or of any right under a copyright, executed by the author on or after January 1, 1978, otherwise than by will, is subject to termination under the following conditions:

(1) In the case of a grant executed by one author, termination of the grant may be effected by that author or, if the author is dead, by the person or persons who, under clause (2) of this subsection, own and are entitled to exercise a total of more than one-half of that author's termination interest. In the case of a grant executed by two or more authors of a joint work, termination of the grant may be effected by a majority of the authors who executed it; if any of such authors is dead, the termination interest of any such author may be exercised as a unit by the person or persons who, under clause (2) of this subsection, own and are entitled to exercise a total of more than one-half of that author's interest.

(2) Where an author is dead, his or her termination interest is owned, and may be exercised, by his widow or her widower and his or her children or grandchildren as follows:

(A) the widow or widower owns the author's entire termination interest unless there are any surviving children or grandchildren of the author, in which case the widow or widower owns one-half of the author's interest;

(B) the author's surviving children, and the surviving children of any dead child of the author, own the author's entire termination interest unless there is a widow or widower, in which case the ownership of one-half of the author's interest is divided among them;

(C) the rights of the author's children and grandchildren are in all cases divided among them and exercised on a per stirpes basis according to the number of such author's children represented; the share of the children of a dead child in a termination interest can be exercised only by the action of a majority of them.

(3) Termination of the grant may be effected at any time during a period of five years beginning at the end of thirty-five years from the date of execution of the grant; or, if the grant covers the right of publication of the work, the period begins at the end of thirty-five years from the date of publication of the work under the grant or at the end of forty years from the date of execution of the grant, whichever term ends earlier.

(4) The termination shall be effected by serving an advance notice in writing, signed by the number and proportion of owners of termination interests required under clauses (1) and (2) of this subsection, or by their duly authorized agents, upon the grantee or the grantee's successor in title.

Notice.

(A) The notice shall state the effective date of the termination, which shall fall within the five-year period specified by clause (3) of this subsection, and the notice shall be served not less than two or more than ten years before that date. A copy of the notice shall be recorded in the Copyright Office before the effective date of termination, as a condition to its taking effect.

(B) The notice shall comply, in form, content, and manner of service, with requirements that the Register of Copyrights shall prescribe by regulation.

(5) Termination of the grant may be effected notwithstanding any agreement to the contrary, including an agreement to make a will or to make any future grant.

(b) EFFECT OF TERMINATION.—Upon the effective date of termination, all rights under this title that were covered by the terminated grants revert to the author, authors, and other persons owning termination interests under clauses (1) and (2) of subsection (a), including those owners who did not join in signing the notice of termination under clause (4) of subsection (a), but with the following limitations:

Limitations.

(1) A derivative work prepared under authority of the grant before its termination may continue to be utilized under the terms of the grant after its termination, but this privilege does not extend to the preparation after the termination of other derivative works based upon the copyrighted work covered by the terminated grant.

(2) The future rights that will revert upon termination of the grant become vested on the date the notice of termination has been served as provided by clause (4) of subsection (a). The rights vest in the author, authors, and other persons named in, and in the proportionate shares provided by, clauses (1) and (2) of subsection (a).

(3) Subject to the provisions of clause (4) of this subsection, a further grant, or agreement to make a further grant, of any right covered by a terminated grant is valid only if it is signed by the same number and proportion of the owners, in whom the right has vested under clause (2) of this subsection, as are required to terminate the grant under clauses (1) and (2) of subsection (a). Such further grant or agreement is effective with respect to all of the persons in whom the right it covers has vested under clause (2) of this subsection, including those who did not join in signing it. If any person dies after rights under a terminated grant have vested in him or her, that person's legal representatives, legatees, or heirs at law represent him or her for purposes of this clause.

(4) A further grant, or agreement to make a further grant, of any right covered by a terminated grant is valid only if it is made after the effective date of the termination. As an exception, however, an agreement for such a further grant may be made between the persons provided by clause (3) of this subsection and the original grantee or such grantee's successor in title, after the notice of termination has been served as provided by clause (4) of subsection (a).

(5) Termination of a grant under this section affects only those rights covered by the grants that arise under this title, and in no way affects rights arising under any other Federal, State, or foreign laws.

(6) Unless and until termination is effected under this section, the grant, if it does not provide otherwise, continues in effect for the term of copyright provided by this title.

17 USC 204.

§ 204. Execution of transfers of copyright ownership

(a) A transfer of copyright ownership, other than by operation of law, is not valid unless an instrument of conveyance, or a note or memorandum of the transfer, is in writing and signed by the owner of the rights conveyed or such owner's duly authorized agent.

(b) A certificate of acknowledgement is not required for the validity of a transfer, but is prima facie evidence of the execution of the transfer if—

(1) in the case of a transfer executed in the United States, the certificate is issued by a person authorized to administer oaths within the United States; or

(2) in the case of a transfer executed in a foreign country, the certificate is issued by a diplomatic or consular officer of the United States, or by a person authorized to administer oaths whose authority is proved by a certificate of such an officer.

§ 205. Recordation of transfers and other documents 17 USC 205.

(a) Conditions for Recordation.—Any transfer of copyright ownership or other document pertaining to a copyright may be recorded in the Copyright Office if the document filed for recordation bears the actual signature of the person who executed it, or if it is accompanied by a sworn or official certification that it is a true copy of the original, signed document.

(b) Certificate of Recordation.—The Register of Copyrights shall, upon receipt of a document as provided by subsection (a) and of the fee provided by section 708, record the document and return it with a certificate of recordation.

(c) Recordation as Constructive Notice.—Recordation of a document in the Copyright Office gives all persons constructive noticc of the facts stated in the recorded document, but only if—

(1) the document, or material attached to it, specifically identifies the work to which it pertains so that, after the document is indexed by the Register of Copyrights, it would be revealed by a reasonable search under the title or registration number of the work; and

(2) registration has been made for the work.

(d) Recordation as Prerequisite to Infringement Suit.—No person claiming by virtue of a transfer to be the owner of copyright or of any exclusive right under a copyright is entitled to institute an infringement action under this title until the instrument of transfer under which such person claims has been recorded in the Copyright Office, but suit may be instituted after such recordation on a cause of action that arose before recordation.

(e) Priority Between Conflicting Transfers.—As between two conflicting transfers, the one executed first prevails if it is recorded, in the manner required to give constructive notice under subsection (c), within one month after its execution in the United States or within two months after its execution outside the United States, or at any time before recordation in such manner of the later transfer. Otherwise the later transfer prevails if recorded first in such manner, and if taken in good faith, for valuable consideration or on the basis of a binding promise to pay royalties, and without notice of the earlier transfer.

(f) Priority Between Conflicting Transfer of Ownership and Nonexclusive License.—A nonexclusive license, whether recorded or not, prevails over a conflicting transfer of copyright ownership if the license is evidenced by a written instrument signed by the owner of the rights licensed or such owner's duly authorized agent, and if—

(1) the license was taken before execution of the transfer; or

(2) the license was taken in good faith before recordation of the transfer and without notice of it.

Chapter 3.—DURATION OF COPYRIGHT

17 USC 301.

§ 301. Preemption with respect to other laws

(a) On and after January 1, 1978, all legal or equitable rights that are equivalent to any of the exclusive rights within the general scope of copyright as specified by section 106 in works of authorship that are fixed in a tangible medium of expression and come within the subject matter of copyright as specified by sections 102 and 103, whether created before or after that date and whether published or unpublished, are governed exclusively by this title. Thereafter, no person is entitled to any such right or equivalent right in any such work under the common law or statutes of any State.

(b) Nothing in this title annuls or limits any rights or remedies under the common law or statutes of any State with respect to—

(1) subject matter that does not come within the subject matter of copyright as specified by sections 102 and 103, including works of authorship not fixed in any tangible medium of expression; or

(2) any cause of action arising from undertakings commenced before January 1, 1978; or

(3) activities violating legal or equitable rights that are not equivalent to any of the exclusive rights within the general scope of copyright as specified by section 106.

(c) With respect to sound recordings fixed before February 15, 1972, any rights or remedies under the common law or statutes of any State shall not be annulled or limited by this title until February 15, 2047. The preemptive provisions of subsection (a) shall apply to any such rights and remedies pertaining to any cause of action arising from undertakings commenced on and after February 15, 2047. Notwithstanding the provisions of section 303, no sound recording fixed before February 15, 1972, shall be subject to copyright under this title before, on, or after February 15, 2047.

(d) Nothing in this title annuls or limits any rights or remedies under any other Federal statute.

17 USC 302.

§ 302. Duration of copyright: Works created on or after January 1, 1978

(a) In General.—Copyright in a work created on or after January 1, 1978, subsists from its creation and, except as provided by the following subsections, endures for a term consisting of the life of the author and fifty years after the author's death.

(b) Joint Works.—In the case of a joint work prepared by two or more authors who did not work for hire, the copyright endures for a term consisting of the life of the last surviving author and fifty years after such last surviving author's death.

(c) Anonymous Works, Pseudonymous Works, and Works Made for Hire.—In the case of an anonymous work, a pseudonymous work, or a work made for hire, the copyright endures for a term of seventy-five years from the year of its first publication, or a term of one hundred years from the year of its creation, whichever expires first. If, before the end of such term, the identity of one or more of the authors of an anonymous or pseudonymous work is revealed in the records of a registration made for that work under subsections (a) or (d) of section 408, or in the records provided by this subsection, the copyright in the work endures for the term specified by subsection (a) or (b), based on the life of the author or authors whose identity has been revealed. Any person having an interest in the copyright in an anonymous or pseudonymous work may at any time record, in records to be maintained by the Copyright Office for that purpose, a statement identifying one or more authors of the work; the statement shall also identify the person filing it, the nature of that person's interest, the source of the information recorded, and the particular work affected, and shall comply in form and content with requirements that the Register of Copyrights shall prescribe by regulation.

(d) Records Relating to Death of Authors.—Any person having an interest in a copyright may at any time record in the Copyright Office a statement of the date of death of the author of the copyrighted work, or a statement that the author is still living on a particular date. The statement shall identify the person filing it, the nature of that person's interest, and the source of the information recorded, and shall comply in form and content with requirements that the Register of Copyrights shall prescribe by regulation. The Register shall maintain current records of information relating to the death of authors of copyrighted works, based on such recorded statements and, to the extent the Register considers practicable, on data contained in any of the records of the Copyright Office or in other reference sources. Recordkeeping.

(e) Presumption as to Author's Death.—After a period of seventy-five years from the year of first publication of a work, or a period of one hundred years from the year of its creation, whichever expires first, any person who obtains from the Copyright Office a certified report that the records provided by subsection (d) disclose nothing to indicate that the author of the work is living, or died less than fifty years before, is entitled to the benefit of a presumption that the author has been dead for at least fifty years. Reliance in good faith upon this presumption shall be a complete defense to any action for infringement under this title.

§ 303. Duration of copyright: Works created but not published or copyrighted before January 1, 1978

17 USC 303.

Copyright in a work created before January 1, 1978, but not theretofore in the public domain or copyrighted, subsists from January 1, 1978, and endures for the term provided by section 302. In no case, however, shall the term of copyright in such a work expire before December 31, 2002; and, if the work is published on or before December 31, 2002, the term of copyright shall not expire before December 31, 2027.

§ 304. Duration of copyright: Subsisting copyrights

17 USC 304.

(a) Copyrights in Their First Term on January 1, 1978.—Any copyright, the first term of which is subsisting on January 1, 1978, shall endure for twenty-eight years from the date it was originally secured: *Provided*, That in the case of any posthumous work or of any periodical, cyclopedic, or other composite work upon which the copyright was originally secured by the proprietor thereof, or of any work copyrighted by a corporate body (otherwise than as assignee or licensee of the individual author) or by an employer for whom such work is made for hire, the proprietor of such copyright shall be entitled to a renewal and extension of the copyright in such work for the further term of forty-seven years when application for such renewal and extension shall have been made to the Copyright Office and duly registered therein within one year prior to the expiration of the original term of copyright: *And provided further*, That in the case of any other copyrighted work, including a contribution by an individual author to a periodical or to a cyclopedic or other composite work, the author of such work, if still living, or the widow, widower, or children of the author, if the author be not living, or if such author, widow, widower, or children be not living, then the author's executors, or in the absence of a will, his or her next of kin shall be entitled to a renewal and extension of the copyright in such work for a further term of forty-seven years when application for such renewal and extension shall have been made to the Copyright Office and duly registered therein within one year prior to the expiration of the original term of copyright: *And provided further*, That in default of the registration of such application for renewal and extension, the copyright in any work shall terminate at the expiration of twenty-eight years from the date copyright was originally secured.

(b) COPYRIGHTS IN THEIR RENEWAL TERM OR REGISTERED FOR RENEWAL BEFORE JANUARY 1, 1978.—The duration of any copyright, the renewal term of which is subsisting at any time between December 31, 1976, and December 31, 1977, inclusive, or for which renewal registration is made between December 31, 1976, and December 31, 1977, inclusive, is extended to endure for a term of seventy-five years from the date copyright was originally secured.

(c) TERMINATION OF TRANSFERS AND LICENSES COVERING EXTENDED RENEWAL TERM.—In the case of any copyright subsisting in either its first or renewal term on January 1, 1978, other than a copyright in a work made for hire, the exclusive or nonexclusive grant of a transfer or license of the renewal copyright or any right under it, executed before January 1, 1978, by any of the persons designated by the second proviso of subsection (a) of this section, otherwise than by will, is subject to termination under the following conditions:

(1) In the case of a grant executed by a person or persons other than the author, termination of the grant may be effected by the surviving person or persons who executed it. In the case of a grant executed by one or more of the authors of the work, termination of the grant may be effected, to the extent of a particular author's share in the ownership of the renewal copyright, by the author who executed it or, if such author is dead, by the person or persons who, under clause (2) of this subsection, own and are entitled to exercise a total of more than one-half of that author's termination interest.

(2) Where an author is dead, his or her termination interest is owned, and may be exercised, by his widow or her widower and his or her children or grandchildren as follows:

(A) the widow or widower owns the author's entire termination interest unless there are any surviving children or grandchildren of the author, in which case the widow or widower owns one-half of the author's interest;

(B) the author's surviving children, and the surviving children of any dead child of the author, own the author's entire termination interest unless there is a widow or widower, in which case the ownership of one-half of the author's interest is divided among them;

(C) the rights of the author's children and grandchildren are in all cases divided among them and exercised on a per stirpes basis according to the number of such author's children represented; the share of the children of a dead child in a termination interest can be exercised only by the action of a majority of them.

(3) Termination of the grant may be effected at any time during a period of five years beginning at the end of fifty-six years from the date copyright was originally secured, or beginning on January 1, 1978, whichever is later.

Advance notice.

(4) The termination shall be effected by serving an advance notice in writing upon the grantee or the grantee's successor in title. In the case of a grant executed by a person or persons other than the author, the notice shall be signed by all of those entitled to terminate the grant under clause (1) of this subsection, or by their duly authorized agents. In the case of a grant executed by one or more of the authors of the work, the notice as to any one author's share shall be signed by that author or his or her duly authorized agent or, if that author is dead, by the number and proportion of the owners of his or her termination interest required under clauses (1) and (2) of this subsection, or by their duly authorized agents.

(A) The notice shall state the effective date of the termination, which shall fall within the five-year period specified by clause (3) of this subsection, and the notice shall be served not less than two or more than ten years before that date. A copy of the notice shall be recorded in the Copyright Office before the effective date of termination, as a condition to its taking effect.

(B) The notice shall comply, in form, content, and manner of service, with requirements that the Register of Copyrights shall prescribe by regulation.

(5) Termination of the grant may be effected notwithstanding any agreement to the contrary, including an agreement to make a will or to make any future grant.

Reversion.

(6) In the case of a grant executed by a person or persons other than the author, all rights under this title that were covered by the terminated grant revert, upon the effective date of termination, to all of those entitled to terminate the grant under clause (1) of this subsection. In the case of a grant executed by one or more of the authors of the work, all of a particular author's rights under this title that were covered by the terminated grant revert, upon the effective date of termination, to that author or, if that author is dead, to the persons owning his or her termination interest under clause (2) of this subsection, including those owners who did not join in signing the notice of termination under clause (4) of this subsection. In all cases the reversion of rights is subject to the following limitations:

Limitations.

(A) A derivative work prepared under authority of the grant before its termination may continue to be utilized under the terms of the grant after its termination, but this privilege does not extend to the preparation after the termination of other derivative works based upon the copyrighted work covered by the terminated grant.

(B) The future rights that will revert upon termination of the grant become vested on the date the notice of termination has been served as provided by clause (4) of this subsection.

(C) Where the author's rights revert to two or more persons under clause (2) of this subsection, they shall vest in those persons in the proportionate shares provided by that clause. In such a case, and subject to the provisions of subclause (D) of this clause, a further grant, or agreement to make a further grant, of a particular author's share with respect to any right covered by a terminated grant is valid only if it is signed by the same number and proportion of the owners, in whom the right has vested under this clause, as are required to terminate the grant under clause (2) of this subsection. Such further grant or agreement is effective with respect to all of the persons in whom the right it covers has vested under this subclause, including those who did not join in signing it. If any person dies after rights under a terminated grant have vested in him or her, that person's legal representatives, legatees, or heirs at law represent him or her for purposes of this subclause.

(D) A further grant, or agreement to make a further grant, of any right covered by a terminated grant is valid only if it is made after the effective date of the termination. As an exception, however, an agreement for such a further grant may be made between the author or any of the persons provided by the first sentence of clause (6) of this subsection, or between the persons provided by subclause (C) of this clause, and the original grantee or such grantee's successor in title, after the notice of termination has been served as provided by clause (4) of this subsection.

(E) Termination of a grant under this subsection affects only those rights covered by the grant that arise under this title, and in no way affects rights arising under any other Federal, State, or foreign laws.

(F) Unless and until termination is effected under this subsection, the grant, if it does not provide otherwise, continues in effect for the remainder of the extended renewal term.

17 USC 305.

§ 305. Duration of copyright: Terminal date

All terms of copyright provided by sections 302 through 304 run to the end of the calendar year in which they would otherwise expire.

Chapter 4.—COPYRIGHT NOTICE, DEPOSIT, AND REGISTRATION

Sec.

17 USC 401.

§ 401. Notice of copyright: Visually perceptible copies

(a) General Requirement.—Whenever a work protected under this title is published in the United States or elsewhere by authority of the copyright owner, a notice of copyright as provided by this section shall be placed on all publicly distributed copies from which the work can be visually perceived, either directly or with the aid of a machine or device.

(b) Form of Notice.—The notice appearing on the copies shall consist of the following three elements:

(1) the symbol © (the letter C in a circle), or the word "Copyright", or the abbreviation "Copr."; and

(2) the year of first publication of the work; in the case of compilations or derivative works incorporating previously published material, the year date of first publication of the compilation or derivative work is sufficient. The year date may be omitted where a pictorial, graphic, or sculptural work, with accompanying text matter, if any, is reproduced in or on greeting cards, postcards, stationery, jewelry, dolls, toys, or any useful articles; and

(3) the name of the owner of copyright in the work, or an abbreviation by which the name can be recognized, or a generally known alternative designation of the owner.

(c) Position of Notice.—The notice shall be affixed to the copies in such manner and location as to give reasonable notice of the claim of copyright. The Register of Copyrights shall prescribe by regulation, as examples, specific methods of affixation and positions of the notice on various types of works that will satisfy this requirement, but these specifications shall not be considered exhaustive.

§ 402. Notice of copyright: Phonorecords of sound recordings

17 USC 402.

(a) General Requirement.—Whenever a sound recording protected under this title is published in the United States or elsewhere by authority of the copyright owner, a notice of copyright as provided by this section shall be placed on all publicly distributed phonorecords of the sound recording.

(b) Form of Notice.—The notice appearing on the phonorecords shall consist of the following three elements:

(1) the symbol ℗ (the letter P in a circle); and

(2) the year of first publication of the sound recording; and

(3) the name of the owner of copyright in the sound recording, or an abbreviation by which the name can be recognized, or a generally known alternative designation of the owner; if the producer of the sound recording is named on the phonorecord labels or containers, and if no other name appears in conjunction with the notice, the producer's name shall be considered a part of the notice.

(c) Position of Notice.—The notice shall be placed on the surface of the phonorecord, or on the phonorecord label or container, in such manner and location as to give reasonable notice of the claim of copyright.

§ 403. Notice of copyright: Publications incorporating United States Government works

17 USC 403.

Whenever a work is published in copies or phonorecords consisting preponderantly of one or more works of the United States Government, the notice of copyright provided by sections 401 or 402 shall also include a statement identifying, either affirmatively or negatively, those portions of the copies or phonorecords embodying any work or works protected under this title.

§ 404. Notice of copyright: Contributions to collective works

17 USC 404.

(a) A separate contribution to a collective work may bear its own notice of copyright, as provided by sections 401 through 403. However, a single notice applicable to the collective work as a whole is sufficient to satisfy the requirements of sections 401 through 403 with respect to the separate contributions it contains (not including advertisements inserted on behalf of persons other than the owner of copyright in the collective work), regardless of the ownership of copyright in the contributions and whether or not they have been previously published.

(b) Where the person named in a single notice applicable to a collective work as a whole is not the owner of copyright in a separate contribution that does not bear its own notice, the case is governed by the provisions of section 406(a).

17 USC 405.

§ 405. Notice of copyright: Omission of notice

(a) EFFECT OF OMISSION ON COPYRIGHT.—The omission of the copyright notice prescribed by sections 401 through 403 from copies or phonorecords publicly distributed by authority of the copyright owner does not invalidate the copyright in a work if—

(1) the notice has been omitted from no more than a relatively small number of copies or phonorecords distributed to the public; or

(2) registration for the work has been made before or is made within five years after the publication without notice, and a reasonable effort is made to add notice to all copies or phonorecords that are distributed to the public in the United States after the omission has been discovered; or

(3) the notice has been omitted in violation of an express requirement in writing that, as a condition of the copyright owner's authorization of the public distribution of copies or phonorecords, they bear the prescribed notice.

(b) EFFECT OF OMISSION ON INNOCENT INFRINGERS.—Any person who innocently infringes a copyright, in reliance upon an authorized copy or phonorecord from which the copyright notice has been omitted, incurs no liability for actual or statutory damages under section 504 for any infringing acts committed before receiving actual notice that registration for the work has been made under section 408, if such person proves that he or she was misled by the omission of notice. In a suit for infringement in such a case the court may allow or disallow recovery of any of the infringer's profits attributable to the infringement, and may enjoin the continuation of the infringing undertaking or may require, as a condition or permitting the continuation of the infringing undertaking, that the infringer pay the copyright owner a reasonable license fee in an amount and on terms fixed by the court.

(c) REMOVAL OF NOTICE.—Protection under this title is not affected by the removal, destruction, or obliteration of the notice, without the authorization of the copyright owner, from any publicly distributed copies or phonorecords.

17 USC 406.

§ 406. Notice of copyright: Error in name or date

(a) ERROR IN NAME.—Where the person named in the copyright notice on copies or phonorecords publicly distributed by authority of the copyright owner is not the owner of copyright, the validity and ownership of the copyright are not affected. In such a case, however, any person who innocently begins an undertaking that infringes the copyright has a complete defense to any action for such infringement if such person proves that he or she was misled by the notice and began the undertaking in good faith under a purported transfer or license from the person named therein, unless before the undertaking was begun—

(1) registration for the work had been made in the name of the owner of copyright; or

(2) a document executed by the person named in the notice and showing the ownership of the copyright had been recorded.

The person named in the notice is liable to account to the copyright owner for all receipts from transfers or licenses purportedly made under the copyright by the person named in the notice.

(b) ERROR IN DATE.—When the year date in the notice on copies or phonorecords distributed by authority of the copyright owner is earlier than the year in which publication first occurred, any period computed from the year of first publication under section 302 is to be computed from the year in the notice. Where the year date is more than one year later than the year in which publication first occurred, the work is considered to have been published without any notice and is governed by the provisions of section 405.

(c) Omission of Name or Date.—Where copies or phonorecords publicly distributed by authority of the copyright owner contain no name or no date that could reasonably be considered a part of the notice, the work is considered to have been published without any notice and is governed by the provisions of section 405.

§ 407. Deposit of copies or phonorecords for Library of Congress 17 USC 407.

(a) Except as provided by subsection (c), and subject to the provisions of subsection (e), the owner of copyright or of the exclusive right of publication in a work published with notice of copyright in the United States shall deposit, within three months after the date of such publication—

(1) two complete copies of the best edition; or

(2) if the work is a sound recording, two complete phonorecords of the best edition, together with any printed or other visually perceptible material published with such phonorecords.

Neither the deposit requirements of this subsection nor the acquisition provisions of subsection (e) are conditions of copyright protection.

(b) The required copies or phonorecords shall be deposited in the Copyright Office for the use or disposition of the Library of Congress. The Register of Copyrights shall, when requested by the depositor and upon payment of the fee prescribed by section 708, issue a receipt for the deposit.

Exemption.

(c) The Register of Copyrights may by regulation exempt any categories of material from the deposit requirements of this section, or require deposit of only one copy or phonorecord with respect to any categories. Such regulations shall provide either for complete exemption from the deposit requirements of this section, or for alternative forms of deposit aimed at providing a satisfactory archival record of a work without imposing practical or financial hardships on the depositor, where the individual author is the owner of copyright in a pictorial, graphic, or sculptural work and (i) less than five copies of the work have been published, or (ii) the work has been published in a limited edition consisting of numbered copies, the monetary value of which would make the mandatory deposit of two copies of the best edition of the work burdensome, unfair, or unreasonable.

Penalties.

(d) At any time after publication of a work as provided by subsection (a), the Register of Copyrights may make written demand for the required deposit on any of the persons obligated to make the deposit under subsection (a). Unless deposit is made within three months after the demand is received, the person or persons on whom the demand was made are liable—

(1) to a fine of not more than $250 for each work; and

(2) to pay into a specially designated fund in the Library of Congress the total retail price of the copies or phonorecords demanded, or, if no retail price has been fixed, the reasonable cost of the Library of Congress of acquiring them; and

(3) to pay a fine of $2,500, in addition to any fine or liability imposed under clauses (1) and (2), if such person willfully or repeatedly fails or refuses to comply with such a demand.

Regulations.

(e) With respect to transmission programs that have been fixed and transmitted to the public in the United States but have not been published, the Register of Copyrights shall, after consulting with the Librarian of Congress and other interested organizations and officials, establish regulations governing the acquisition, through deposit or otherwise, of copies or phonorecords of such programs for the collections of the Library of Congress.

(1) The Librarian of Congress shall be permitted, under the standards and conditions set forth in such regulations, to make a fixation of a transmission program directly from a transmission to the public, and to reproduce one copy or phonorecord from such fixation for archival purposes.

(2) Such regulations shall also provide standards and procedures by which the Register of Copyrights may make written demand, upon the owner of the right of transmission in the United States, for the deposit of a copy or phonorecord of a specific transmission program. Such deposit may, at the option of the owner of the right of transmission in the United States, be accomplished by gift, by loan for purposes of reproduction, or by sale at a price not to exceed the cost of reproducing and supplying the copy or phonorecord. The regulations established under this clause shall provide reasonable periods of not less than three months for compliance with a demand, and shall allow for extensions of such periods and adjustments in the scope of the demand or the methods for fulfilling it, as reasonably warranted by the circumstances. Willful failure or refusal to comply with the conditions prescribed by such regulations shall subject the owner of the right of transmission in the United States to liability for an amount, not to exceed the cost of reproducing and supplying the copy or phonorecord in question, to be paid into a specially designated fund in the Library of Congress.

(3) Nothing in this subsection shall be construed to require the making or retention, for purposes of deposit, of any copy or phonorecord of an unpublished transmission program, the transmission of which occurs before the receipt of a specific written demand as provided by clause (2).

(4) No activity undertaken in compliance with regulations prescribed under clauses (1) or (2) of this subsection shall result in liability if intended solely to assist in the acquisition of copies or phonorecords under this subsection.

17 USC 408.

§ 408. Copyright registration in general

(a) Registration Permissive.—At any time during the subsistence of copyright in any published or unpublished work, the owner of copyright or of any exclusive right in the work may obtain registration of the copyright claim by delivering to the Copyright Office the deposit specified by this section, together with the application and fee specified by sections 409 and 708. Subject to the provisions of section 405(a), such registration is not a condition of copyright protection.

(b) Deposit for Copyright Registration.—Except as provided by subsection (c), the material deposited for registration shall include—

(1) in the case of an unpublished work, one complete copy or phonorecord;

(2) in the case of a published work, two complete copies or phonorecords of the best edition;

(3) in the case of a work first published outside the United States, one complete copy or phonorecord as so published;

(4) in the case of a contribution to a collective work, one complete copy or phonorecord of the best edition of the collective work.

Copies or phonorecords deposited for the Library of Congress under section 407 may be used to satisfy the deposit provisions of this section, if they are accompanied by the prescribed application and fee, and by any additional identifying material that the Register may, by regulation, require. The Register shall also prescribe regulations establishing requirements under which copies or phonorecords acquired for the Library of Congress under subsection (e) of section 407, otherwise than by deposit, may be used to satisfy the deposit provisions of this section. Regulations.

(c) ADMINISTRATIVE CLASSIFICATION AND OPTIONAL DEPOSIT.—

(1) The Register of Copyrights is authorized to specify by regulation the administrative classes into which works are to be placed for purposes of deposit and registration, and the nature of the copies or phonorecords to be deposited in the various classes specified. The regulations may require or permit, for particular classes, the deposit of identifying material instead of copies or phonorecords, the deposit of only one copy or phonorecord where two would normally be required, or a single registration for a group of related works. This administrative classification of works has no significance with respect to the subject matter of copyright or the exclusive rights provided by this title.

(2) Without prejudice to the general authority provided under clause (1), the Register of Copyrights shall establish regulations specifically permitting a single registration for a group of works by the same individual author, all first published as contributions to periodicals, including newspapers, within a twelve-month period, on the basis of a single deposit, application, and registration fee, under all of the following conditions— Regulations.

(A) if each of the works as first published bore a separate copyright notice, and the name of the owner of copyright in the work, or an abbreviation by which the name can be recognized, or a generally known alternative designation of the owner was the same in each notice; and

(B) if the deposit consists of one copy of the entire issue of the periodical, or of the entire section in the case of a newspaper, in which each contribution was first published; and

(C) if the application identifies each work separately, including the periodical containing it and its date of first publication.

(3) As an alternative to separate renewal registrations under subsection (a) of section 304, a single renewal registration may be made for a group of works by the same individual author, all first published as contributions to periodicals, including newspapers, upon the filing of a single application and fee, under all of the following conditions:

(A) the renewal claimant or claimants, and the basis of claim or claims under section 304(a), is the same for each of the works; and

(B) the works were all copyrighted upon their first publication, either through separate copyright notice and registration or by virtue of a general copyright notice in the periodical issue as a whole; and

(C) the renewal application and fee are received not more than twenty-eight or less than twenty-seven years after the thirty-first day of December of the calendar year in which all of the works were first published; and

(D) the renewal application identifies each work separately, including the periodical containing it and its date of first publication.

(d) CORRECTIONS AND AMPLIFICATIONS.—The Register may also establish, by regulation, formal procedures for the filing of an application for supplementary registration, to correct an error in a copyright registration or to amplify the information given in a registration. Such application shall be accompanied by the fee provided by section 708, and shall clearly identify the registration to be corrected or amplified. The information contained in a supplementary registration augments but does not supersede that contained in the earlier registration.

(e) PUBLISHED EDITION OF PREVIOUSLY REGISTERED WORK.—Registration for the first published edition of a work previously registered in unpublished form may be made even though the work as published is substantially the same as the unpublished version.

17 USC 409.

§ 409. Application for copyright registration

The application for copyright registration shall be made on a form prescribed by the Register of Copyrights and shall include—

(1) the name and address of the copyright claimant;

(2) in the case of a work other than an anonymous or pseudonymous work, the name and nationality or domicile of the author or authors, and, if one or more of the authors is dead, the dates of their deaths;

(3) if the work is anonymous or pseudonymous, the nationality or domicile of the author or authors;

(4) in the case of a work made for hire, a statement to this effect;

(5) if the copyright claimant is not the author, a brief statement of how the claimant obtained ownership of the copyright;

(6) the title of the work, together with any previous or alternative titles under which the work can be identified;

(7) the year in which creation of the work was completed;

(8) if the work has been published, the date and nation of its first publication;

(9) in the case of a compilation or derivative work, an identification of any preexisting work or works that it is based on or incorporates, and a brief, general statement of the additional material covered by the copyright claim being registered;

(10) in the case of a published work containing material of which copies are required by section 601 to be manufactured in the United States, the names of the persons or organizations who performed the processes specified by subsection (c) of section 601 with respect to that material, and the places where those processes were performed; and

(11) any other information regarded by the Register of Copyrights as bearing upon the preparation or identification of the work or the existence, ownership, or duration of the copyright.

17 USC 410.

§ 410. Registration of claim and issuance of certificate

(a) When, after examination, the Register of Copyrights determines that, in accordance with the provisions of this title, the material deposited constitutes copyrightable subject matter and that the other legal and formal requirements of this title have been met, the Register shall register the claim and issue to the applicant a certificate of registration under the seal of the Copyright Office. The certificate shall contain the information given in the application, together with the number and effective date of the registration.

(b) In any case in which the Register of Copyrights determines that, in accordance with the provisions of this title, the material deposited does not constitute copyrightable subject matter or that the claim is invalid for any other reason, the Register shall refuse registration and shall notify the applicant in writing of the reasons for such refusal.

(c) In any judicial proceedings the certificate of a registration made before or within five years after first publication of the work shall constitute prima facie evidence of the validity of the copyright and of the facts stated in the certificate. The evidentiary weight to be accorded the certificate of a registration made thereafter shall be within the discretion of the court. Prima facie evidence.

(d) The effective date of a copyright registration is the day on which an application, deposit, and fee, which are later determined by the Register of Copyrights or by a court of competent jurisdiction to be acceptable for registration, have all been received in the Copyright Office. Effective date.

§ 411. Registration as prerequisite to infringement suit 17 USC 411.

(a) Subject to the provisions of subsection (b), no action for infringement of the copyright in any work shall be instituted until registration of the copyright claim has been made in accordance with this title. In any case, however, where the deposit, application, and fee required for registration have been delivered to the Copyright Office in proper form and registration has been refused, the applicant is entitled to institute an action for infringement if notice thereof, with a copy of the complaint, is served on the Register of Copyrights. The Register may, at his or her option, become a party to the action with respect to the issue of registrability of the copyright claim by entering an appearance within sixty days after such service, but the Register's failure to become a party shall not deprive the court of jurisdiction to determine that issue.

(b) In the case of a work consisting of sounds, images, or both, the first fixation of which is made simultaneously with its transmission, the copyright owner may, either before or after such fixation takes place, institute an action for infringement under section 501, fully subject to the remedies provided by sections 502 through 506 and sections 509 and 510, if, in accordance with requirements that the Register of Copyrights shall prescribe by regulation, the copyright owner—

(1) serves notice upon the infringer, not less than ten or more than thirty days before such fixation, identifying the work and the specific time and source of its first transmission, and declaring an intention to secure copyright in the work; and

(2) makes registration for the work within three months after its first transmission.

§ 412. Registration as prerequisite to certain remedies for infringement 17 USC 412.

In any action under this title, other than an action instituted under section 411(b), no award of statutory damages or of attorney's fees, as provided by sections 504 and 505, shall be made for—

(1) any infringement of copyright in an unpublished work commenced before the effective date of its registration; or

(2) any infringement of copyright commenced after first publication of the work and before the effective date of its registration, unless such registration is made within three months after the first publication of the work.

Chapter 5.—COPYRIGHT INFRINGEMENT AND REMEDIES

17 USC 501.

§ 501. Infringement of copyright

(a) Anyone who violates any of the exclusive rights of the copyright owner as provided by sections 106 through 118, or who imports copies or phonorecords into the United States in violation of section 602, is an infringer of the copyright.

(b) The legal or beneficial owner of an exclusive right under a copyright is entitled, subject to the requirements of sections 205(d) and 411, to institute an action for any infringement of that particular right committed while he or she is the owner of it. The court may require such owner to serve written notice of the action with a copy of the complaint upon any person shown, by the records of the Copyright Office or otherwise, to have or claim an interest in the copyright, and shall require that such notice be served upon any person whose interest is likely to be affected by a decision in the case. The court may require the joinder, and shall permit the intervention, of any person having or claiming an interest in the copyright.

(c) For any secondary transmission by a cable system that embodies a performance or a display of a work which is actionable as an act of infringement under subsection (c) of section 111, a television broadcast station holding a copyright or other license to transmit or perform the same version of that work shall, for purposes of subsection (b) of this section, be treated as a legal or beneficial owner if such secondary transmission occurs within the local service area of that television station.

(d) For any secondary transmission by a cable system that is actionable as an act of infringement pursuant to section 111(c)(3), the following shall also have standing to sue: (i) the primary transmitter whose transmission has been altered by the cable system; and (ii) any broadcast station within whose local service area the secondary transmission occurs.

17 USC 502.

§ 502. Remedies for infringement: Injunctions

(a) Any court having jurisdiction of a civil action arising under this title may, subject to the provisions of section 1498 of title 28, grant temporary and final injunctions on such terms as it may deem reasonable to prevent or restrain infringement of a copyright.

(b) Any such injunction may be served anywhere in the United States on the person enjoined; it shall be operative throughout the United States and shall be enforceable, by proceedings in contempt or otherwise, by any United States court having jurisdiction of that person. The clerk of the court granting the injunction shall, when requested by any other court in which enforcement of the injunction is sought, transmit promptly to the other court a certified copy of all the papers in the case on file in such clerk's office.

§ 503. Remedies for infringement: Impounding and disposition of infringing articles 17 USC 503.

(a) At any time while an action under this title is pending, the court may order the impounding, on such terms as it may deem reasonable, of all copies or phonorecords claimed to have been made or used in violation of the copyright owner's exclusive rights, and of all plates, molds, matrices, masters, tapes, film negatives, or other articles by means of which such copies or phonorecords may be reproduced.

(b) As part of a final judgment or decree, the court may order the destruction or other reasonable disposition of all copies or phonorecords found to have been made or used in violation of the copyright owner's exclusive rights, and of all plates, molds, matrices, masters, tapes, film negatives, or other articles by means of which such copies or phonorecords may be reproduced.

§ 504. Remedies for infringement: Damages and profits 17 USC 504.

(a) In General.—Except as otherwise provided by this title, an infringer of copyright is liable for either—

(1) the copyright owner's actual damages and any additional profits of the infringer, as provided by subsection (b); or

(2) statutory damages, as provided by subsection (c).

(b) Actual Damages and Profits.—The copyright owner is entitled to recover the actual damages suffered by him or her as a result of the infringement, and any profits of the infringer that are attributable to the infringement and are not taken into account in computing the actual damages. In establishing the infringer's profits, the copyright owner is required to present proof only of the infringer's gross revenue, and the infringer is required to prove his or her deductible expenses and the elements of profit attributable to factors other than the copyrighted work.

(c) Statutory Damages.—

(1) Except as provided by clause (2) of this subsection, the copyright owner may elect, at any time before final judgment is rendered, to recover, instead of actual damages and profits, an award of statutory damages for all infringements involved in the action, with respect to any one work, for which any one infringer is liable individually, or for which any two or more infringers are liable jointly and severally, in a sum of not less than $250 or more than $10,000 as the court considers just. For the purposes of this subsection, all the parts of a compilation or derivative work constitute one work.

(2) In a case where the copyright owner sustains the burden of proving, and the court finds, that infringement was committed willfully, the court in its discretion may increase the award of statutory damages to a sum of not more than $50,000. In a case where the infringer sustains the burden of proving, and the court finds, that such infringer was not aware and had no reason to believe that his or her acts constituted an infringement of copyright, the court it its discretion may reduce the award of statutory damages to a sum of not less than $100. The court shall remit statutory damages in any case where an infringer believed and had reasonable grounds for believing that his or her use of the copyrighted work was a fair use under section 107, if the infringer was: (i) an employee or agent of a nonprofit educational institution, library, or archives acting within the scope of his or her employment who, or such institution, library, or archives itself, which infringed by reproducing the work in copies or phonorecords; or (ii) a public broadcasting entity which or a person who, as a regular part of the nonprofit activities of a public

broadcasting entity (as defined in subsection (g) of section 118) infringed by performing a published nondramatic literary work or by reproducing a transmission program embodying a performance of such a work.

17 USC 505.

§ 505. Remedies for infringement: Costs and attorney's fees

In any civil action under this title, the court in its discretion may allow the recovery of full costs by or against any party other than the United States or an officer thereof. Except as otherwise provided by this title, the court may also award a reasonable attorney's fee to the prevailing party as part of the costs.

17 USC 506.

§ 506. Criminal offenses

(a) CRIMINAL INFRINGEMENT.—Any person who infringes a copyright willfully and for purposes of commercial advantage or private financial gain shall be fined not more than $10,000 or imprisoned for not more than one year, or both: *Provided*, *however*, That any person who infringes willfully and for purposes of commercial advantage or private financial gain the copyright in a sound recording afforded by subsections (1), (2), or (3) of section 106 or the copyright in a motion picture afforded by subsections (1), (3), or (4) of section 106 shall be fined not more than $25,000 or imprisoned for not more than one year, or both, for the first such offense and shall be fined not more than $50,000 or imprisoned for not more than two years, or both, for any subsequent offense.

(b) FORFEITURE AND DESTRUCTION.—When any person is convicted of any violation of subsection (a), the court in its judgment of conviction shall, in addition to the penalty therein prescribed, order the forfeiture and destruction or other disposition of all infringing copies or phonorecords and all implements, devices, or equipment used in the manufacture of such infringing copies or phonorecords.

(c) FRAUDULENT COPYRIGHT NOTICE.—Any person who, with fraudulent intent, places on any article a notice of copyright or words of the same purport that such person knows to be false, or who, with fraudulent intent, publicly distributes or imports for public distribution any article bearing such notice or words that such person knows to be false, shall be fined not more than $2,500.

(d) FRAUDULENT REMOVAL OF COPYRIGHT NOTICE.—Any person who, with fraudulent intent, removes or alters any notice of copyright appearing on a copy of a copyrighted work shall be fined not more than $2,500.

(e) FALSE REPRESENTATION.—Any person who knowingly makes a false representation of a material fact in the application for copyright registration provided for by section 409, or in any written statement filed in connection with the application, shall be fined not more than $2,500.

17 USC 507.

§ 507. Limitations on actions

(a) CRIMINAL PROCEEDINGS.—No criminal proceeding shall be maintained under the provisions of this title unless it is commenced within three years after the cause of action arose.

(b) CIVIL ACTIONS.—No civil action shall be maintained under the provisions of this title unless it is commenced within three years after the claim accrued.

17 USC 508.

§ 508. Notification of filing and determination of actions

(a) Within one month after the filing of any action under this title, the clerks of the courts of the United States shall send written notification to the Register of Copyrights setting forth, as far as is shown by the papers filed in the court, the names and addresses of the parties and the title, author, and registration number of each work involved in the action. If any other copyrighted work is later included in the action by amendment, answer, or other pleading, the clerk shall also send a notification concerning it to the Register within one month after the pleading is filed.

(b) Within one month after any final order or judgment is issued in the case, the clerk of the court shall notify the Register of it, sending with the notification a copy of the order or judgment together with the written opinion, if any, of the court.

(c) Upon receiving the notifications specified in this section, the Register shall make them a part of the public records of the Copyright Office.

§ 509. Seizure and forfeiture 17 USC 509.

(a) All copies or phonorecords manufactured, reproduced, distributed, sold, or otherwise used, intended for use, or possessed with intent to use in violation of section 506(a), and all plates, molds, matrices, masters, tapes, film negatives, or other articles by means of which such copies or phonorecords may be reproduced, and all electronic, mechanical, or other devices for manufacturing, reproducing, or assembling such copies or phonorecords may be seized and forfeited to the United States.

(b) The applicable procedures relating to (i) the seizure, summary and judicial forfeiture, and condemnation of vessels, vehicles, merchandise, and baggage for violations of the customs laws contained in title 19, (ii) the disposition of such vessels, vehicles, merchandise, and baggage or the proceeds from the sale thereof, (iii) the remission or mitigation of such forfeiture, (iv) the compromise of claims, and (v) the award of compensation to informers in respect of such forfeitures, shall apply to seizures and forfeitures incurred, or alleged to have been incurred, under the provisions of this section, insofar as applicable and not inconsistent with the provisions of this section; except that such duties as are imposed upon any officer or employee of the Treasury Department or any other person with respect to the seizure and forfeiture of vessels, vehicles, merchandise; and baggage under the provisions of the customs laws contained in title 19 shall be performed with respect to seizure and forfeiture of all articles described in subsection (a) by such officers, agents, or other persons as may be authorized or designated for that purpose by the Attorney General. 19 USC 1 et seq.

§ 510. Remedies for alteration of programing by cable systems 17 USC 510.

(a) In any action filed pursuant to section 111(c)(3), the following remedies shall be available:

(1) Where an action is brought by a party identified in subsections (b) or (c) of section 501, the remedies provided by sections 502 through 505, and the remedy provided by subsection (b) of this section; and

(2) When an action is brought by a party identified in subsection (d) of section 501, the remedies provided by sections 502 and 505, together with any actual damages suffered by such party as a result of the infringement, and the remedy provided by subsection (b) of this section.

(b) In any action filed pursuant to section 111(c)(3), the court may decree that, for a period not to exceed thirty days, the cable system shall be deprived of the benefit of a compulsory license for one or more distant signals carried by such cable system.

Chapter 6.—MANUFACTURING REQUIREMENTS AND IMPORTATION

17 USC 601.

§ 601. Manufacture, importation, and public distribution of certain copies

(a) Prior to July 1, 1982, and except as provided by subsection (b), the importation into or public distribution in the United States of copies of a work consisting preponderantly of nondramtic literary material that is in the English language and is protected under this title is prohibited unless the portions consisting of such material have been manufactured in the United States or Canada.

(b) The provisions of subsection (a) do not apply—

(1) where, on the date when importation is sought or public distribution in the United States is made, the author of any substantial part of such material is neither a national nor a domiciliary of the United States or, if such author is a national of the United States, he or she has been domiciled outside the United States for a continuous period of at least one year immediately preceding that date; in the case of a work made for hire, the exemption provided by this clause does not apply unless a subsustantial part of the work was prepared for an employer or other person who is not a national or domiciliary of the United States or a domestic corporation or enterprise;

(2) where the United States Customs Service is presented with an import statement issued under the seal of the Copyright Office, in which case a total of no more than two thousand copies of any one such work shall be allowed entry; the import statement shall be issued upon request to the copyright owner or to a person designated by such owner at the time of registration for the work under section 408 or at any time thereafter;

(3) where importation is sought under the authority or for the use, other than in schools, of the Government of the United States or of any State or political subdivision of a State;

(4) where importation, for use and not for sale, is sought—

(A) by any person with respect to no more than one copy of any work at any one time;

(B) by any person arriving from outside the United States, with respect to copies forming part of such person's personal baggage; or

(C) by an organization operated for scholarly, educational, or religious purposes and not for private gain, with respect to copies intended to form a part of its library;

(5) where the copies are reproduced in raised characters for the use of the blind; or

(6) where, in addition to copies imported under clauses (3) and (4) of this subsection, no more than two thousand copies of any one such work, which have not been manufactured in the United States or Canada, are publicly distributed in the United States; or

(7) where, on the date when importation is sought or public distribution in the United States is made—

(A) the author of any substantial part of such material is an individual and receives compensation for the transfer or license of the right to distribute the work in the United States; and

(B) the first publication of the work has previously taken place outside the United States under a transfer or license granted by such author to a transferee or licensee who was not a national or domiciliary of the United States or a domestic corporation or enterprise; and

(C) there has been no publication of an authorized edition of the work of which the copies were manufactured in the United States; and

(D) the copies were reproduced under a transfer or license granted by such author or by the transferee or licensee of the right of first publication as mentioned in subclause (B), and the transferee or the licensee of the right of reproduction was not a national or domiciliary of the United States or a domestic corporation or enterprise.

(c) The requirement of this section that copies be manufactured in the United States or Canada is satisfied if—

(1) in the case where the copies are printed directly from type that has been set, or directly from plates made from such type, the setting of the type and the making of the plates have been performed in the United States or Canada; or

(2) in the case where the making of plates by a lithographic or photoengraving process is a final or intermediate step preceding the printing of the copies, the making of the plates has been performed in the United States or Canada; and

(3) in any case, the printing or other final process of producing multiple copies and any binding of the copies have been performed in the United States or Canada.

(d) Importation or public distribution of copies in violation of this section does not invalidate protection for a work under this title. However, in any civil action or criminal proceeding for infringement of the exclusive rights to reproduce and distribute copies of the work, the infringer has a complete defense with respect to all of the nondramatic literary material comprised in the work and any other parts of the work in which the exclusive rights to reproduce and distribute copies are owned by the same person who owns such exclusive rights in the nondramatic literary material, if the infringer proves—

(1) that copies of the work have been imported into or publicly distributed in the United States in violation of this section by or with the authority of the owner of such exclusive rights; and

(2) that the infringing copies were manufactured in the United States or Canada in accordance with the provisions of subsection (c); and

(3) that the infringement was commenced before the effective date of registration for an authorized edition of the work, the copies of which have been manufactured in the United States or Canada in accordance with the provisions of subsection (c).

(e) In any action for infringement of the exclusive rights to reproduce and distribute copies of a work containing material required by this section to be manufactured in the United States or Canada, the copyright owner shall set forth in the complaint the names of the persons or organizations who performed the processes specified by subsection (c) with respect to that material, and the places where those processes were performed.

§ 602. Infringing importation of copies or phonorecords 17 USC 602.

(a) Importation into the United States, without the authority of the owner of copyright under this title, of copies or phonorecords of a work that have been acquired outside the United States is an infringement of the exclusive right to distribute copies or phonorecords under section 106, actionable under section 501. This subsection does not apply to—

(1) importation of copies or phonorecords under the authority or for the use of the Government of the United States or of any State or political subdivision of a State, but not including copies or phonorecords for use in schools, or copies of any audiovisual work imported for purposes other than archival use;

(2) importation, for the private use of the importer and not for distribution, by any person with respect to no more than one copy or phonorecord of any one work at any one time, or by any person arriving from outside the United States with respect to copies or phonorecords forming part of such person's personal baggage; or

(3) importation by or for an organization operated for scholarly, educational, or religious purposes and not for private gain, with respect to no more than one copy of an audiovisual work solely for its archival purposes, and no more than five copies or phonorecords of any other work for its library lending or archival purposes, unless the importation of such copies or phonorecords is part of an activity consisting of systematic reproduction or distribution, engaged in by such organization in violation of the provisions of section 108(g)(2).

(b) In a case where the making of the copies or phonorecords would have constituted an infringement of copyright if this title had been applicable, their importation is prohibited. In a case where the copies or phonorecords were lawfully made, the United States Customs Service has no authority to prevent their importation unless the provisions of section 601 are applicable. In either case, the Secretary of the Treasury is authorized to prescribe, by regulation, a procedure under which any person claiming an interest in the copyright in a particular work may, upon payment of a specified fee, be entitled to notification by the Customs Service of the importation of articles that appear to be copies or phonorecords of the work.

Regulations.

17 USC 603.

§ 603. Importation prohibitions: Enforcement and disposition of excluded articles

Regulations.

(a) The Secretary of the Treasury and the United States Postal Service shall separately or jointly make regulations for the enforcement of the provisions of this title prohibiting importation.

(b) These regulations may require, as a condition for the exclusion of articles under section 602—

(1) that the person seeking exclusion obtain a court order enjoining importation of the articles; or

Surety bond.

(2) that the person seeking exclusion furnish proof, of a specified nature and in accordance with prescribed procedures, that the copyright in which such person claims an interest is valid and that the importation would violate the prohibition in section 602; the person seeking exclusion may also be required to post a surety bond for any injury that may result if the detention or exclusion of the articles proves to be unjustified.

(c) Articles imported in violation of the importation prohibitions of this title are subject to seizure and forfeiture in the same manner as property imported in violation of the customs revenue laws. Forfeited articles shall be destroyed as directed by the Secretary of the Treasury or the court, as the case may be; however, the articles may be returned to the country of export whenever it is shown to the satisfaction of the Secretary of the Treasury that the importer had no reasonable grounds for believing that his or her acts constituted a violation of law.

Chapter 7.—COPYRIGHT OFFICE

§ 701. The Copyright Office: General responsibilities and organization

17 USC 701.

(a) All administrative functions and duties under this title, except as otherwise specified, are the responsibility of the Register of Copyrights as director of the Copyright Office of the Library of Congress. The Register of Copyrights, together with the subordinate officers and employees of the Copyright Office, shall be appointed by the Librarian of Congress, and shall act under the Librarian's general direction and supervision.

Seal.

(b) The Register of Copyrights shall adopt a seal to be used on and after January 1, 1978, to authenticate all certified documents issued by the Copyright Office.

Report to Librarian of Congress.

(c) The Register of Copyrights shall make an annual report to the Librarian of Congress of the work and accomplishments of the Copyright Office during the previous fiscal year. The annual report of the Register of Copyrights shall be published separately and as a part of the annual report of the Librarian of Congress.

(d) Except as provided by section 706(b) and the regulations issued thereunder, all actions taken by the Register of Copyrights under this title are subject to the provisions of the Administrative Procedure Act of June 11, 1946, as amended (c. 324, 60 Stat. 237, title 5, United States Code, Chapter 5, Subchapter II and Chapter 7). 5 USC 551, 701.

§ 702. Copyright Office regulations

17 USC 702.

The Register of Copyrights is authorized to establish regulations not inconsistent with law for the administration of the functions and duties made the responsibility of the Register under this title. All regulations established by the Register under this title are subject to the approval of the Librarian of Congress.

§ 703. Effective date of actions in Copyright Office

17 USC 703.

In any case in which time limits are prescribed under this title for the performance of an action in the Copyright Office, and in which the last day of the prescribed period falls on a Saturday, Sunday, holiday, or other nonbusiness day within the District of Columbia or the Federal Government, the action may be taken on the next succeeding business day, and is effective as of the date when the period expired.

§ 704. Retention and disposition of articles deposited in Copyright Office

17 USC 704.

(a) Upon their deposit in the Copyright Office under sections 407 and 408, all copies, phonorecords, and identifying material, including those deposited in connection with claims that have been refused registration, are the property of the United States Government.

Regulations.

(b) In the case of published works, all copies, phonorecords, and identifying material deposited are available to the Library of Congress for its collections, or for exchange or transfer to any other library. In the case of unpublished works, the Library is entitled, under regulations that the Register of Copyrights shall prescribe, to select any deposits for its collections or for transfer to the National Archives of the United States or to a Federal records center, as defined in section 2901 of title 44.

(c) The Register of Copyrights is authorized, for specific or general categories of works, to make a facsimile reproduction of all or any part of the material deposited under section 408, and to make such reproduction a part of the Copyright Office records of the registration, before transferring such material to the Library of Congress as provided by subsection (b), or before destroying or otherwise disposing of such material as provided by subsection (d).

(d) Deposits not selected by the Library under subsection (b), or identifying portions or reproductions of them, shall be retained under the control of the Copyright Office, including retention in Government storage facilities, for the longest period considered practicable and desirable by the Register of Copyrights and the Librarian of Congress. After that period it is within the joint discretion of the Register and the Librarian to order their destruction or other disposition; but, in the case of unpublished works, no deposit shall be knowingly or intentionally destroyed or otherwise disposed of during its term of copyright unless a facsimile reproduction of the entire deposit has been made a part of the Copyright Office records as provided by subsection (c).

(e) The depositor of copies, phonorecords, or identifying material under section 408, or the copyright owner of record, may request retention, under the control of the Copyright Office, of one or more of such articles for the full term of copyright in the work. The Register of Copyrights shall prescribe, by regulation, the conditions under which such requests are to be made and granted, and shall fix the fee to be charged under section 708(a)(11) if the request is granted.

17 USC 705.

§ 705. Copyright Office records: Preparation, maintenance, public inspection, and searching

(a) The Register of Copyrights shall provide and keep in the Copyright Office records of all deposits, registrations, recordations, and other actions taken under this title, and shall prepare indexes of all such records.

(b) Such records and indexes, as well as the articles deposited in connection with completed copyright registrations and retained under the control of the Copyright Office, shall be open to public inspection.

Report.

(c) Upon request and payment of the fee specified by section 708, the Copyright Office shall make a search of its public records, indexes, and deposits, and shall furnish a report of the information they disclose with respect to any particular deposits, registrations, or recorded documents.

17 USC 706.

§ 706. Copies of Copyright Office records

(a) Copies may be made of any public records or indexes of the Copyright Office; additional certificates of copyright registration and copies of any public records or indexes may be furnished upon request and payment of the fees specified by section 708.

(b) Copies or reproductions of deposited articles retained under the control of the Copyright Office shall be authorized or furnished only under the conditions specified by the Copyright Office regulations.

17 USC 707

§ 707. Copyright Office forms and publications

(a) Catalog of Copyright Entries.—The Register of Copyrights shall compile and publish at periodic intervals catalogs of all copyright registrations. These catalogs shall be divided into parts in accordance with the various classes of works, and the Register has discretion to determine, on the basis of practicability and usefulness, the form and frequency of publication of each particular part.

(b) OTHER PUBLICATIONS.—The Register shall furnish, free of charge upon request, application forms for copyright registration and general informational material in connection with the functions of the Copyright Office. The Register also has the authority to publish compilations of information, bibliographies, and other material he or she considers to be of value to the public.

(c) DISTRIBUTION OF PUBLICATIONS.—All publications of the Copyright Office shall be furnished to depository libraries as specified under section 1905 of title 44, and, aside from those furnished free of charge, shall be offered for sale to the public at prices based on the cost of reproduction and distribution.

§ 708. Copyright Office fees

17 USC 708.

(a) The following fees shall be paid to the Register of Copyrights:

(1) for the registration of a copyright claim or a supplementary registration under section 408, including the issuance of a certificate of registration, $10;

(2) for the registration of a claim to renewal of a subsisting copyright in its first term under section 304(a), including the issuance of a certificate of registration, $6;

(3) for the issuance of a receipt for a deposit under section 407, $2;

(4) for the recordation, as provided by section 205, of a transfer of copyright ownership or other document of six pages or less, covering no more than one title, $10; for each page over six and each title over one, 50 cents additional;

(5) for the filing, under section 115(b), of a notice of intention to make phonorecords, $6;

(6) for the recordation, under section 302(c), of a statement revealing the identity of an author of an anonymous or pseudonymous work, or for the recordation, under section 302(d), of a statement relating to the death of an author, $10 for a document of six pages or less, covering no more than one title; for each page over six and for each title over one, $1 additional;

(7) for the issuance, under section 601, of an import statement, $3;

(8) for the issuance, under section 706, of an additional certificate of registration, $4;

(9) for the issuance of any other certification, $4; the Register of Copyrights has discretion, on the basis of their cost, to fix the fees for preparing copies of Copyright Office records, whether they are to be certified or not;

(10) for the making and reporting of a search as provided by section 705, and for any related services, $10 for each hour or fraction of an hour consumed;

(11) for any other special services requiring a substantial amount of time or expense, such fees as the Register of Copyrights may fix on the basis of the cost of providing the service.

(b) The fees prescribed by or under this section are applicable to the United States Government and any of its agencies, employees, or officers, but the Register of Copyrights has discretion to waive the requirement of this subsection in occasional or isolated cases involving relatively small amounts. Waiver.

(c) The Register of Copyrights shall deposit all fees in the Treasury of the United States in such manner as the Secretary of the Treasury directs. The Register may, in accordance with regulations that Regulations.

he or she shall prescribe, refund any sum paid by mistake or in excess of the fee required by this section; however, before making a refund in any case involving a refusal to register a claim under section 410(b), the Register may deduct all or any part of the prescribed registration fee to cover the reasonable administrative costs of processing the claim.

17 USC 709.

§ 709. Delay in delivery caused by disruption of postal or other services

In any case in which the Register of Copyrights determines, on the basis of such evidence as the Register may by regulation require, that a deposit, application, fee, or any other material to be delivered to the Copyright Office by a particular date, would have been received in the Copyright Office in due time except for a general disruption or suspension of postal or other transportation or communications services, the actual receipt of such material in the Copyright Office within one month after the date on which the Register determines that the disruption or suspension of such services has terminated, shall be considered timely.

17 USC 710.

§ 710. Reproduction for use of the blind and physically handicapped: Voluntary licensing forms and procedures

Regulation.

The Register of Copyrights shall, after consultation with the Chief of the Division for the Blind and Physically Handicapped and other appropriate officials of the Library of Congress, establish by regulation standardized forms and procedures by which, at the time applications covering certain specified categories of nondramatic literary works are submitted for registration under section 408 of this title, the copyright owner may voluntarily grant to the Library of Congress a license to reproduce the copyrighted work by means of Braille or similar tactile symbols, or by fixation of a reading of the work in a phonorecord, or both, and to distribute the resulting copies or phonorecords solely for the use of the blind and physically handicapped and under limited conditions to be specified in the standardized forms.

Chapter 8.—COPYRIGHT ROYALTY TRIBUNAL

Sec.

17 USC 801.

§ 801. Copyright Royalty Tribunal: Establishment and purpose

(a) There is hereby created an independent Copyright Royalty Tribunal in the legislative branch.

(b) Subject to the provisions of this chapter, the purposes of the Tribunal shall be—

(1) to make determinations concerning the adjustment of reasonable copyright royalty rates as provided in sections 115 and 116, and to make determinations as to reasonable terms and rates of royalty payments as provided in section 118. The rates applicable under sections 115 and 116 shall be calculated to achieve the following objectives:

(A) To maximize the availability of creative works to the public;

(B) To afford the copyright owner a fair return for his creative work and the copyright user a fair income under existing economic conditions;

(C) To reflect the relative roles of the copyright owner and the copyright user in the product made available to the public with respect to relative creative contribution, technological contribution, capital investment, cost, risk, and contribution to the opening of new markets for creative expression and media for their communication;

(D) To minimize any disruptive impact on the structure of the industries involved and on generally prevailing industry practices.

(2) to make determinations concerning the adjustment of the copyright royalty rates in section 111 solely in accordance with the following provisions:

(A) The rates established by section 111(d)(2)(B) may be adjusted to reflect (i) national monetary inflation or deflation or (ii) changes in the average rates charged cable subscribers for the basic service of providing secondary transmissions to maintain the real constant dollar level of the royalty fee per subscriber which existed as of the date of enactment of this Act: *Provided*, That if the average rates charged cable system subscribers for the basic service of providing secondary transmissions are changed so that the average rates exceed national monetary inflation, no change in the rates established by section 111(d)(2)(B) shall be permitted: *And provided further*, That no increase in the royalty fee shall be permitted based on any reduction in the average number of distant signal equivalents per subscriber. The Commission may consider all factors relating to the maintenance of such level of payments including, as an extenuating factor, whether the cable industry has been restrained by subscriber rate regulating authorities from increasing the rates for the basic service of providing secondary transmissions.

(B) In the event that the rules and regulations of the Federal Communications Commission are amended at any time after April 15, 1976, to permit the carriage by cable systems of additional television broadcast signals beyond the local service area of the primary transmitters of such signals, the royalty rates established by section 111(d)(2)(B) may be adjusted to insure that the rates for the additional distant signal equivalents resulting from such carriage are reasonable in the light of the changes effected by the amendment to such rules and regulations. In determining the reasonableness of rates proposed following an amendment of Federal Communications Commission rules and regulations, the Copyright Royalty Tribunal shall consider, among other factors, the economic impact on copyright owners and users: *Provided*, That no adjustment in royalty rates shall be made under this subclause with respect to any distant signal equivalent or fraction thereof represented by (i) carriage of any signal permitted under the rules and regulations of the Federal Communications Commission in effect on April 15, 1976, or the carriage of a signal of the same type (that is, independent, network, or noncommercial educational) substituted for such permitted signal, or (ii) a television broadcast signal first carried after April 15, 1976, pursuant to an individual waiver of the rules and regulations of the Federal Communications Commission, as such rules and regulations were in effect on April 15, 1976.

(C) In the event of any change in the rules and regulations of the Federal Communications Commission with respect to syndicated and sports program exclusivity after April 15, 1976, the rates established by section 111(d)(2)(B) may be adjusted to assure that such rates are reasonable in light of the changes to such rules and regulations, but any such adjustment shall apply only to the affected television broadcast signals carried on those systems affected by the change.

(D) The gross receipts limitations established by section 111(d)(2)(C) and (D) shall be adjusted to reflect national monetary inflation or deflation or changes in the average rates charged cable system subscribers for the basic service of providing secondary transmissions to maintain the real constant dollar value of the exemption provided by such section; and the royalty rate specified therein shall not be subject to adjustment; and

(3) to distribute royalty fees deposited with the Register of Copyrights under sections 111 and 116, and to determine, in cases where controversy exists, the distribution of such fees.

Notice.

(c) As soon as possible after the date of enactment of this Act, and no later than six months following such date, the President shall publish a notice announcing the initial appointments provided in section 802, and shall designate an order of seniority among the initially-appointed commissioners for purposes of section 802(b).

17 USC 802.

§ 802. Membership of the Tribunal

(a) The Tribunal shall be composed of five commissioners appointed by the President with the advice and consent of the Senate for a term of seven years each; of the first five members appointed, three shall be designated to serve for seven years from the date of the notice specified in section 801(c), and two shall be designated to serve for five years from such date, respectively. Commissioners shall be compensated at the highest rate now or hereafter prescribe for grade 18 of the General Schedule pay rates (5 U.S.C. 5332).

(b) Upon convening the commissioners shall elect a chairman from among the commissioners appointed for a full seven-year term. Such chairman shall serve for a term of one year. Thereafter, the most senior commissioner who has not previously served as chairman shall serve as chairman for a period of one year, except that, if all commissioners have served a full term as chairman, the most senior commissioner who has served the least number of terms as chairman shall be designated as chairman.

(c) Any vacancy in the Tribunal shall not affect its powers and shall be filled, for the unexpired term of the appointment, in the same manner as the original appointment was made.

17 USC 803.

§ 803. Procedures of the Tribunal

(a) The Tribunal shall adopt regulations, not inconsistent with law, governing its procedure and methods of operation. Except as otherwise provided in this chapter, the Tribunal shall be subject to the provisions of the Administrative Procedure Act of June 11, 1946, as amended (c. 324, 60 Stat. 237, title 5, United States Code, chapter 5, subchapter II and chapter 7).

5 USC 551, 701.

Publication in Federal Register.

(b) Every final determination of the Tribunal shall be published in the Federal Register. It shall state in detail the criteria that the Tribunal determined to be applicable to the particular proceeding, the various facts that it found relevant to its determination in that proceeding, and the specific reasons for its determination.

§ 804. Institution and conclusion of proceedings 17 USC 804.

(a) With respect to proceedings under section 801(b)(1) concerning the adjustment of royalty rates as provided in sections 115 and 116, and with respect to proceedings under section 801(b)(2)(A) and (D)—

(1) on January 1, 1980, the Chairman of the Tribunal shall cause to be published in the Federal Register notice of commencement of proceedings under this chapter; and

(2) during the calendar years specified in the following schedule, any owner or user of a copyrighted work whose royalty rates are specified by this title, or by a rate established by the Tribunal, may file a petition with the Tribunal declaring that the petitioner requests an adjustment of the rate. The Tribunal shall make a determination as to whether the applicant has a significant interest in the royalty rate in which an adjustment is requested. If the Tribunal determines that the petitioner has a significant interest, the Chairman shall cause notice of this determination, with the reasons therefor, to be published in the Federal Register, together with notice of commencement of proceedings under this chapter.

(A) In proceedings under section 801(b)(2) (A) and (D), such petition may be filed during 1985 and in each subsequent fifth calendar year.

(B) In proceedings under section 801(b)(1) concerning the adjustment of royalty rates as provided in section 115, such petition may be filed in 1987 and in each subsequent tenth calendar year.

(C) In proceedings under section 801(b)(1) concerning the adjustment of royalty rates under section 116, such petition may be filed in 1990 and in each subsequent tenth calendar year.

(b) With respect to proceedings under subclause (B) or (C) of section 801(b)(2), following an event described in either of those subsections, any owner or user of a copyrighted work whose royalty rates are specified by section 111, or by a rate established by the Tribunal, may, within twelve months, file a petition with the Tribunal declaring that the petitioner requests an adjustment of the rate. In this event the Tribunal shall proceed as in subsection (a)(2), above. Any change in royalty rates made by the Tribunal pursuant to this subsection may be reconsidered in 1980, 1985, and each fifth calendar year thereafter, in accordance with the provisions in section 801(b)(2) (B) or (C), as the case may be.

(c) With respect to proceedings under section 801(b)(1), concerning the determination of reasonable terms and rates of royalty payments as provided in section 118, the Tribunal shall proceed when and as provided by that section.

(d) With respect to proceedings under section 801(b)(3), concerning the distribution of royalty fees in certain circumstances under sections 111 or 116, the Chairman of the Tribunal shall, upon determination by the Tribunal that a controversy exists concerning such distribution, cause to be published in the Federal Register notice of commencement of proceedings under this chapter.

(e) All proceedings under this chapter shall be initiated without delay following publication of the notice specified in this section, and the Tribunal shall render its final decision in any such proceeding within one year from the date of such publication.

17 USC 805.

§ 805. Staff of the Tribunal

(a) The Tribunal is authorized to appoint and fix the compensation of such employees as may be necessary to carry out the provisions of this chapter, and to prescribe their functions and duties.

(b) The Tribunal may procure temporary and intermittent services to the same extent as is authorized by section 3109 of title 5. 5 USC 3109.

17 USC 806.

§ 806. Administrative support of the Tribunal

(a) The Library of Congress shall provide the Tribunal with necessary administrative services, including those related to budgeting, accounting, financial reporting, travel, personnel, and procurement. The Tribunal shall pay the Library for such services, either in advance or by reimbursement from the funds of the Tribunal, at amounts to be agreed upon between the Librarian and the Tribunal.

(b) The Library of Congress is authorized to disburse funds for the Tribunal, under regulations prescribed jointly by the Librarian of Congress and the Tribunal and approved by the Comptroller General. Such regulations shall establish requirements and procedures under which every voucher certified for payment by the Library of Congress under this chapter shall be supported with a certification by a duly authorized officer or employee of the Tribunal, and shall prescribe the responsibilities and accountability of said officers and employees of the Tribunal with respect to such certifications.

17 USC 807.

§ 807. Deduction of costs of proceedings

Before any funds are distributed pursuant to a final decision in a proceeding involving distribution of royalty fees, the Tribunal shall assess the reasonable costs of such proceeding.

17 USC 808.

§ 808. Reports

In addition to its publication of the reports of all final determinations as provided in section 803(b), the Tribunal shall make an annual report to the President and the Congress concerning the Tribunal's work during the preceding fiscal year, including a detailed fiscal statement of account.

17 USC 809.

§ 809. Effective date of final determinations

Any final determination by the Tribunal under this chapter shall become effective thirty days following its publication in the Federal Register as provided in section 803(b), unless prior to that time an appeal has been filed pursuant to section 810, to vacate, modify, or correct such determination, and notice of such appeal has been served on all parties who appeared before the Tribunal in the proceeding in question. Where the proceeding involves the distribution of royalty fees under sections 111 or 116, the Tribunal shall, upon the expiration of such thirty-day period, distribute any royalty fees not subject to an appeal filed pursuant to section 810.

17 USC 810.

§ 810. Judicial review

Any final decision of the Tribunal in a proceeding under section 801(b) may be appealed to the United States Court of Appeals, within thirty days after its publication in the Federal Register by an aggrieved party. The judicial review of the decision shall be had, in accordance with chapter 7 of title 5, on the basis of the record before the Tribunal. No court shall have jurisdiction to review a final decision of the Tribunal except as provided in this section. 5 USC 701.

TRANSITIONAL AND SUPPLEMENTARY PROVISIONS

17 USC note prec. 101.

SEC. 102. This Act becomes effective on January 1, 1978, except as otherwise expressly provided by this Act, including provisions of the first section of this Act. The provisions of sections 118, 304(b), and chapter 8 of title 17, as amended by the first section of this Act, take effect upon enactment of this Act.

SEC. 103. This Act does not provide copyright protection for any work that goes into the public domain before January 1, 1978. The exclusive rights, as provided by section 106 of title 17 as amended by the first section of this Act, to reproduce a work in phonorecords and to distribute phonorecords of the work, do not extend to any nondramatic musical work copyrighted before July 1, 1909. 17 USC note prec. 101.

SEC. 104. All proclamations issued by the President under section 1(e) or 9(b) of title 17 as it existed on December 31, 1977, or under previous copyright statutes of the United States, shall continue in force until terminated, suspended, or revised by the President. 17 USC note prec. 101.

SEC. 105. (a) (1) Section 505 of title 44 is amended to read as follows:

"§ 505. Sale of duplicate plates 44 USC 505.

"The Public Printer shall sell, under regulations of the Joint Committee on Printing to persons who may apply, additional or duplicate stereotype or electrotype plates from which a Government publication is printed, at a price not to exceed the cost of composition, the metal, and making to the Government, plus 10 per centum, and the full amount of the price shall be paid when the order is filed.".

(2) The item relating to section 505 in the sectional analysis at the beginning of chapter 5 of title 44, is amended to read as follows:

"505. Sale of duplicate plates.".

(b) Section 2113 of title 44 is amended to read as follows:

"§ 2113. Limitation on liability 44 USC 2113.

"When letters and other intellectual productions (exclusive of patented material, published works under copyright protection, and unpublished works for which copyright registration has been made) come into the custody or possession of the Administrator of General Services, the United States or its agents are not liable for infringement of copyright or analogous rights arising out of use of the materials for display, inspection, research, reproduction, or other purposes.".

(c) In section 1498(b) of title 28, the phrase "section 101(b) of title 17" is amended to read "section 504(c) of title 17". 28 USC 1498.

(d) Section 543(a)(4) of the Internal Revenue Code of 1954, as amended, is amended by striking out "(other than by reason of section 2 or 6 thereof)". 26 USC 543.

(e) Section 3202(a) of title 39 is amended by striking out clause (5). Section 3206 of title 39 is amended by deleting the words "subsections (b) and (c)" and inserting "subsection (b)" in subsection (a), and by deleting subsection (c). Section 3206(d) is renumbered (c). 39 USC 3202, 3206.

(f) Subsection (a) of section 290(e) of title 15 is amended by deleting the phrase "section 8" and inserting in lieu thereof the phrase "section 105". 15 USC 290e.

(g) Section 131 of title 2 is amended by deleting the phrase "deposit to secure copyright," and inserting in lieu thereof the phrase "acquisition of material under the copyright law,". 2 USC 131.

SEC. 106. In any case where, before January 1, 1978, a person has lawfully made parts of instruments serving to reproduce mechanically a copyrighted work under the compulsory license provisions of section 1(e) of title 17 as it existed on December 31, 1977, such person may continue to make and distribute such parts embodying the same mechanical reproduction without obtaining a new compulsory license 17 USC 115 note.

under the terms of section 115 of title 17 as amended by the first section of this Act. However, such parts made on or after January 1, 1978, constitute phonorecords and are otherwise subject to the provisions of said section 115.

17 USC 304 note. SEC. 107. In the case of any work in which an ad interim copyright is subsisting or is capable of being secured on December 31, 1977, under section 22 of title 17 as it existed on that date, copyright protection is hereby extended to endure for the term or terms provided by section 304 of title 17 as amended by the first section of this Act.

17 USC 401 note. SEC. 108. The notice provisions of sections 401 through 403 of title 17 as amended by the first section of this Act apply to all copies or phonorecords publicly distributed on or after January 1, 1978. However, in the case of a work published before January 1, 1978, compliance with the notice provisions of title 17 either as it existed on December 31, 1977, or as amended by the first section of this Act, is adequate with respect to copies publicly distributed after December 31, 1977.

17 USC 410 note. SEC. 109. The registration of claims to copyright for which the required deposit, application, and fee were received in the Copyright Office before January 1, 1978, and the recordation of assignments of copyright or other instruments received in the Copyright Office before January 1, 1978, shall be made in accordance with title 17 as it existed on December 31, 1977.

17 USC 407 note. SEC. 110. The demand and penalty provisions of section 14 of title 17 as it existed on December 31, 1977, apply to any work in which copyright has been secured by publication with notice of copyright on or before that date, but any deposit and registration made after that date in response to a demand under that section shall be made in accordance with the provisions of title 17 as amended by the first section of this Act.

SEC. 111. Section 2318 of title 18 of the United States Code is amended to read as follows:

18 USC 2318.

"§ 2318. Transportation, sale or receipt of phonograph records bearing forged or counterfeit labels

"(a) Whoever knowingly and with fraudulent intent transports, causes to be transported, receives, sells, or offers for sale in interstate or foreign commerce any phonograph record, disk, wire, tape, film, or other article on which sounds are recorded, to which or upon which is stamped, pasted, or affixed any forged or counterfeited label, knowing the label to have been falsely made, forged, or counterfeited shall be fined not more than $10,000 or imprisoned for not more than one year, or both, for the first such offense and shall be fined not more than $25,000 or imprisoned for not more than two years, or both, for any subsequent offense.

"(b) When any person is convicted of any violation of subsection (a), the court in its judgment of conviction shall, in addition to the penalty therein prescribed, order the forfeiture and destruction or other disposition of all counterfeit labels and all articles to which counterfeit labels have been affixed or which were intended to have had such labels affixed.".

"(c) Except to the extent they are inconsistent with the provisions of this title, all provisions of section 509, title 17, United States Code, are applicable to violations of subsection (a).".

17 USC 501 note. SEC. 112. All causes of action that arose under title 17 before January 1, 1978, shall be governed by title 17 as it existed when the cause of action arose.

SEC. 113. (a) The Librarian of Congress (hereinafter referred to as the "Librarian") shall establish and maintain in the Library of Congress a library to be known as the American Television and Radio Archives (hereinafter referred to as the "Archives"). The purpose of the Archives shall be to preserve a permanent record of the television and radio programs which are the heritage of the people of the United States and to provide access to such programs to historians and scholars without encouraging or causing copyright infringement.

American Television and Radio Archives Act.
2 USC 170.

(1) The Librarian, after consultation with interested organizations and individuals, shall determine and place in the Archives such copies and phonorecords of television and radio programs transmitted to the public in the United States and in other countries which are of present or potential public or cultural interest, historical significance, cognitive value, or otherwise worthy of preservation, including copies and phonorecords of published and unpublished transmission programs—

(A) acquired in accordance with sections 407 and 408 of title 17 as amended by the first section of this Act; and

(B) transferred from the existing collections of the Library of Congress; and

(C) given to or exchanged with the Archives by other libraries, archives, organizations, and individuals; and

(D) purchased from the owner thereof.

(2) The Librarian shall maintain and publish appropriate catalogs and indexes of the collections of the Archives, and shall make such collections available for study and research under the conditions prescribed under this section.

(b) Notwithstanding the provisions of section 106 of title 17 as amended by the first section of this Act, the Librarian is authorized with respect to a transmission program which consists of a regularly scheduled newscast or on-the-spot coverage of news events and, under standards and conditions that the Librarian shall prescribe by regulation—

(1) to reproduce a fixation of such a program, in the same or another tangible form, for the purposes of preservation or security or for distribution under the conditions of clause (3) of this subsection; and

(2) to compile, without abridgment or any other editing, portions of such fixations according to subject matter, and to reproduce such compilations for the purpose of clause (1) of this subsection; and

(3) to distribute a reproduction made under clause (1) or (2) of this subsection—

(A) by loan to a person engaged in research; and

(B) for deposit in a library or archives which meets the requirements of section 108(a) of title 17 as amended by the first section of this Act,

in either case for use only in research and not for further reproduction or performance.

(c) The Librarian or any employee of the Library who is acting under the authority of this section shall not be liable in any action for copyright infringement committed by any other person unless the Librarian or such employee knowingly participated in the act of infringement committed by such person. Nothing in this section shall be construed to excuse or limit liability under title 17 as amended by the first section of this Act for any act not authorized by that title or this section, or for any act performed by a person not authorized to act under that title or this section.

Citation of section.

(d) This section may be cited as the "American Television and Radio Archives Act".

Appropriation authorization. 17 USC note prec. 101.

SEC. 114. There are hereby authorized to be appropriated such funds as may be necessary to carry out the purposes of this Act.

Severability. 17 USC note prec. 101.

SEC. 115. If any provision of title 17, as amended by the first section of this Act, is declared unconstitutional, the validity of the remainder of this title is not affected.

Approved October 19, 1976.

LEGISLATIVE HISTORY:

HOUSE REPORTS: No. 94-1476 (Comm. on the Judiciary) and No. 94-1733 (Comm. of Conference).

SENATE REPORT No. 94-473 (Comm. on the Judiciary).

CONGRESSIONAL RECORD, Vol. 122 (1976):

Feb. 6, 16-19, considered and passed Senate.

Sept. 22, considered and passed Senate, amended.

Sept. 30, Senate and House agreed to conference report.

Note.—A change has been made in the slip law format to provide for one-time preparation of copy to be used for publication of both slip laws and the United States Statutes at Large volumes. Comments from users are invited by the Office of the Federal Register, National Archives and Records Service, Washington, D.C. 20408.

O

Highlights of the New Copyright Law

INTRODUCTION

President Gerald R. Ford signed, on October 19, 1976, the bill for the general revision of the United States copyright law, which became Public Law 94-553 (90 Stat. 2541). The new statute specifies that, with particular exceptions, its provisions are to enter into force on **January 1, 1978.** The new law will supersede the copyright act of 1909, as amended, which will however remain in force until the new enactment takes effect.

HIGHLIGHTS

Some of the highlights of the new statute are listed below. For detailed information about specific changes or new provisions, write to the Copyright Office.

Single National System

Instead of the present dual system of protecting works under the common law before they are published and under the Federal statute after publication, the new law will establish a single system of statutory protection for all copyrightable works, whether published or unpublished.

Duration of Copyright

For works already under statutory protection, the new law retains the present term of copyright of 28 years from first publication (or from registration in some cases), renewable by certain persons for a second period of protection, but it increases the length of the second period to 47 years. Copyrights in their first term **must still be renewed** to receive the full new maximum term of 75 years, but copyrights in their second term between December 31, 1976 and December 31, 1977, are automatically extended up to the maximum of 75 years without the need for further renewal.

For works created after January 1, 1978, the new law provides a term lasting for the author's life, plus an additional 50 years after the author's death. For works made for hire, and for anonymous and pseudonymous works (unless the author's identity is revealed in Copyright Office records), the new term will be 75 years from publication or 100 years from creation, whichever is shorter.

For unpublished works that are already in existence on January 1, 1978, but that are not protected by statutory copyright and have not yet gone into the public domain, the new Act will generally provide automatic Federal copyright protection for the same life-plus-50 or 75/100-year terms prescribed for new works. Special dates of termination are provided for copyrights in older works of this sort.

The new Act does not restore copyright protection for any work that has gone into the public domain.

Termination of Transfers

Under the present law, after the first term of 28 years the renewal copyright reverts in certain situations to the author or other specified beneficiaries. The new law drops the renewal feature except for works already in their first term of statutory protection when the new law takes effect. Instead, for transfers of rights made by an author or certain of the author's heirs after January 1, 1978, the new Act generally permits the author or certain heirs to terminate the transfer after 35 years by serving written notice on the transferee within specified time limits.

For works already under statutory copyright protection, a similar right of termination is provided with respect to transfers covering the newly-added years extending the present maximum term of the copyright from 56 to 75 years. Within certain time limits, an author or specified heirs of the author are generally entitled to file a notice terminating the author's transfers covering any part of the period (usually 19 years) that has now been added to the end of the second term of copyright in a work already under protection when the new law comes into effect.

Government Publications

The new law continues the prohibition in the present law against copyright in "publications of the

United States Government" but clarifies its scope by defining works covered by the prohibition as those prepared by an officer or employee of the U.S. Government as part of that person's official duties.

Fair Use

The new law adds a provision to the statute specifically recognizing the principle of "fair use" as a limitation on the exclusive rights of copyright owners, and indicates factors to be considered in determining whether particular uses fall within this category.

Reproduction by Libraries and Archives

In addition to the provision for "fair use," the new law specifies circumstances under which the making or distribution of single copies of works by libraries and archives for noncommercial purposes do not constitute a copyright infringement.

Copyright Royalty Tribunal

The new law creates a Copyright Royalty Tribunal whose purpose will be to determine whether copyright royalty rates, in certain categories where such rates are established in the law, are reasonable and, if not, to adjust them; it will also in certain circumstances determine the distribution of those statutory royalty fees deposited with the Register of Copyrights.

Sound Recordings

The new law retains the provisions added to the present copyright law in 1972, which accord protection against the unauthorized duplication of sound recordings. The new law does not create a performance right for sound recordings as such.

Recording Rights in Music

The new law makes a number of changes in the present system providing compulsory licensing for the recording of music. Among other things it raises the statutory royalty from the present rate of 2 cents to a rate of 2 and ¾ cents or ½ cent per minute of playing time, whichever amount is larger.

Exempt Performances

The new law removes the present general exemption of public performance of nondramatic literary and musical works where the performance is not "for profit." Instead, it provides several specific exemptions for certain types of nonprofit uses, including performances in classrooms and instructional broadcasting. The law also gives broadcasting organizations a limited privilege of making "ephemeral recordings" of their broadcasts.

Public Broadcasting

Under the new Act, noncommercial transmissions by public broadcasters of published musical and graphic works will be subject to a compulsory license. Copyright owners and public broadcasting entities that do not reach voluntary agreement will be subject to the terms and rates prescribed by the Copyright Royalty Tribunal.

Jukebox Exemption

The new law removes the present exemption for performances of copyrighted music by jukeboxes. It will substitute a system of compulsory licenses based upon the payment by jukebox operators of an annual royalty fee to the Register of Copyrights for later distribution by the Copyright Royalty Tribunal to the copyright owners.

Cable Television

The new law provides for the payment, under a system of compulsory licensing, of certain royalties for the secondary transmission of copyrighted works on cable television systems (CATV). The amounts are to be paid to the Register of Copyrights for later distribution to the copyright owners by the Copyright Royalty Tribunal.

Notice of Copyright

The old law now requires, as a mandatory condition of copyright protection, that the published copies of a work bear a copyright notice. The new enactment calls for a notice on published copies, but omission or errors will not immediately result in forfeiture of the copyright, and can be corrected within certain time limits. Innocent infringers misled by the omission or error will be shielded from liability.

Deposit and Registration

As under the present law, registration will not be a condition of copyright protection but will be a prerequisite to an infringement suit. Subject to certain exceptions, the remedies of statutory damages and attorney's fees will not be available for infringements occurring before registration. Copies or phonorecords of works published with the notice of copyright that are not registered are required to be deposited for the collections of the Library of Congress, not as a condition of copyright protection, but under provisions of the law making the copyright owner subject to certain penalties for failure to deposit after a demand by the Register of Copyrights.

Manufacturing Clause

Certain works must now be manufactured in the United States to have copyright protection here. The new Act would terminate this requirement completely after July 1, 1982. For the period between January 1, 1978 and July 1, 1982, it makes several modifications that will narrow the coverage of the manufacturing clause, will permit the importation of 2,000 copies manufactured abroad instead of the present limit of 1,500 copies, and will equate manufacture in Canada with manufacture in the United States.

BACKGROUND

The present movement for general revision of the copyright law began in 1955 with a program that produced, under the supervision of the Copyright Office, a series of 35 extensive studies of major copyright problems. This was followed by a report of the Register of Copyrights on general revision in 1961, by the preparation in the Copyright Office of a preliminary proposed draft bill, and by a series of meetings with a Panel of Consultants consisting of copyright experts, the majority of them from outside the Government. Following a supplementary report by the Register and a bill introduced in Congress primarily for consideration and comment, the first legislative hearings were held before a subcommittee of the House Judiciary Committee on the basis of a bill introduced in 1965. Also in the same year a companion bill was introduced in the Senate.

In 1967, after the subcommittee had held extensive hearings, the House of Representatives passed a revision bill whose major features were similar to the bill just enacted.

There followed another series of extensive hearings before a subcommittee of the Senate Judiciary Committee but, owing chiefly to an extended impasse on the complex and controversial subject of cable television, the revision bill was prevented from reaching the Senate floor.

Indeed it was not until 1974 that the copyright revision bill was enacted by the Senate. However, that bill, although in its general terms the same as the measure approved by the House in 1967, was different in a number of particulars. In February 1976 the Senate again passed the bill in essentially the same form as the one it had previously passed. Thereafter the House, following further hearings and consideration by the Judiciary subcommittee, passed the bill on September 22, 1976. There followed a meeting of a conference committee of the two Houses, which resolved the differences between the two bills and reported a single version that was enacted by each body and presented to the President.

FURTHER INFORMATION

During the period before January 1, 1978, the Copyright Office will prepare regulations in accordance with the new statute and will also revise its application forms, instructions, and other printed matter to meet the needs under the new law. In addition, the Office plans to hold extensive meetings with interested parties in order to make the transition from the old law to the new as smooth and efficient as possible.

Additional copies of the new statute are available free of charge by writing to the Copyright Office, Library of Congress, Washington, D.C. 20559. You may also have your name added to the Copyright Office Mailing List by sending a written request to the Copyright Office.

Duration of Copyright Under the New Law

INTRODUCTION

The copyright law (Title 17 of the U.S. Code) has been amended by the enactment of a statute for its general revision. The new enactment, Public Law 94-553, was signed by the President on October 19, 1976. The following is a general summary of the provisions of the new statute dealing with duration of copyright. For detailed information, write to the Copyright Office.

WORKS ALREADY UNDER STATUTORY COPYRIGHT PROTECTION

For works already under statutory protection, the new law retains the present term of copyright of 28 years from first publication (or from registration in some cases), renewable by certain persons for a second period of protection, but it increases the length of the second period to 47 years. The maximum total term of copyright protection for works already protected by the Federal statute is increased from 56 years (a first term of 28 years plus a renewal term of 28 years) to 75 years (a first term of 28 years plus a renewal term of 47 years).

The specific situation for such works depends on whether the copyright is in its first term or has already been renewed when the new law comes into effect:

- **Copyrights in their first term on January 1, 1978.** Copyrights in their first term on January 1, 1978, will still have to be renewed during the last (28th) year of the original copyright term to receive the maximum statutory duration. If a valid renewal registration is made at the proper time, the second term will last for 47 years (19 years longer than the present 28-year renewal term).

- **Copyrights in their second term between December 31, 1976 and December 31, 1977.**[1] Copyrights that have already been renewed and are in their second term at any time between December 31, 1976, and December 31, 1977, inclusive, do not need to be renewed again. They are automatically extended to last for a total term of 75 years from the date they were originally secured.

> **NOTE:** This extension applies not only to copyrights less than 56 years old, but also to older copyrights that have previously been extended in duration under a series of Congressional enactments beginning in 1962. As in the case of all other copyrights subsisting in their second term between December 31, 1976, and December 31, 1977, these copyrights will expire at the end of the calendar year in which the 75th anniversary of the original date of copyright occurs.

WORKS CREATED ON OR AFTER JANUARY 1, 1978

For works created on or after January 1, 1978, the new law provides a term lasting for the author's life, plus an additional 50 years after the author's death. For works made for hire, and for anonymous and pseudonymous works (unless the author's identity is revealed in Copyright Office records), the new term will be 75 years from publication or 100 years from creation, whichever is shorter.

[1] A special situation arises where a first-term copyright becomes eligible for renewal during the calendar year 1977. If renewal registration is made before January 1, 1978, the duration of the copyright is extended to the full period of 75 years without the need for a further renewal. If renewal registration has not been made by January 1, 1978, renewal for the second 47-year term can be made under the new law at any time between January 1, 1978, and December 31, 1978.

WORKS IN EXISTENCE BUT NOT COPYRIGHTED ON JANUARY 1, 1978

For unpublished works that are already in existence on January 1, 1978, but that are not protected by statutory copyright and have not yet gone into the public domain, the new Act will generally provide automatic Federal copyright protection for the same life-plus-50 or 75/100-year terms provided for new works.

However, all works in this category are guaranteed at least 25 years of statutory protection; the law specifies that in no case will copyright in a work of this sort expire before December 31, 2002, and if the work is published before that date the term is extended by another 25 years, through the end of 2027.

SPECIAL POINTS TO REMEMBER

Please note the following:

- Copyrights in their first term on January 1, 1978, must still be renewed; if not, they expire at the end of 28 years from the date they were secured.
- Copyrights in their second term on January 1, 1978, are automatically extended up to a maximum of 75 years, without the need for further renewal.
- Works already in the public domain cannot be protected under the new law. The Act provides no

procedure for restoring protection for works in which copyright has been lost for any reason.

- The new law provides that all terms of copyright will run through the end of the calendar year in which they would otherwise expire. This will not only affect the duration of copyrights, but also the time-limits for renewal registrations.

TERMINATION OF GRANTS

For works already under statutory copyright protection on January 1, 1978, the new Act contains special provisions allowing an author, or specified heirs of the author, to file a notice terminating any grant of rights made by the author and covering any part of the period (usually 19 years) that has now been added to the end of the renewal copyright. This right to reclaim ownership of all or part of the extended term is optional; it can be exercised only by certain specified persons in accordance with prescribed conditions and within strict time limits.

With respect to copyrights that are nearly 56 years old, or that are already older than 56 years, the option of serving an advance notice of termination may already be a possibility.

> **NOTE:** Copies of the new statute are available free of charge by writing to the Copyright Office, Library of Congress, Washington, D.C. 20559. You may also have your name added to the Copyright Office Mailing List by sending us a written request.

The Copyright Office

Basic Function

The basic function of the Copyright Office is the administration of the copyright law of the United States (Title 17 of the U.S. Code). The Office examines claims to copyright in a wide variety of literary, artistic and musical works, registers those claims that meet the requirements of the law, and catalogs all registrations. It conducts correspondence about the claims and supplies general information concerning copyright law and registration procedures. Recently the Office has been handling over 1 million pieces of mail and has been making more than 400,000 registrations each year.

Location and Mailing Address

The Copyright Office is located in Building No. 2, Crystal City Mall, Jefferson Davis Highway, Arlington, Virginia. All mail to the Office should be addressed to the **Register of Copyrights, Library of Congress, Washington, D.C. 20559.** The Copyright Office has no branches in other cities. The Public Information Office is open to the public between 8 a.m. and 4 p.m., Mondays through Fridays (except legal holidays).

Patents and Trademarks

Inquiries concerning the scope and requirements of the Federal patent and trademark laws should be addressed to the **Commissioner of Patents and Trademarks, Washington, D.C. 20231.** The Copyright Office does not deal with these matters.

Relationship to the Library of Congress

The administration of the copyright law was entrusted to the Library of Congress by an act of Congress in 1870, and the Copyright Office has been a separate department of the Library since 1897. The collections of the Library have been greatly enriched by its acquisition of a substantial proportion of the copies deposited for registration over the years; in fact, the Act of 1870 and the copyright system have been called "the keystone of the Library of Congress as the National Library of the United States." During fiscal year 1976 the Copyright Office transferred nearly 400,000 copies to the Library for its collections or for exchange with other libraries.

Catalog Card Numbers

The Copyright Office is operationally separate from other departments and units of the Library of Congress and has no authority to provide Library of Congress catalog cards or to assign catalog card numbers. Correspondence concerning Library of Congress catalog cards and the preassignment of catalog card numbers should be addressed to: **CIP Office, Processing Department, Library of Congress, Washington, D.C. 20540.**

Records and Catalogs of the Copyright Office

When a claim is found acceptable for registration a numbered certificate of copyright registration is mailed to the copyright owner or a designated recipient, and the application is bound in book form as an official record of the registration. The Office catalogs each registration, and maintains a card catalog. This catalog now includes over 31 million cards covering more than 16 million registrations. In addition, a *Catalog of Copyright Entries,* divided by subject matter, has been published in book form since 1891. The Office also maintains extensive records and card catalogs covering assignments and other documents relating to the ownership and rights under a copyright. The deposit copies not acquired by the Library of Congress are retained by the Copyright Office for varying periods of time, in some cases indefinitely.

Searching in the Copyright Office

The official records of the Copyright Office, including its card catalogs, are open to public inspection without charge between 8 a.m. and 4 p.m., Mondays through Fridays (except legal holidays). Persons who wish information from the official records and who cannot do their own searching in the Washington area may use the printed *Catalog of Copyright Entries,* copies of which are in many major libraries. Or they may have the Copyright Office make the search and furnish an official report for the hourly search fee of $5.

Certified Copies

When the Copyright Office certifies a copy of one of its records, it attaches a statement attesting that the document is a true copy of the record in question and affixes the official Copyright Office seal. The certification may be valuable in proving the authenticity of the document.

Limitations on the Information Furnished

The Copyright Office is not permitted to offer legal advice or opinions on copyright matters. However, on questions involving the methods of securing copyright, the procedures for making registration, and the practices of the Office, its policy is to be as helpful as possible in furnishing general information. The Office publishes a number of circulars on copyright subjects, including a booklet (Circular 1) entitled "General Information on Copyright." This and other circulars, together with a copy of any of the 20 application forms for copyright registration, may be obtained free of charge from the Copyright Office upon request.

NOTABLE DATES IN AMERICAN COPYRIGHT

May 31, 1790. First copyright law enacted under the U.S. Constitution. Term of 14 years with privilege of renewal for 14 years. Books, maps, and charts protected. Copyright registration to be made in the U.S. District Court where the author or proprietor resided.

June 9, 1790. First copyright entry: *The Philadelphia Spelling Book*.

April 29, 1802. Prints added to protected works.

February 3, 1831. First general revision of the copyright law. Music added to protected works. First term of copyright extended to 28 years with privilege of renewal for 14 years.

August 18, 1856. Dramatic compositions added to protected works.

March 3, 1865. Photographs added to protected works.

July 8, 1870. Second general revision of the copyright law. Copyright activities, including deposit and registration, centralized in the Library of Congress. Works of art added to protected works. Translations and dramatizations mentioned. Indexing of the record of registrations begun.

March 3, 1891. First U.S. copyright law authorizing establishment of copyright relations with foreign countries. Periodicals mentioned. Records of works registered, now called the *Catalog of Copyright Entries,* published in book form for the first time in July 1891.

January 6, 1897. Music protected against unauthorized public performance.

February 19, 1897. Copyright Office established as a separate department of the Library of Congress. Position of Register of Copyrights created.

July 1, 1909. Effective date of third general revision of the copyright law, the basis of the present law. Admission of certain classes of unpublished works to copyright registration. Term of statutory protection for a work first copyrighted in published form measured from the date of publication rather than the date of recordation of the title of the work. Renewal term extended from 14 to 28 years.

August 24, 1912. Motion pictures, previously registered as photographs, added to classes of protected works.

July 13, 1914. President proclaims U.S. adherence to Buenos Aires Copyright Convention of 1910, establishing convention protection between the United States and certain Latin American nations.

July 1, 1940. Effective date of transfer of jurisdiction for the registration of commercial prints and labels from the Patent Office to the Register of Copyrights.

July 30, 1947. Copyright law codified into positive law as Title 17 of the U.S. Code.

January 1, 1953. Recording and performing rights extended to nondramatic literary works.

September 16, 1955. Effective date of the coming into force in the United States of the Universal Copyright Convention as signed at Geneva, Switzerland, on September 6, 1952, which had been proclaimed by the President, and related changes in Title 17 of the U.S. Code.

September 19, 1962. First of nine special acts extending terms of subsisting renewal copyrights pending Congressional action on general copyright law revision.

February 15, 1972. Effective date of act extending limited copyright protection to sound recordings fixed and first published on or after this date.

March 10, 1974. United States becomes the eighth member of the Convention for the Protection of Producers of Phonograms Against Unauthorized Duplication of Their Phonograms which came into force on April 18, 1973.

July 10, 1974. United States becomes a member of the Universal Copyright Convention as revised at Paris, France, on July 24, 1971.

December 31, 1974. Ninth in the series of legislative enactments extending all subsisting copyrights in their second term through December 31, 1976.

October 19, 1976. Fourth general revision of the copyright law signed by the President.

January 1, 1978. Effective date of principal provisions of the new copyright law. In general, the term of protection for works created on or after this date consists of the life of the author and 50 years after the author's death.

REGISTERS OF COPYRIGHTS

THORVALD SOLBERG	
Register	1897–1930
WILLIAM L. BROWN	
Acting Register	1930–1934
Register	1934–1936
CLEMENT L. BOUVÉ	
Register	1936–1943
RICHARD C. DEWOLFE	
Acting Register	1944–1945
SAM BASS WARNER	
Register	1945–1951
ARTHUR FISHER	
Acting Register	1951
Register	1951–1960
ABRAHAM L. KAMINSTEIN	
Register	1960–1971
GEORGE D. CARY	
Register	1971–1973
ABE A. GOLDMAN	
Acting Register	1973
BARBARA RINGER	
Register	1973 to the present

ILLUSTRATED
by
DON
RICO

COPYRIGHT
&
PIRACY
by
WALTER E. HURST
© COPYRIGHT MCMLXXV Walter E. Hurst
2

PLEASE NOTE
COPYRIGHT OWNER IS:
WALTER E. HURST
COPYRIGHT CLAIMANT IS:
WALTER E. HURST
EMPLOYER IS:
WALTER E. HURST
EMPLOYEE FOR HIRE IS:
DON RICO
4

DEFINITION OF "COPYRIGHT":
The right of literary property as recognized and sanctioned by positive law. An intangible, incorporeal right granted by statute to the author or originator of certain literary or artistic productions, whereby he is invested, for a limited period, with the sole and exclusive privilege of multiplying copies of the same and publishing and selling them.

DEFINITION OF "COPYRIGHT"
"Copyright: the exclusive right given by law for a certain term of years to an author, composer, etc., (or his assignee) to print, publish and sell copies of his original work."
OXFORD ENGLISH DICTIONARY

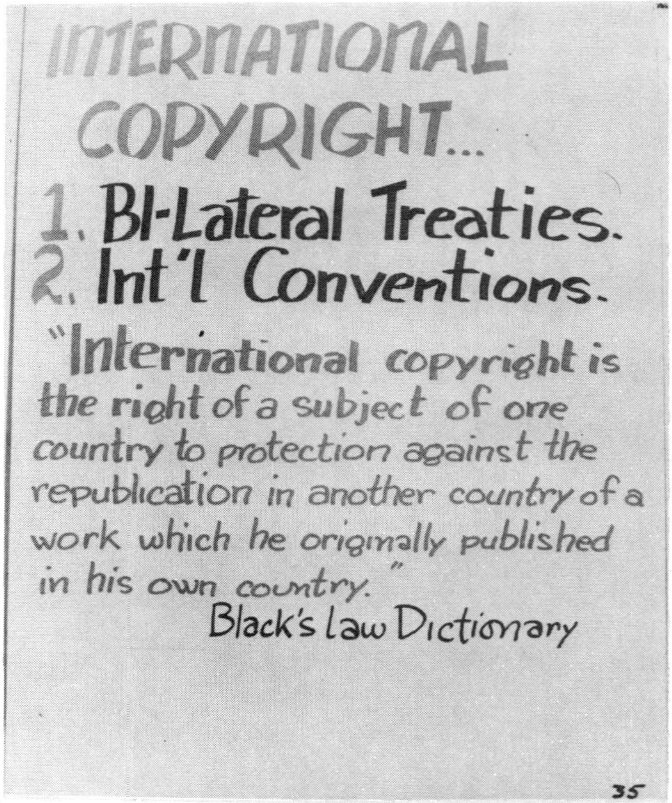
INTERNATIONAL COPYRIGHT...
1. BI-Lateral Treaties.
2. Int'l Conventions.
"International copyright is the right of a subject of one country to protection against the republication in another country of a work which he originally published in his own country."
Black's Law Dictionary
35

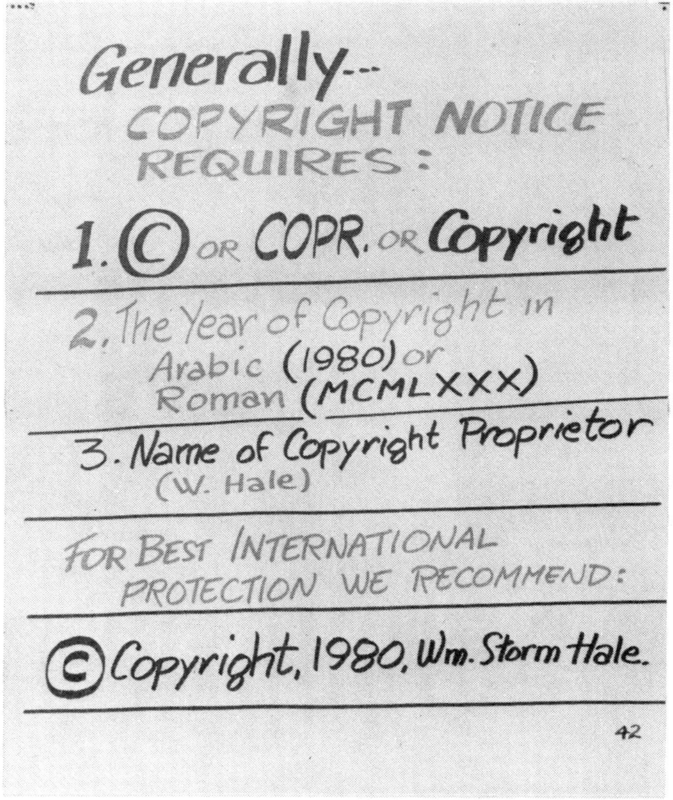
Generally---
COPYRIGHT NOTICE REQUIRES:
1. © OR COPR. OR Copyright
2. The Year of Copyright in Arabic (1980) or Roman (MCMLXXX)
3. Name of Copyright Proprietor (W. Hale)
FOR BEST INTERNATIONAL PROTECTION WE RECOMMEND:
© Copyright, 1980, Wm. Storm Hale.
42

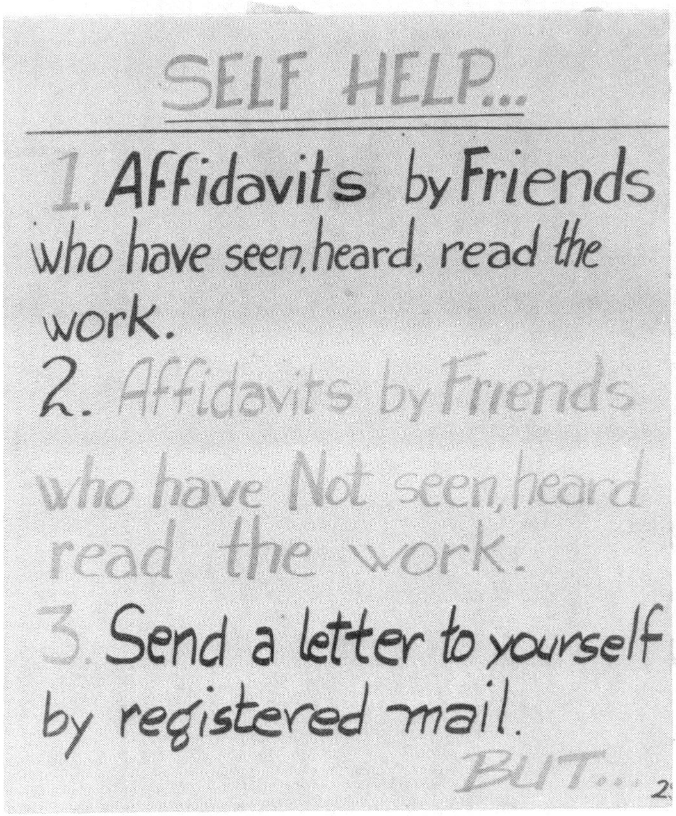
SELF HELP...
1. Affidavits by Friends who have seen, heard, read the work.
2. Affidavits by Friends who have Not seen, heard read the work.
3. Send a letter to yourself by registered mail.
BUT...

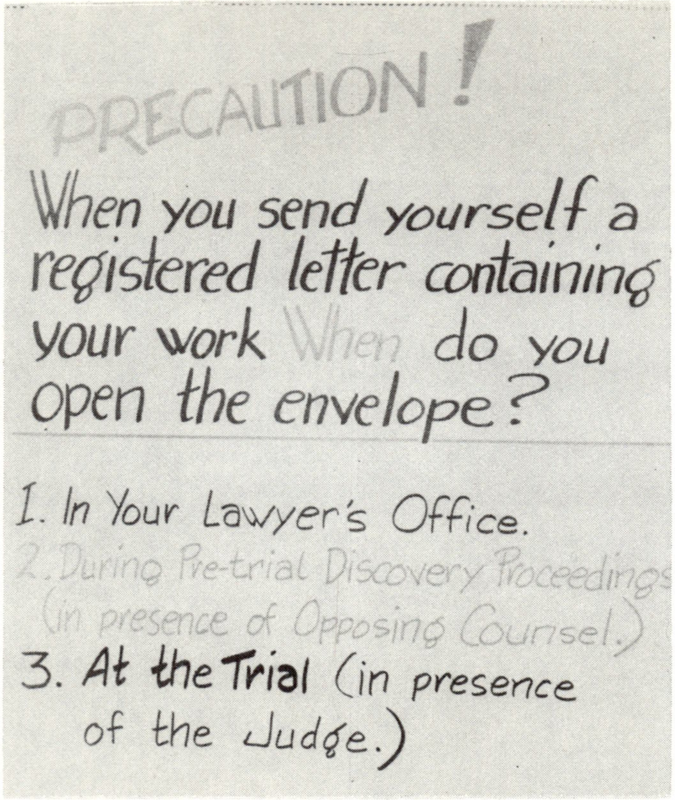
PRECAUTION!
When you send yourself a registered letter containing your work When do you open the envelope?
1. In Your Lawyer's Office.
2. During Pre-trial Discovery Proceedings (in presence of Opposing Counsel.)
3. At the Trial (in presence of the Judge.)

Registration of Unpublished Works
1. U.S. Copyright Office
2. By States
3. Your Own Office
4. Writers Guild
28

PHYSICAL OWNERSHIP DOES NOT MEAN THE RIGHT TO REPRODUCE!
I'M GOING TO REPRODUCE THE LOVE LETTERS YOU SENT ME.
THAT'S A NO-NO! YOU MAY POSSESS THEM PHYSICALLY— BUT YOU DON'T HAVE THE RIGHT TO REPRODUCE THEM!
MERE POSSESSION OF ANY MANUSCRIPT DOES NOT OWNERSHIP OF ANY LITERARY PROPERTY THEREIN...
32

THUS...
The Right to Publish and Copyright Private Letters Generally Belongs to the Writer or his legal Representative and NOT to the Recipient.
33

© COPYRIGHT

AVOID BEING A PIRATE.
WHAT IS A PIRATE?
SOMEONE WHO COMMITS PIRACY.
WHAT IS PIRACY?
PLAGIARISM...USING A COPYRIGHT-PROTECTED WORK WITHOUT THE REQUIRED PERMISSION.
DR

© COPYRIGHT
EXAMPLE OF PIRACY # 1
I'LL BE HAPPY TO PHOTOCOPY TEN COPIES OF WALTER HURST'S "MOTION PICTURE DISTRIBUTION" FOR EACH OF YOU.
OTHER LIBRARIANS
MOTION PICTURE DISTRIBUTION by Walter E. HURST
LIBRARIAN
A TO X Copier
©MCMLXXVII-Walter.E.Hurst
DR

EXAMPLE OF PIRACY #2

EXAMPLE OF PIRACY #3

WHAT IS A COPYRIGHT ROYALTY TRIBUNAL?

The COPYRIGHT ROYALTY TRIBUNAL MAKES DETERMINATIONS CONCERNING ADJUSTMENT OF ROYALTY RATES: PAID BY A CABLE SYSTEM WHOSE SECONDARY TRANSMISSIONS ARE SUBJECT TO COMPULSORY LICENSING UNDER SUBSECTION (C) OF §111

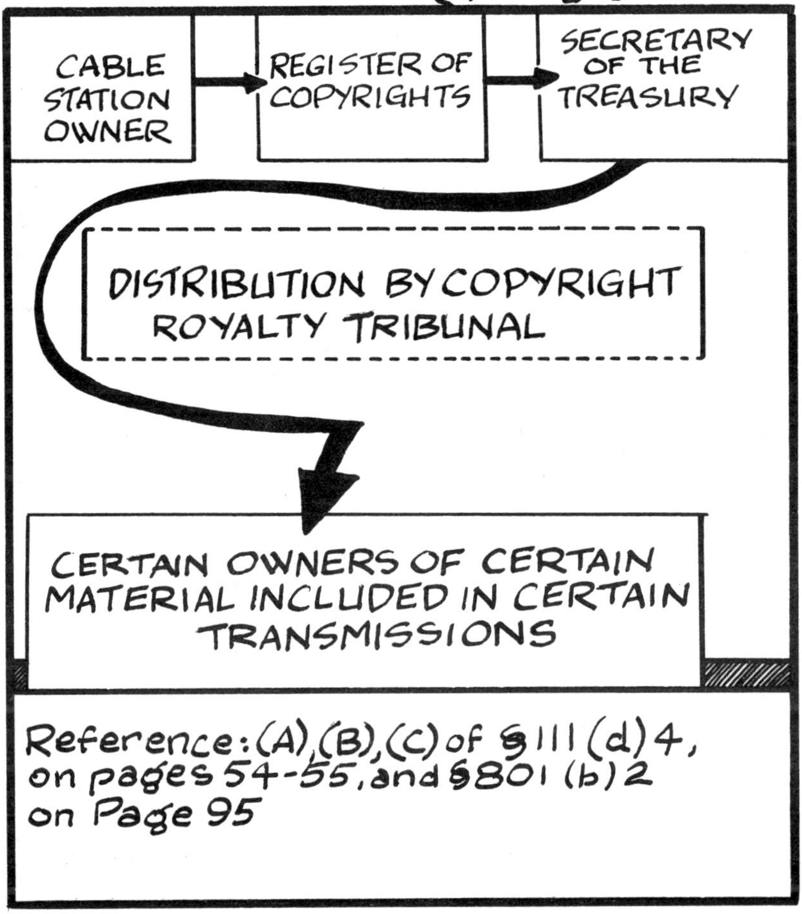

THE COPYRIGHT ROYALTY TRIBUNAL MAKES DETERMINATIONS OF REASONABLE RATES CONCERNING COIN-OPERATED MACHINE FEES.

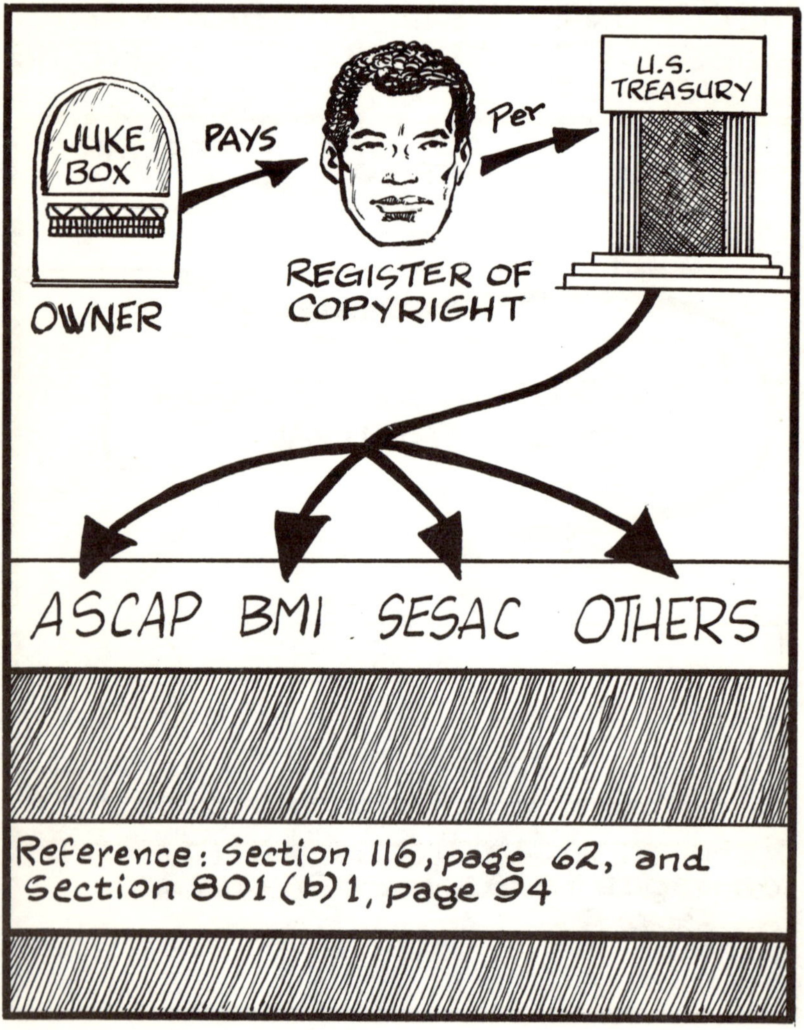

FUNCTIONS:
TO MAKE DETERMINATIONS OF REASONABLE RATES CONCERNING MECHANICAL LICENSES (AMOUNT RECORD COMPANY PAYS PUBLISHER PER RECORD)
RECORD CO.
Publisher →
Reference: Section 115, Page 61, and Section 801 (b)1, Page 94

CHAPTER 1

YOU AND COPYRIGHT

101. We don't know you.

102. Please fill in the questions (if you own this book) in this book.

103. Your filling in the answers won't help us know you because we won't read your answers.

104. Your filling in the answers may help you to understand copyright.

105. This chapter illustrates how we talk to listeners in our presence.

106. Imagine that we are smiling and addressing you.

107. Do you want to learn:

    (a) Some copyright law <u>theory</u>? ( )YES ( )NO.
    (b) Some practical aspects of <u>making money</u> with copyright? ( )YES ( )NO.
    (c) Some practical information about <u>registering</u> your copyrights with the Copyright Office? ( )YES ( )NO.
    (d) Something about the U.S. Copyright Acts from 1909 through 1977? ( )YES ( )NO.
    (e) Something about the U.S. Copyright Act of 1976 effective January 1, 1978? ( )YES ( )NO.

CHAPTER 2

TITLES

201. Have you looked at the title of this book? ( )YES ( )NO.

202. What is the title of this book?___________.

203. If you had to fill out a Copyright Office registration form concerning this book, and the form asked "2. TITLE" what would you fill in as the title of this book?_________________________.

204. Did you notice that your answers to Question #202 and #203 are identical? ( )YES ( )NO.

205. You would be surprised how many people have one title on their book (or magazine, or painting or song) but list another title on the applicable Copyright Office form.

206. Lots of works which are eligible to receive copyright protection sometimes don't have titles (for example; prints, photographs, paintings, sculptures).

207. Some of these people, when faced with a Copyright Office form that asks for TITLE of the work, throw up their hands and say, "My work does not have a title. What should I do?"

208. The answer is: Make up a title. You could call it "Custer's Last Stand" (describes the work) "Photograph Of Aunt Liz In 1980 (classifies the work, subject and date), "Rico's Prints Of Heroes And Villians, Number 10" (Author's name, type of work, and subject matter).

209. Please remember that your title is going on

file in the Copyright Office in the Library of Congress and elsewhere, and will be published in a Catalog Of The Copyright Office (and possibly elsewhere).

210. You might take pity on yourself and others who someday are trying to match titles and the works they belong to by writing the title in, on, or under your work.

CHAPTER 3

THE COPYRIGHT NOTICE.
(The First Part: © Copyright)

301. Please look at the page on the reverse side of the title page in this book.

302. "REVERSE...8, The back or rear of anything...." THE RANDOM HOUSE DICTIONARY OF THE ENGLISH LANGUAGE, (The Unabridged Edition, page 1226, 1967).

303. Somewhere on the reverse side of the title page of this book you will see a copyright notice.

304. Look for a sequence that has three elements.

305. The first element concerns the word COPYRIGHT and the symbol ©. The symbol © stands for COPYRIGHT.

306. We like using the full word COPYRIGHT because the word is so impressive. It is a word found in many dictionaries.

307. We like using the symbol © because it is powerful internationally.

308. A copyright notice, such as "COPYRIGHT 1977 by WALTER E. HURST" is a good notice for works Walter E. Hurst wants to protect in the United States.

309. A copyright notice such as "© 1977 by Walter E. Hurst" is a good notice for works Walter E. Hurst wants to protect in the United States <u>and</u> in the Universal Copyright Convention countries.

310. Some people don't know that © stands for COPYRIGHT. Some would-be pirates may pretend that they don't know that © stands for COPYRIGHT.

311. To obtain maximum protection, we use the symbol ©. To provide maximum information, we use the full word COPYRIGHT.

CHAPTER 4

THE COPYRIGHT NOTICE
(The Second Part: The Year)

401. Please look at the page in this book which is on the reverse side of the title page.

402. Please write down the entire "Copyright Notice".

____________________	__________	________________
© COPYRIGHT	YEAR	COPYRIGHT OWNER

403. Sometimes the YEAR is written with Arabic numbrals: 1,2,3,4,5,6,7,8,9,0.

404. Sometimes the YEAR is written with Roman Numerals: I,V,X,L,C,M.

405. 1978 = MCMLXXVIII
1000 = M
900 = CM
70 = LXX
8 = VIII

406. M = 1000
C = 100
CM = 900
L = 50
X = 10
XX = 20
LXX = 70
V = 5
I = 1
III = 3
VIII = 8

407. Why are Arabic figures used?

(a) They are simple to use.

(b) The customer is supposed to read the year.
(c) To show that the book is recent.
(d) Later, to show the user that the work is old and the user should buy a current edition.
(e) The writer of the Copyright Notice does not know Roman numerals.

408. Why are Roman figures used?

(a) To hide the date.
(b) It looks mysterious.
(c) The writer of the Copyright Notice does not know Arabic figures.

409. If a work is to be published in late 1977, should the copyright notice show 1977 or 1978? ANSWER: 1977.

410. If a book first published in 1978 is partially revised and added to in 1979, what years should the copyright notice show? ANSWER: 1978, 1979. Example: © Copyright 1978, 1979 by Seven Arts Press, Inc. Another example: © Copyright MCMLXXVIII, MCMLXXIX by Seven Arts Press, Inc.

411. The various Copyright Office forms ask for date of publication of published works.

412. The date you show on the Copyright Office form should be consistent with the year in the copyright notice.

413. FOR EXAMPLE:

(a) Year in copyright notice: © 1979 by Seven Arts Press, Inc.
(b) Date of publication in the Copyright Office registration form: December 1, 1979.

414. Don't be caught:

(a) Being a wise guy by putting an incorrect <u>future</u> date in your copyright notice, then,
(b) Giving evidence against yourself by putting the correct date on your registration form.

415. You may lose your copyright by placing a future year in lieu of the correct year.

416. You may be subjected to criminal action for lying to the United States, if you intentionally put wrong information on a government document, (the Copyright Office registration form).

417. Thus, you should have both:

(a) A correct date of publication and,
(b) A correct year in the copyright notice.

CHAPTER 5

THE COPYRIGHT NOTICE
(The Third Part: The Name)

501. Please look at the page in this book which is on the reverse side of the title page.

502. Notice the name portion of the copyright notice: WALTER E. HURST.

503. Is the copyright notice:

Part 1: © COPYRIGHT
Part 2: MCMLXXVII
Part 3: Walter E. Hurst

504. Check that against:

(a) The name of the publisher: Seven Arts Press, Inc.
(b) The name(s) of any co-authors: William Storm Hale.
(c) The name(s) of any editor: Sharon Marshall.
(d) The name(s) of any illustrator: Don Rico.
(e) The name(s) of any contributor. Is there an an introduction, preface or foreword?
(f) The name(s) of anyone quoted in the book.

505. Copyright belongs to the creator. (The writer, the artist, the songwriter.)

506. The book was created by Walter E. Hurst. Therefore, the copyright notice lists the name of Walter E. Hurst.

507. When the Copyright Office registration form for this book is filled out, the first question: COPYRIGHT CLAIMANT(S) AND ADDRESS(ES) will contain the name and address of Walter E. Hurst.

CHAPTER 6

COPYRIGHT OWNER

601. "COPYRIGHT OWNER", with respect to any one of the exclusive rights comprised in a copyright, refers to the owner of that particular right.

602. As far as this book is concerned, the "Copyright Owner" is Walter E. Hurst.

603. But, Walter E. Hurst did not write the entire book....

CHAPTER 7

WORK MADE FOR HIRE
SUPPLEMENTARY WORK
INSTRUCTIONAL TEXT

701. A "work made for hire" is -

(a) A work prepared by an employee within the scope of his or her employment;
(b) A work specially ordered or commissioned for use as a contribution to a collective work, as a part of a motion picture or other audiovisual work, as a compilation, as an instructional text, as answer material for a test, or as an atlas, if the parties expresssly agree in a written instrument signed by them that the work shall be considered a work made for hire. For the purpose of the foregoing sentence, a "supplementary work" is a work prepared for publication as a secondary adjunct to a work by another author for the purpose of introducing, concluding, illustrating, explaining, revision, commenting upon, or assisting in the use of the other work, such as forewords, afterwords, pictorial illustrations, maps, charts, tables, editorial notes, musical arrangements, answer material for tests, bibliographies, appendixes, and indexes, and an "instructional text" is a literary, pictorial, or graphic work prepared for publication with the purpose of use in systematic instructional activities. SOURCE: Section 101 of the Copyright Act of 1976.

702. Don Rico did "supplementary work" for this book.

703. Don Rico prepared illustrations specially ordered for use as supplementary work.

704. A contract between a COPYRIGHT OWNER and a WORKER FOR HIRE might state: (see next page)

"The undersigned COPYRIGHT OWNER and the undersigned WORKER FOR HIRE hereby expressly agree in writing that the work performed and to be performed by WORKER FOR HIRE (in illustrating) (in adding written material) the following work (a textbook, an encyclopedia, a motion picture) tentatively entitled (COPYRIGHT or QUESTIONS AND ANSWERS CONCERNING COPYRIGHT or AN INTRODUCTION TO COPYRIGHT LAW AND HOW TO REGISTER COPYRIGHTS) shall be considered a work made for hire.

Date of Contract______________________________

Place of Contract_____________________________

Signature of
WORKER FOR HIRE_______________________________

Name, Address & Social Security
Number of WORKER FOR HIRE_____________________

____

Signature of
COPYRIGHT OWNER_______________________________

Name, Address & Social Security
Number of COPYRIGHT OWNER_____________________

____

WORK MADE FOR HIRE:
(1) A work prepared by an employee within the scope of his employment.
EDITORIAL
Reference 17 USC 101

WORK MADE FOR HIRE:
(2) A work specially ordered or commissioned for use as a contribution... if the parties expressly agree in a written instrument signed by them.
Reference: 17USC101 (See Definitions)

CHAPTER 8

COPYRIGHT ASSIGNMENTS

801. Please look at copyright notices of some of the books near you.

802. Please write down the title, copyright notice, author and publisher of one book in which the copyright notice was in the name of the author. For example:

(a) Title: YOUR INCOME TAX COMIC BOOK (MR. INFORMATION BATTLES FOR THE TAXPAYER).
(b) Copyright notice: Copyright © MCMLXXVI by Walter E. Hurst.
(c) Authors: Walter E. Hurst & Don Rico.
(d) Seven Arts Press, Inc.

803. Please write down the title, copyright notice, author and publisher of one book in which the author was the publisher.
For example:

(a) Title: LAW DICTIONARY FOR LAYPERSONS & LISTENERS - ABOUT 1000 DEFINITIONS.
(b) Copyright notice: Copyright © MCMLXXVIII by Seven Arts Press, Inc.
(c) Author: Seven Arts Press, Inc.
(d) Publisher: Seven Arts Press, Inc.

804. In this case, all workers on the project were employees-for-hire and their employer is deemed to be the original author of the dictionary.

805. Often, the staff of many publishers of dictionaries, encyclopedias, newspapers and magazines are employees-for-hire (workers-for-hire), and the "person" (sole proprietorship, partnership, corporation, government) who pays for the work is

deemed to be the original author.

806. It is fairly easy to grasp the concept that the copyright belongs to an employer when the words are written by salaried employees, researchers, reporters, re-write men and editors (employee-for-hire, worker-for-hire).

807. It is fairly easy to grasp the concept that the copyright belongs to the company which commissions the work and pays for it when there is an express contract between the parties setting forth the circumstances and the express agreement between the parties (worker-for-hire).

808. Please write down the title, copyright notice, author and publisher of one book in which the copyright notice contains the name of the publisher. For example:

(a) Title: TRADEMARKS (HOW TO REGISTER YOUR TRADEMARK & OTHER INTRODUCTORY INFORMATION).
(b) Copyright notice: ©Copyright MCMLXXIX by Seven Arts Press, Inc.
(c) Author: Walter E. Hurst
(d) Publisher: Seven Arts Press, Inc.

809. In this case, the original copyright creator is the author.

810. But the copyright claimant is the publisher.

811. How did this situation come about?

812. The author assigned his copyright to the publisher.

813. The author (as assignor) assigned his copyright to the publisher (as assignee).

814. Sample contract: The undersigned author hereby assigns all his rights in the work tentatively entitled TRADEMARKS (HOW TO REGISTER YOUR TRADEMARK & OTHER INTRODUCTORY INFORMATION) to the undersigned publisher.

Date:____________________________

Place:___________________________

The undersigned author: (signature)__________

Author's name, address, social security number:

____

The undersigned publisher: (name of publisher)

Signature of person signing for publisher:______

____

Name & title (such as President) of signer:_____

____

Address of publisher:____________________________

Employer identification or ISBN:_________________

CHAPTER 9

BE WARY OF SAMPLE, SIMPLE & ALL CONTRACTS

901. The sample contract just set forth was simple; it was too simple. The assingment was one of "all rights in the work".

902. Under the 1909 Copyright Act, the duration of copyright was for a first period of 28 years and a second period of 28 years.

903. One case held that since the assignment of copyright in the case did not expressly mention the renewal period, the assignment did not include the renewal period.

904. Another case held that since the contract and assignment in the case did not expressly mention the author was assigning his rights to use the hero of the book (Sam Spade) in future books, that author retained the right to use the hero in future books.

905. Contracts tend to become longer and longer as draftsmen utilize existing form contracts from form books as basic drafts, modify the form contract to fit the circumstances of the particular situation, and then add whatever they may think of.

906. Here is the assignment clause of a contract used in the music industry before December 31, 1977, concerning a song:

> The COMPOSER hereby sells, assigns, transfers and delivers to the PUBLISHER, its successors and assigns, the original musical composition written and composed by _____, at present entitled _____ which title may be changed by the PUBLISHER; including the title, words, and music thereof, and all rights therein; and all copyrights and the rights to secure copyrights and any extensions and renewals of copyrights in the same and in any arrangements and adaptations thereof, throughout the world; and any and all other rights that the COMPOSER now has or to which he may be entitled or that he hereafter could or might secure with

respect to this composition, if these presents had not been made, throughout the world; and to have and to hold the same absolutely unto the PUBLISHER its successors and assigns.

907. The contracts and portions of contracts set forth in this book are for your education; they are not necesarily fair or unfair, enforceable or unenforceable.

908. The contracts and portions of contracts set forth in this book are for your education. Please educate yourself by reading them from time to time.

CHAPTER 10

"PEOPLE WANT TO SCREW LAWYERS"

1001. An author once said to a publisher: "I want to write a book on law for laypersons. I want to teach a little legal vocabulary and procedure. With this knowledge, the layperson can better understand what the lawyer is saying and what he wants. The layperson will be in a good position to help his lawyer."

1002. The publisher replied: "People don't want to help their lawyers. People want to screw their lawyers! People want to screw their lawyers out of legal fees. Write a book on HOW TO HANDLE YOUR OWN DIVORCE, HOW TO START YOUR OWN CORPORATION, HOW TO HANDLE YOUR OWN BANKRUPTCY."

1003. The author responded: "Lawyers, legal secretaries and para-legals who use and follow such books make mistakes the first few times and often even after the first few times. There are so many variations from the norm, that making mistakes on the first draft is almost inevitable. Some of these books are terrific in teaching people basics, and with this knowledge the layperson can better understand what the lawyer is saying and what he wants. But, the layperson is rarely knowledgeable enough after reading a book to handle his legal problems without a lawyer."

1004. The publisher replied: "You are right. But, people don't know that. All people want to do is screw their lawyers, and in wanting that, many people screw themselves."

CHAPTER 11

THE COPYRIGHT OFFICE

1101. The basic funciton of the U.S. Copyright Office is the administration of the copyright law.

1102. The Copyright Office <u>examines</u> claim to copyright in a wide variety of works.

1103. Please take a look at the headings of the free forms furnished by the Copyright Office to anyone who requests forms; the heading says "Application for Registration of a Claim to Copyright".

1104. You can write a letter to the Copyright Office:

REGISTER OF COPYRIGHTS
Library of Congress
Washington, D.C. 20559

Dear Register:

Please send me free:

1. Circular 1. General information about copyright.
2. Circular 2. Publications of the Copyright Office.

Yours truly,

XXXXXXX

P.S. I am interested in registering a claim to copyright in (book, song, map, etc.) Please send appropriate registration forms and circulars.

1105. The Copyright Office registers those claims that meet "the requirements of law".

1106. One reason why we are offering you information on subjects such as COPYRIGHT NOTICE, WORKERS FOR HIRE and ASSIGNMENTS is to teach you about "the requirements of law.

1107. If you know "the requirements of law", then you have a better chance to meet "the requirements of law".

1108. The Copyright Office catalogs all registrations.

1109. The Copyright Office conducts correspondence about the claims and supplies general information concerning copyright law and registration procedures.

1110. When a claim is found acceptable for registration, a numbered certificate of copyright registration is mailed to the copyright claimant or a designated recipient.

1111. Please look on any form APPLICATION FOR REGISTRATION OF A CLAIM TO COPYRIGHT for two items: 1. Name and address of person or organization to whom correspondence, or refund, if any, should be sent. 2. Send Certificate To: Name, Address.

1112. When a copyright claimant handles his own paperwork concerning registration of claims to copyright, the copyright claimant may put his name and address in both places.

1113. When an attorney handles the paperwork for a claimant, the attorney may want to fill in his name and address under "Name and address of person or organization to whom correspondence, or refund, if any, should be sent". That would enable the attorney to swiftly correspond with the Copyright Office in the event the Copyright Office bounces back claims.

1114. Some attorneys list the applicants name and address, and other attorneys list their own name and address under SEND CERTIFICATE TO: Name and address.

1115. When the attorney receives the certificates, the attorney can photocopy it for his files, and forward the original certificate to the copyright claimant.

1116. The form intially filled out by or for the copyright claimant is a four page form. Pages 1 & 2 are the APPLICATION FOR REGISTRATION OF A CLAIM TO COPY-

RIGHT. Pages 3 & 4 are the CERTIFICATE REGISTRATION OF A CLAIM TO COPYRIGHT.

1117. When the Copyright Office approves the APPLICATION FOR REGISTRATION OF A CLAIM TO COPYRIGHT, the Copyright Office keeps pages 1 & 2 and returns to the claimant pages 3 & 4 (the CERTIFICATE, REGISTRATION OF A CLAIM TO COPYRIGHT).

1118. The Copyright Office catalogs each registration and maintains a card catalog.

CHAPTER 12

CATALOG OF COPYRIGHT ENTRIES

1201. A CATALOG OF COPYRIGHT ENTRIES, divided by subject matter, has been published in a pamphlet or book form since 1891.

1202. The "Third Series" has been published concerning Copyright Office registration since 1947.

1203. Theoretically, copies of the CATALOG OF COPYRIGHT ENTRIES can be orderd from the Superintendent of Documents, U.S. Government Printing Office, Washington, D.C. 20402.

1204. However, not all copies of all parts of all catalogs are kept in print. Occasionally, babies can be conceived, born and attend kindergarden between the times of some orders and the time the orderer receives the catalogs. Usually, though, orders are filled faster than the end of the second trimester of a human pregnancy.

1205. The cost of each catalog part is low, and the copyright specialist may find catalogs useful to make swift incomplete searches.

1206. The catalogs parts for the Third Series include:

- Part 1. Books and Pamphlets including Serials and Contributions to Periodicals.
- Part 2. Periodicals.
- Part 3-4. Dramas and Works prepared for oral delivery.
- Part 5. Music.
- Part 6. Maps and Atlases.
- Part 7-11A. Works of Art, Reproductions of Works of Art, Scientific and Technical Drawings, Photographic Works, Prints and Pictorial Illustrations.
- Part 11B. Commercial Prints and Labels.
- Part 12-13. Motion Pictures.
- Part 14. Sound Recordings.

1207. There are several CATALOG OF COPYRIGHT ENTRIES, CUMULATIVE SERIES:

(a) Motion Pictures 1894-1912.
(b) " " 1912-1939.
(c) " " 1940-1949.
(d) " " 1950-1959.
(e) " " 1960-1969.

1208. These catalogs list original registrations with the Copyright Office.

1209. The duration of the intital period of statutory protection under the 1909 law: 28 Years.

1210. If no renewal certificate was filed, the work was protected only for the intial 28 year period.

1211. Many persons are interested in learning the names of the motion pictures which were protected only for the intial 28 years.

1212. Seven Arts Press, Inc. published a book which is a reprint of the CATALOG OF COPYRIGHT ENTRIES, MOTION PICTURES 1894-1912 and 1912-1939.

1213. This book, entitled FILM SUPERLIST: 20,000 MOTION PICTURES IN THE U.S. PUBLIC DOMAIN, shows the renewal registration numbers and dates of the films for which renewals were filed.

1214. The reader of FILM SUPERLIST can readily see the names of the films for which no renewal was filed.

1215. Thousands of the public domain films listed in FILM SUPERLIST can be purchased from various sources (such as Historical Films and from some advertisers in Classical Film Collector).

The CATALOG OF COPYRIGHT ENTRIES is published by authority of sections 210 and 211 of Title 17 of the *United States Code*. Section 210 provides in part: "The current catalog of copyright entries and the index volumes herein provided for shall be admitted in any court as prima facie evidence of the facts stated therein as regards any copyright registration."

Orders, payable in advance, for all parts of the *Catalog of Copyright Entries* should be sent to the Superintendent of Documents, U.S. Government Printing Office, Washington, D.C. 20402. Orders may be placed for individual issues, as subscriptions for one or more parts, or for the complete *Catalog*, for periods of one, two, or three years. All orders should state clearly the title and the inclusive dates of the part wanted; checks or money orders should be made payable to the Superintendent of Documents.

The Copyright Office welcomes inquiries, suggestions, and comments on the content and organization of the *Catalog*. Such communications should be addressed to the Chief of the Cataloging Division, Copyright Office, Library of Congress, Washington D.C. 20559.

The record of each copyright registration listed in the *Catalog* includes a description of the work copyrighted and data relating to the copyright claim (the name of the copyright claimant as given in the application for registration, the copyright date, the copyright registration number, etc.). For each registration listed, except for renewals, there has been deposited a copy or copies of the work in accordance with the provisions contained in sections 12, 13, 14, or 215 of Title 17 of the *United States Code*.

Each part listed in the following table records registrations in the class or classes indicated by the alphabetical symbols. The second and third letters, if any, that follow the initial letter are added by the Copyright Office for the purpose of statistical analysis.

CHAPTER 13

REGISTRATION CLASSES (1947-1977)

1301. There is a system.

1302. Copyright protects certain types of works, such as books and songs and maps and sound recordings and others.

1303. The Copyright Office created slightly different forms for different classes.

1304. Many of the questions on the various forms are the same or similar.

1305. Form E concerning songs asks:

COPYRIGHT CLAIMANT(S) AND ADDRESS(ES).
TITLE.
AUTHORS.
DATE OF PUBLICATION.
PLACE OF PUBLICATION.
PREVIOUS REGISTRATION OR PUBLICATION.
DEPOSIT ACCOUNT.
SEND CORRESPONDENCE TO.
SEND CERTIFICATE TO.

1306. Form A, concerning books, asks almost the same questions, deletes the question about PREVIOUS REGISTRATION OR PUBLICATIONS, adds an inquiry about BOOKS IN ENGLISH PREVIOUSLY MANUFACTURED AND PUBLISHED ABROAD, adds a CERTIFICATION concerning place of manufacture of the book.

1307. The 1909 law (section 16), the "manufacturing clause", provided that certain books had to be manufactured in the United States to receive regular Copyright protection. The 1976 law limited this manufacturing requirement to 1982.

1308. Please look at the reverse side of the title page of this book and other books for the magic phrase "Manufactured in The United States".

1309. While most forms are alike in most respects, each form is slightly different to accomodate the requirements of law concerning that type of work.

1310. One of the differences in forms is caused by the theoretical and practical difference concerning "published" and "unpublished" works.

CHAPTER 14

"PUBLISHED" AND "UNPUBLISHED"

1401. Return with us to the days of history when things were simpler. Before an author's work was published, it had to be conceived, written, set to type, printed. Then on some day, the publisher would make copies of the book available to the public. Often the same entrepreneur was printer and bookbinder and publisher and bookseller. As a matter of timing, before the book was made public it was unpublished; on the day it made public, the book was published.

1402. Judge made law, called common law, recognized the concept of copyright hundreds of years ago.

1403. Judges recognized that a writer of an unpublished work such as a letter, had a right to copy and a right to stop others from copying the letter.

1404. Statutory law, such as statutes passed by Parliament, protected published books.

1405. For a long time the two sources of law, judge made law and statutory law worked side by side protecting works before publication (judge made law) and after publication (statutory law).

1406. The United States Constitution, Article 1, stated that Congress could pass laws to protect writings.

1407. Congress interpreted the Constitution to expand the meanings of "writings" to include photographs, songs, plays, labels, sound recordings, etc.

1408. Congress provided that copyright claimants could register their claims to copyright at various places; the right place now is the Copyright Office.

1409. Naturally, when any claim is registered some kind of form must be filled out. The least the form must ask is the name and address of the copyright claimant and some identification of the work being registered.

1410. Along with the registration form must come the appropriate filing fee.

1411. Along with the form and the fee must come information concerning the work being registered.

1412. That information is easy with books. The Copyright Office wants two identical copies of the best education of the work.

1414. That information is easy when sheet music is offered for sale to the public. The Copyright Office wants two identical copies of the best edition of the published sheet music.

1415. The appropriate Copyright Office form for each respective kind of published work asks for date of publication and place of publication.

1416. Date of publication is the date the work was first made available to the public.

1417. The form wants to know when the work was, not when the work will be, published.

1418. The earliest day on which an application can state the work was published, is the day on which the Copyright Office form was filled out.

1419. Place of Publication is generally: United States of America.

1420. Some people publish simultaneously in the United States and Canada. Those people would write: Place of Publication: United States of America and Canada.

1421. The above described system of FIRST PUBLISH, THEN REGISTER AND SEND two copies works fine with many kinds of works.

1422. (By the way, the published work must have proper copyright notice.) Thus the sequence is: FIRST Add Copyright Notice In The Copy To Be Reproduced (printed, etc) SECOND Reproduce. THIRD publish. FOURTH Register.

1423. The system works nicely for routinely published works, such as: (1977 forms)

(a) Published books manufactured in the United States of America. Form A.
(b) A periodical manufactured in the United States of America. Form B.
(c) A contribution to a periodical manufactured in the United States of America. Form BB.
(d) Other routinely mass printed works.

1424. But, in addition to mass reproduced printed works, the Copyright Act of 1909 (as amended from time to time to include works such as labels, sound recordings, etc.) permits registration of certain <u>unpublished</u> works.

1425. Not all unpublished works can be registered. For example, while unpublished music can be registered, unpublished book manuscripts can not. (1977 system).

1426. In some cases, the Copyright Office requests one complete copy of the unpublished work.

1427. That requirement is fairly easy to meet in the case of dramatic works (class D). Plays, etc., are routinely typed and photocopied.

1428. But, what is sent to the Copyright Office to protect one-of-a-kind works like a painting or a sculpture?

1429. For the answer, see the appropriate Copyright Office form. A photocopy sounds logical. Two photocopies sound logical. See the form and instructions concerning the number and size of photographs.

1430. See the forms for other possible alternatives.

1431. BUT WATCH OUT FOR THAT QUESTION CONCERNING PUBLICATION.

1432. For example, Form E can be used to protect both published and unpublished music.

1433. Unpublished works don't need COPYRIGHT NOTICES on them.

1434. Published works need COPYRIGHT NOTICES on them.

1435. Don't claim that a work was published if that work does not have proper COPYRIGHT NOTICE on the copies you are sending to the Copyright Office.

1436. The Copyright Act of 1976 classifies works differently from the classifications in use during 1976 (based on the Copyright Act of 1909, as amended).

1437. Categories under the 1976 Act, (listed in Section 102) include:

(a) Literary works.
(b) Musical works, including any accompanying words.
(c) Dramatic works, including any accompanying music.
(d) Pantomimes and choreographic works.
(e) Pictorial, graphic and sculptural works.
(f) Motion pictures and other audiovisual works.
(g) Sound recordings.

1438. Some of the forms used in 1976 and 1977 may be added to or altered for use in and after 1978.

1439. The basic concepts concerning pre-publication and publications should be absorbed by the reader.

1440. Section 104(a) refers to the works protected by the 1976 Act and states that these works "while unpublished, are subject to the protection under this title ...".

1441. The new statute (effective January 1, 1978) protects both published and unpublished works.

CHAPTER 15

FEES

1501. The $6.00 fee accompanying applications for registrations for claims to copyright was raised to $10.00 by the 1976 Act.

1502. Fees under the new Act include:

> (SEE PAGE 93 OF THIS BOOK: SECTION 708, OF THE GENERAL REVISION OF COPYRIGHT LAW, TITLE 17 OF THE UNITED STATES CODE.)

CHAPTER 16

FEES AND MUSIC

1601. A songwriter can register an unpublished song and pay one filing fee for registering that song.

1602. The form will list just that one song by title, and will list appropriate information concerning copyright claimant and songwriter(s).

1603. Information concerning that song will be processed routinely on Copyright Office cards, in that part of the Catalogs of the Copyright Office which concerns music.

1604. Sometimes a songwriter may want to register many unpublished songs.

1605. A songwriter may want to publish a book containing many of his unpublished songs.

1606. The songwriter should investigate the requirements of registering a book.

1607. While an unpublished song can be registered, an unpublished book can not be registered.

1608. A book must be published to be registered.

1609. A book has a title. A songwriter may use his name in the title. For example: Hale's First Song Book. For another example: Songs by William Storm Hale, Book One.

1610. A book must have copyright notice. For example: COPYRIGHT © 1977 by William Storm Hale.

1611. A book must be published before registration.

1612. That means that the book must be offered to the public through direct offers "Would you like to buy this book", through postings "Buy A Copy Of "HALE'S FIRST SONG BOOK" by William Storm Hale, Only $25.00 Per Copy".

1613. Many books have a Table of Contents. Many books have an Index. Many books have an Introduction or a Preface.

1614. If a songwriter is going to publish a book containing his songs, he should consider questions such as:

(a) How many copies should I print?
(b) How should I bind the pages together?
(c) What kind of cover should I have?
(d) What is my market for the book?
(e) Should I try to sell the book through retail music stores?
(f) Should I loan copies of the book to potential users of songs?
(g) Should I get a re-sale certificate?
(h) Do I need a city or county license to be a book publisher?
(i) Am I really publishing a book or am I trying to pull a fraud on the Copyright Office?

1615. Just to make you aware of a complication. Form A, which concerns books, asks for the name and other information about the author. There is room for 3 authors. Were all the songs in the song book written by three or fewer writers?

1616. A music publisher may be faced with the same desire to register many songs at one time for one fee.

1617. The songwriter and music publisher may want to consider the size of the lead sheet containing the song.

1618. Many lead sheets are prepared on normal "letter size" 8 1/2" x 11" pages.

1619. Other lead sheets are prepared on bigger normal music size pages, 9 1/2" x 3".

1620. If a book is "bound" on the left side, then there should be a margin on the left side of the page.

1621. A book need not be bound to be a book. For example, a book may be a 3 ring loose-leaf book with 3 holes in the music paper.

1622. Thus the songwriter or music publisher who plans to publish a book may plan ahead by having lead sheets prepared on 8 1/2" x 11" music manuscript paper containing 3 holes and a margin on the left.

1623. If a song in the book is later published as sheet music, the copyright notice on the sheet music should include the year in which the book was published.

1624. If a song as published on sheet music differs (additions, deletions, new arrangement, new or different lyrics, etc.) from the song as published in the book, the copyright notice on the sheet music should list both years (that of the book and that of the sheet music).

1625. There are disadvantages to the song book idea.

1626. It may be simpler to register each song separately.

1627. The part of the Catalog of Copyright Entries which list songs does not list books and does not list the individual songs contained in books; the part only lists songs registered as songs.

CHAPTER 17

UNIVERSAL COPYRIGHT CONVENTION

1701. The United States Congress can make laws for the United States.

1702. American copyright owners want copyright protection in the United States.

1703. Many foreign copyright owners want copyright protection in the United States.

1704. There are various treaties and presidential proclamations; but the most important of the international dealings for Americans is the Universal Copyright Convention.

1705. Generally, the basic approach of each country which is a member of the Universal Copyright Convention is the theory that each respective nation will treat foreigners the way it treats its own citizens.

1706. The copyright notice requires the symbol c, the year, and the name of the copyright proprietor.

1707. Under the 1909-1977 law, the year date in the copyright notice is not required to secure U.S. copyright protection for works registered in Classes F through K. However, the year date of first publication is required in the notice to secure protection under the Universal Copyright Convention.

CHAPTER 18

INFORMATION PRINTED ON COPYRIGHT OFFICE REGISTRATION FORMS

1801. It is time for small print.

1802. The APPLICATION FOR REGISTRATION OF A CLAIM TO COPYRIGHT forms contain lots of pertinent information.

1803. You will see a pattern: Theoretical information, registration, Deposit of copies, photographs, etc.
If an earlier registration is made of unpublished material, and the material is later published, another registration should be made.

1804. The new law has different periods of protection for works (depending upon different circumstances).

1805. One of the circumstances may be the death of the creator (for example, in the event a copyright is for the life of the creator plus 50 years).

1806. Copyright assignors, assignees, licensors, licensees, may want to include information concerning creators in each assignment and license: date of birth, place of birth, social security number, drivers license number, and state (also, for dead creators: date and place of death, county and state of probate).

1807. Some of that information will be needed in the Copyright Office and in publishers offices.

CHAPTER 19

COPYRIGHT DEPOSITS AND ALTERNATE DEPOSITS.

1901. The general idea behind the old and the new copyright law is that material deposited for registration generally consists of:

(a) in the case of an unpublished work, one complete copy.
(b) in the case of a published work, two complete copies of the best edition.
(c) in the case of a work published outside the United States, one complete copy.
(d) in the case of a contribution to a collective work, one complete copy of the best edition of the collective work.
(e) in certain cases, (e.g. paintings) deposit may be made of identifying material (such as photographs of the work) instead of copies.
(f) sub-paragraphs may apply to phonorecords.

1902. The Register may, by regulations, change deposit requirements. For example, under the old law, a promise to deposit two copies of a movie on demand was accepted in lieu of actual deposit of two copies at the time of registration.

1903. For exact information concerning your work (book, song, painting) see the current applicable form.

CHAPTER 20

OLD BOOKS, COPYRIGHT AND THE PUBLIC DOMAIN

2001. Literary works, which have been protected by copyright, fall into the public domain after the duration of copyright protection.

2002. During the period of copyright protection, the right to copy belongs to the creator, the creator's assignees and licensees.

2003. When a literary work is in the public domain, the work is no longer protected by copyright.

2004. The book entitled THE QUESTION OF COPYRIGHT, edited by G. H. Putnam, copyright 1891 by G. H. Putnam's Sons, contained articles by R. R. Bowker, Brander Matthews and others.

2005. R. R. Bowker's article on "THE NATURE AND ORIGIN OF COPYRIGHT" is now in the public domain, and is reprinted in this book.

2006. Brander Matthew's article on THE EVOLUTION OF COPYRIGHT is now in the public domain, and is reprinted in this book.

2007. Thanks to the fact that the writings of these excellent creators are in the public domain, the writings are again available for reading by you, the public.

CHAPTER 21

SUPREME COURT DECISIONS

2101. Occasionally, copyright cases reach the United States Supreme Court; decisions are published by various publishers and are narrated on cassettes by Seven Arts Press, Inc. (Seven Arts Tape Library). The Superintendent of Documents publishes UNITED STATES REPORTS. A price list can be obtained from the U.S. Government Printing Office, Washington, D.C. 20402.

2102. UNITED STATES REPORTS are in the public domain.

2103. We are reproducing odd pages selected from various volumes of the UNITED STATES REPORTS. Please notice how easily the cases can be read (once a few words are understood). Beware of thinking that just because a case may be good law at the time it was decided, that the case is still good law. It is quite possible that:

(a) the Supreme Court later reversed or modified the earlier case,
(b) a later statute created new law because Congress did not like an earlier Supreme Court case.

AUTHOR'S RIGHT

TO RENEWAL

FRED FISHER MUSIC CO. ET AL. *v.* M. WITMARK & SONS.

CERTIORARI TO THE CIRCUIT COURT OF APPEALS FOR THE SECOND CIRCUIT.

No. 327. Argued January 14, 15, 1943.—Decided April 5, 1943.

Under the Copyright Act of 1909, as amended, an author's right to obtain a renewal and extension of his copyright is assignable by him by an agreement made before the expiration of the original copyright term. P. 656.

125 F. 2d 949, affirmed.

CERTIORARI, 317 U. S. 611, to review the affirmance of a decree of the District Court, 38 F. Supp. 72, granting an interlocutory injunction in a case of alleged copyright infringement.

Mr. John Schulman, with whom *Mr. Arthur Garfield Hays* was on the brief, for petitioners.

Mr. Robert W. Perkins, with whom *Mr. Stuart H. Aarons* was on the brief, for respondent.

MR. JUSTICE FRANKFURTER delivered the opinion of the Court.

This case presents a question never settled before, even though it concerns legislation having a history of more than two hundred years. The question itself can be stated very simply. Under § 23 of the Copyright Act of

1909, 35 Stat. 1075, as amended,[1] a copyright in a musical composition lasts for twenty-eight years from the date of its first publication, and the author can renew the copyright, if he is still living, for a further term of twenty-eight years by filing an application for renewal within a year before the expiration of the first twenty-eight year period. Section 42 of the Act provides that a copyright

---

[1] The relevant provisions of the Copyright Act read as follows:

SEC. 23. That the copyright secured by this Act shall endure for twenty-eight years from the date of first publication, whether the copyrighted work bears the author's true name or is published anonymously or under an assumed name: *Provided,* That in the case of any posthumous work or of any periodical, cyclopedic, or other composite work upon which the copyright was originally secured by the proprietor thereof, or of any work copyrighted by a corporate body (otherwise than as assignee or licensee of the individual author) or by an employer for whom such work is made for hire, the proprietor of such copyright shall be entitled to a renewal and extension of the copyright in such work for the further term of twenty-eight years when application for such renewal and extension shall have been made to the copyright office and duly registered therein within one year prior to the expiration of the original term of copyright: *And provided further,* That in the case of any other copyrighted work, including a contribution by an individual author to a periodical or to a cyclopedic or other composite work, the author of such work, if still living, or the widow, widower, or children of the author, if the author be not living, or if such author, widow, widower, or children be not living, then the author's executors, or in the absence of a will, his next of kin shall be entitled to a renewal and extension of the copyright in such work for a further term of twenty-eight years when application for such renewal and extension shall have been made to the copyright office and duly registered therein within one year prior to the expiration of the original term of copyright: *And provided further,* That in default of the registration of such application for renewal and extension, the copyright in any work shall determine at the expiration of twenty-eight years from first publication.

SEC. 42. That copyright secured under this or previous Acts of the United States may be assigned, granted, or mortgaged by an instrument in writing signed by the proprietor of the copyright, or may be bequeathed by will.

"may be assigned . . . by an instrument in writing signed by the proprietor of the copyright . . ." Concededly, the author can assign the original copyright and, after he has secured it, the renewal copyright as well. The question is—does the Act prevent the author from assigning his interest in the renewal copyright before he has secured it?

This litigation arises from a controversy over the renewal rights in the popular song "When Irish Eyes Are Smiling." It was written in 1912 by Ernest R. Ball, Chauncey Olcott, and George Graff, Jr., each of whom was under contract to a firm of music publishers, M. Witmark & Sons. Pursuant to the contracts, Witmark on August 12, 1912, applied for and obtained the copyright in the song. On May 19, 1917, Graff and Witmark made a further agreement, under which, for the sum of $1,600, Graff assigned to Witmark "all rights, title and interest" in a number of songs, including "When Irish Eyes Are Smiling." The contract provided for the conveyance of "all copyrights and renewals of copyrights and the right to secure all copyrights and renewals of copyrights in the [songs], and any and all rights therein that I [Graff] or my heirs, executors, administrators or next of kin may at any time be entitled to." To that end, Witmark was given an irrevocable power of attorney to execute in Graff's name all documents "necessary to secure to [Witmark] the renewals and extensions of the copyrights in said compositions and all rights therein for the terms of such renewals and extensions." In addition, Graff agreed that, "upon the expiration of the first term of any copyright," he would execute and deliver to Witmark "all papers necessary in order to secure to it the renewals and extensions of all copyrights in said compositions and all rights therein for the terms of such renewals and extensions." This agreement was duly recorded in the Copyright Office.

On August 12, 1939, the first day of the twenty-eighth year of the copyright in "When Irish Eyes Are Smiling," Witmark applied for and registered the renewal copyright in Graff's name.[2] On the same day, exercising its power of attorney under the agreement of May 19, 1917, Witmark also assigned to itself Graff's interest in the renewal. Eleven days later, Graff himself applied for and registered the renewal copyright in his own name; and on October 24, 1939, he assigned his renewal interest to another music publishing firm, Fred Fisher Music Co., Inc. Both Graff and Fisher knew of the prior registration of the renewal by Witmark and of the latter's assignment to itself. Relying upon the validity of the assignment made to it on October 24, 1939, and without obtaining permission from Witmark, Fisher published and sold copies of "When Irish Eyes Are Smiling," representing to the trade that it owned the renewal rights in the song. Witmark thereupon brought this suit to enjoin these activities. The District Court granted a preliminary injunction *pendente lite* solely upon the ground that there was no statutory bar against an author's assignment of his interest in the renewal before it was secured. 38 F. Supp. 72. The court considered no evidence and made no findings upon the question whether equitable relief should be denied on other grounds, such as inadequacy of consideration and the like.[3] Upon appeal to the Circuit

[2] Ball and Olcott were no longer living at the time, and under § 23 of the Act their interests in the renewal passed to their widows. Witmark is also the assignee of Mrs. Olcott's interest in the renewal copyright, and Mrs. Ball has assigned her interest to another music publisher. The validity of neither assignment is involved in this suit.

[3] In opposing the motion for a preliminary injunction, Graff submitted an affidavit stating he "was in desperate financial straits" when he entered into the agreement of May 19, 1917. The District Court made no findings upon and did not otherwise deal with the issue that this allegation may raise.

Court of Appeals for the Second Circuit under § 129 of the Judicial Code, 28 U. S. C. § 227, permitting appeals from interlocutory decrees, the order was affirmed. 125 F. 2d 949. The Circuit Court of Appeals limited itself, as did the parties before it, to the question of statutory construction, wholly apart from the particular circumstances of the case. The court expressly left open "other contentions which the parties may wish and be entitled to raise on the merits, including possibly claims of inadequacy of consideration." 125 F. 2d at 954. The petition for certiorari in this Court stated that the "sole question is whether . . . an agreement to assign his renewal, made by an author in advance of the twenty-eighth year of the original term of copyright, is valid and enforceable." Because of the obvious importance of this question of the proper construction of the Copyright Act, we brought the case here. 317 U. S. 611.

Plainly, there is only one question before us—does the Copyright Act nullify an agreement by an author, made during the original copyright term, to assign his renewal? The explicit words of the statute give the author an unqualified right to renew the copyright. No limitations are placed upon the assignability of his interest in the renewal. If we look only to what the Act says, there can be no doubt as to the answer. But each of the parties finds support for its conclusion in the historical background of copyright legislation, and to that we must turn to discover whether Congress meant more than it said.

Anglo-American copyright legislation begins in 1709 with the Statute of 8 Anne, c. 19. That act gave the author and his assigns the exclusive copyright for fourteen years from publication, and after the expiration of such term, if the author was still living, the copyright could be renewed for another fourteen years. The statute did not expressly provide that the author could assign his renewal interest during the original copyright term. But the

English courts held that the author's right of renewal, although contingent upon his surviving the original fourteen-year period, could be assigned, and that if he did survive the original term he was bound by the assignment. *Carnan* v. *Bowles,* 2 Bro. C. C. 80; *Rundell* v. *Murray,* Jac. 311; see Maugham, Law of Literary Property (1828) 73; Curtis on Copyright (1847) 235. Subsequent English legislation eliminated the problem by providing for one continuous term of copyright. In 1814 the statute was amended to provide that the author and his assigns should have the copyright for twenty-eight years, "and also, if the author shall be living at the end of that period, for the residue of his natural life." 54 Geo. III, c. 156. In 1842 the copyright term was extended to forty-two years or the life of the author and seven years, whichever should prove longer. 5 & 6 Vict., c. 45; see Macgillivray, Law of Copyright (1902) 56–57. The English law today, with minor qualifications not relevant here, gives the author and his assigns the exclusive copyright for the life of the author and fifty years after his death. Copyright Act of 1911, 1 & 2 Geo. V, c. 34; see Oldfield, Law of Copyright (1912) 60–66; Robertson, Law of Copyright (1912) 44–50; Copinger, Law of Copyright (7th ed. 1936) 78–86.

In this country, the copyright laws enacted by the original thirteen states prior to 1789 were based largely upon the Statute of Anne. In 1783 the Continental Congress passed a resolution calling upon the states to adopt copyright legislation for the protection of authors and publishers. The resolution recommended that copyright be given to authors and publishers "for a certain time, not less than fourteen years from the first publication; and to secure to the said authors, if they shall survive the term first mentioned, and to their executors, administrators and assigns, the copyright of such books for another term of time not less than fourteen years." Journals of the Continental Congress, 1774–1789 (1922), vol. xxiv, pp. 326–27. When the resolution was adopted, laws governing copyrights were on the statute-books of at least three states, Connecticut, Massachusetts, and Maryland. The Connecticut and Maryland statutes substantially followed the Statute of Anne: in both states copyright was granted for a term of fourteen years, renewable for another term of the same length if the author survived the original term. Connecticut, Acts & Laws (Green, 1783) 617–19; Maryland, Laws (Green, 1783) c. 34. The Maryland statute employed the phraseology of the Statute of Anne, providing simply that the privilege of renewal belonged to the author. The Connecticut statute, however, explicitly incorporated the construction made by the English courts, and conferred the right of renewal upon the author and "his heirs and assigns." The Massachusetts statute created a single copyright term of twenty-one years. Massachusetts, Acts & Laws (Edes, 1783) 236.

In response to the resolution of the Congress, nine of the ten other states enacted copyright legislation. Only Delaware did not adopt a copyright statute. Five states accepted the recommendation of the Congress and followed the Statute of Anne: two copyright terms of fourteen years, the second term contingent upon the author's surviving the first. New Jersey, Acts of the General Assembly (Collins, 1783) c. 21; Pennsylvania, Laws (Bradford, 1784) c. 125; South Carolina, Acts, Ordinances and Resolves (Miller, 1784) 49–51; Candler, Colonial Records of Georgia (1911), vol. xix, part 2, pp. 485–89; Laws of New York, 1786, c. 54. Four of these, like the earlier Connecticut statute, explicitly provided that the right of renewal could be exercised by the author's heirs and assigns, namely, New Jersey, Pennsylvania, Georgia, and New York. The four remaining states enacted statutes providing for single terms of varying lengths, ranging from fourteen to twenty-one years. New Hampshire,

Laws (Melcher, 1789) 161–62; Rhode Island, Acts and Resolves (Carter, 1783) 6–7; Virginia, Acts (Dunlap & Hayes, 1785) 8–9; North Carolina, Laws 1785, c. 24.

Exercising the power granted by Article 1, § 8 of the Constitution—"To promote the Progress of Science and useful Arts, by securing for limited Times to Authors and Inventors the exclusive Right to their respective Writings and Discoveries"—the first Congress enacted a copyright statute, the Act of May 31, 1790, 1 Stat. 124. As might have been expected, this Act reflected its historical antecedents. The author was given the copyright for fourteen years and "if, at the expiration of the said term, the author or authors, or any of them, be living, and a citizen or citizens of these United States, or resident therein, the same exclusive right shall be continued to him or them, his or their executors, administrators or assigns, for the further term of fourteen years." 1 Stat. 124. In view of the language and history of this provision, there can be no doubt that if the present case had arisen under the Act of 1790, there would be no statutory restriction upon the assignability of the author's renewal interest. The petitioners contend, however, that such a limitation was introduced by subsequent legislation, particularly the Copyright Acts of 1831 and 1909.

The Act of February 3, 1831, 4 Stat. 436, amended the 1790 Act in two important respects: the original term was increased from fourteen to twenty-eight years, and the renewal term, although still only fourteen years long, could pass to the author's widow or children if he did not survive the original term. The renewal provision, like the Statute of Anne, did not refer to the author's "assigns." The purpose of these changes, as stated in the report of the Committee on the Judiciary of the House of Representatives was "chiefly to enlarge the period for the enjoyment of copy-right, and thereby to place authors in this country more nearly upon an equality with authors in other countries. . . . In the United States, by the existing laws, a copy-right is secured to the author, in the first instance, for fourteen years; and if, at the end of that period, he be living, then for fourteen years more; but, if he be not then living, the copy-right is determined, although, by the very event of the death of the author, his family stand in more need of the only means of subsistence ordinarily left to them." Register of Debates, vol. 7, appendix CXIX.

Plainly, therefore, the Copyright Act of 1831 merely enlarged the benefits of the copyright; it extended the length of the original term and gave the author's widow and children that which theretofore they did not possess, namely, the right of renewal to which the author would have been entitled if he had survived the original term. The petitioners attach much significance to a sentence appearing in the report of the committee: "The question is, whether the author or the bookseller should receive the reward." *Ibid.* The meaning of this sentence, read in its context, is quite clear. By providing that, if the author should not survive the original term, his renewal interest should, instead of falling into the public domain, pass to his widow and children, Congress was of course preferring the author to the bookseller. But neither expressly nor impliedly did the Act of 1831 impose any restraints upon the right of the author himself to assign his contingent interest in the renewal. That the Act contained no such limitation was accepted without question both by the courts, see *Pierpont* v. *Fowle,* 19 Fed. Cas. 652 (C. C. Mass. 1846), and *Paige* v. *Banks,* 13 Wall. 608, with which compare *White-Smith Music Pub. Co.* v. *Goff,* 187 F. 247, 250–53, and by commentators, see Curtis on Copyright (1847) 235; 2 Morgan, Law of Literature (1875) 229–30; Spalding, Law of Copyright (1878) 111; Drone on Copyright (1879) 326–32; Bowker on Copyright (1886) 20, 34; 2 Kent's Commentaries (12th ed.

1873) 510; Solberg, Copyright Protection and Statutory Formalities (1904) 24. Representative Ellsworth,[4] who submitted the committee report on the bill that became the Copyright Act of 1831, himself stated unequivocally that an agreement to assign the renewal was binding upon the author. See Ellsworth, Copy-Right Manual (1862) 29.

We come, finally, to the Copyright Act of March 4, 1909, 35 Stat. 1075, which, except for some minor amendments not relevant here, is the statute in effect at the present time. In December, 1905, President Theodore Roosevelt urged the Congress to undertake a revision of the copyright laws. H. Doc. 1, 59th Cong., 1st Sess., p. LII. In response to this message the Librarian of Congress, under whose authority the Copyright Office functions, invited persons interested in copyright legislation to attend a conference for the purpose of devising a satisfactory measure. Several conferences were held in 1905 and 1906, resulting in a bill which was introduced in the House and Senate by the chairman of the Committee on Patents in each body. This bill (H. R. 19853 and S. 6330, 59th Cong., 1st Sess.) provided, in the case of books and musical compositions, for a single copyright term lasting for the life of the author and for fifty years thereafter. Joint hearings by the House and Senate Committees were held on this bill, but no action was taken by the Fifty-ninth Congress. At the next session of Congress, this and other bills to revise the copyright laws were again introduced. Extensive public hearings were held. The result of this elaborate legislative consideration of the problem of copyright was a bill (H. R. 28192; S. 9440) which became the Copyright Act of 1909. As stated in the report of the House committee, this bill "differs in many respects from

[4] William Wolcott Ellsworth, the son of Oliver Ellsworth, third Chief Justice of the United States. See Biographical Directory of the American Congress, 1774–1927 (1928) 943.

any of the bills previously introduced. Your committee believes that in all its essential features it fairly meets and solves the difficult problems with which the committee had to deal . . ." H. Rep. 2222, 60th Cong., 2d Sess., p. 4. Under the bill, copyright was given for twenty-eight years, with a renewal period of the same duration. The report of the House committee indicates the reasons for this provision. This section of the report, to which much importance has been attached by the judges of the court below and by the parties, must be read in the light of the specific problem with which the Congress was presented: should there be one long term, as was provided for in the bill resulting from the conferences held by the Librarian of Congress, or should there be two shorter terms? The House and Senate committees chose the latter alternative. They were aware that an assignment by the author of his "copyright" in general terms did not include conveyance of his renewal interest. See *Pierpont* v. *Fowle,* 19 Fed. Cas. 652 (C. C. Mass. 1846); 2 Morgan, Law of Literature (1875) 229–30; Macgillivray, Law of Copyright (1902) 267. During the hearings of the Joint Committee, Representative Currier the chairman of the House committee, referred to the difficulties encountered by Mark Twain:

"Mr. Clemens told me that he sold the copyright for Innocents Abroad for a very small sum, and he got very little out of the Innocents Abroad until the twenty-eight-year period expired, and then his contract did not cover the renewal period, and in the fourteen years of the renewal period he was able to get out of it all of the profits." (Hearings before the Committees on Patents of the Senate and House of Representatives on Pending Bills to Amend and Consolidate the Acts respecting Copyright, 60th Cong., 1st Sess., p. 20.)

By providing for two copyright terms, each of relatively short duration, Congress enabled the author to sell his "copyright" without losing his renewal interest. If the author's copyright extended over a single, longer term, his sale of the "copyright" would terminate his entire interest. That this is the basic consideration of policy underlying the renewal provision of the Copyright Act of 1909 clearly appears from the report of the House committee which submitted the legislation (the Senate committee adopted the report of the House committee, see Sen. Rep. 1108, 60th Cong., 2d Sess.):

"Section 23 deals with the term of the copyright. Under existing law the copyright term is twenty-eight years, with the right of renewal by the author, or by the author's widow or children if he be dead, for a further term of fourteen years. The act of 1790 provided for an original term of fourteen years, with the right of renewal for fourteen years. The act of 1831 extended the term to its present length. It was urged before the committee that it would be better to have a single term without any right of renewal, and a term of life and fifty years was suggested. Your committee, after full consideration, decided that it was distinctly to the advantage of the author to preserve the renewal period. It not infrequently happens that the author sells his copyright outright to a publisher for a comparatively small sum. If the work proves to be a great success and lives beyond the term of twenty-eight years, your committee felt that it should be the exclusive right of the author to take the renewal term, and the law should be framed *as is the existing law* [italics ours], so that he could not be deprived of that right.

"The present term of twenty-eight years, with the right of renewal for fourteen years, in many cases is insufficient. The terms, taken together, ought to be long enough to give the author the exclusive right to his work for such a period that there would be no probability of its being taken away from him in his old age, when, perhaps, he needs it the most. A very small percentage of the copyrights are ever renewed. All use of them ceases in most cases long before the expiration of twenty-eight years. In the comparatively few cases where the work survives the original term the author ought to be given an adequate renewal term. In the exceptional case of a brilliant work of literature, art, or musical composition it continues to have a value for a long period, but this value is dependent upon the merit of the composition. Just in proportion as the composition is meritorious and deserving will it continue to be profitable, provided the copyright is extended so long; and it is believed that in all such cases where the merit is very high this term is certainly not too long.

"Your committee do not favor and the bill does not provide for any extension of the original term of twenty-eight years, but it does provide for an extension of the renewal term from fourteen years to twenty-eight years; and it makes some change in existing law as to those who may apply for the renewal. Instead of confining the right of renewal to the author, if still living, or to the widow or children of the author, if he be dead, we provide that the author of such work, if still living, may apply for the renewal, or the widow, widower, or children of the author, if the author be not living, or if such author, widow, widower, or children be not living, then the author's executors, or, in the absence of a will, his next of kin. It was not the intention to permit the administrator to apply for the renewal, but to permit the author who had no wife or children to bequeath by will the right to apply for the renewal." (H. Rep. 2222, 60th Cong., 2d Sess., pp. 14–15.)

The report cannot be tortured, by reading it without regard to the circumstances in which it was written, into an expression of a legislative purpose to nullify agreements by authors to assign their renewal interests. If

Congress, speaking through its responsible members, had any intention of altering what theretofore had not been questioned, namely, that there were no statutory restraints upon the assignment by authors of their renewal rights, it is almost certain that such purpose would have been manifested. The legislative materials reveal no such intention.

We agree with the court below, therefore, that neither the language nor the history of the Copyright Act of 1909 lend support to the conclusion that the "existing law" prior to 1909, under which authors were free to assign their renewal interests if they were so disposed, was intended to be altered. We agree, also, that there are no compelling considerations of policy which could justify reading into the Act a construction so at variance with its history. The policy of the copyright law, we are told, is to protect the author—if need be, from himself—and a construction under which the author is powerless to assign his renewal interest furthers this policy. We are asked to recognize that authors are congenitally irresponsible, that frequently they are so sorely pressed for funds that they are willing to sell their work for a mere pittance, and therefore assignments made by them should not be upheld. It is important that we distinguish between two problems implied in these situations: whether, despite the contrary direction given to this legislation by the momentum of history, we are to impute to Congress the enactment of an absolute statutory bar against assignments of authors' renewal interests, and secondly, whether, although there be no such statutory bar, a particular assignment should be denied enforcement by the courts because it was made under oppressive circumstances. The first question alone is presented here, and we make no intimations upon the other. It is one thing to hold that the courts should not make themselves instruments of injustice by lending their aid to the enforcement of an agreement where the author was under such coercion of circumstances that enforcement would be unconscionable. Cf. *Union Pacific R. Co.* v. *Public Service Comm'n,* 248 U. S. 67, 70; *Lonergan* v. *Buford,* 148 U. S. 581, 589–91; *Snyder* v. *Rosenbaum,* 215 U. S. 261, 265–66; *Post* v. *Jones,* 19 How. 150, 160; *The Elfrida,* 172 U. S. 186, 193–94. It is quite another matter to hold, as we are asked in this case, that regardless of the circumstances surrounding a particular assignment, no agreements by authors to assign their renewal interests are binding.

It is not for courts to judge whether the interests of authors clearly lie upon one side of this question rather than the other. If an author cannot make an effective assignment of his renewal, it may be worthless to him when he is most in need. Nobody would pay an author for something he cannot sell. We cannot draw a principle of law from the familiar stories of garret-poverty of some men of literary genius. Even if we could do so, we cannot say that such men would regard with favor a rule of law preventing them from realizing on their assets when they are most in need of funds. Nor can we be unmindful of the fact that authors have themselves devised means of safeguarding their interests. We do not have such assured knowledge about authorship, and particularly about song writing, or the psychology of gifted writers and composers, as to justify us as judges in importing into Congressional legislation a denial to authors of the freedom to dispose of their property possessed by others. While authors may have habits making for intermittent want, they may have no less a spirit of independence which would resent treatment of them as wards under guardianship of the law.

We conclude, therefore, that the Copyright Act of 1909 does not nullify agreements by authors to assign their renewal interests. We are fortified in this conclusion by reference to the actual practices of authors and publishers with respect to assignments of renewals, as disclosed by the records of the Copyright Office. Since the enactment of the Copyright Act of 1870, 16 Stat. 198, 213, assignments of copyrights must be recorded in the office of the Register of Copyrights. The records of the Copyright Office, we are advised, show that during the period from July, 1870, to July, 1871, the first period in which assignments were recorded in the Office, 223 assignments were registered. Of these 14 were assignments of renewal interests. Similarly, during the first six months of 1909, immediately preceding the enactment of the Copyright Act of that year, 304 assignments were recorded, and of these 62 were assignments of renewal interests. In the six-month period following the enactment of the Copyright Act of 1909, there was no significant change: 404 assignments, of which 68 were transfers of renewals. And, to round out the picture, in the most recent complete volume of records (covering the period from January 27, 1943, to February 12, 1943), 135 assignments were recorded, and of these 29 were assignments of renewals. Many assignments have thus been entered into in good faith upon the assumption that they were valid and enforceable.

In addition to all other books and pamphlets relevant to our problem, we have consulted all of the twenty treatises on the American law of copyright available at the Library of Congress. Eight of these state, without qualification, that an author can effectively agree to assign his renewal interest before it has been secured;[5] two state

[5] Curtis on Copyright (1847) 235; Drone on Copyright (1879) 326–32; Howell, Copyright Law (1942) 108; 2 Morgan, Law of Literature (1875) 229–30; Spalding, Law of Copyright (1878) 111; Macgillivray, Law of Copyright (1902) 266–67; Wittenberg, Protection and Marketing of Literary Property (1937) 45; Ladas, International Protection of Literary and Artistic Property (1938) 772–73.

the rule with some reservations;[6] ten are either silent or ambiguous.[7] And the forms of assignment of copyright in treatises and standard form-books generally contain a provision designed to transfer the renewal interest.[8]

The available evidence indicates, therefore, that renewal interests of authors have been regarded as assignable both before and after the Copyright Act of 1909. To hold at this late date that, as a matter of law, such interests are not assignable would be to reject all relevant aids to construction.

Affirmed.

MR. JUSTICE RUTLEDGE took no part in the consideration or decision of this case.

MR. JUSTICE BLACK, MR. JUSTICE DOUGLAS, and MR. JUSTICE MURPHY conclude that the analysis of the language and history of the copyright law in the dissenting opinion of Judge Frank in the court below, 125 F. 2d 949, 954, demonstrates a Congressional purpose to re-

---

[6] DeWolf, Outline of Copyright Law (1925) 65–66; Weil, American Copyright Law (1917) 365–66.

[7] Amdur, Copyright Law and Practice (1936) 540–41; Frohlich and Schwartz, Law of Motion Pictures (1918) 548–49; Marchetti, Law of Stage, Screen, and Radio (1936) 67; Bowker, Copyright—Its History and Its Law (1912) 117, 438; Bump, Law of Patents, Trade-marks, Labels, and Copyrights (2d ed. 1884); Elfreth, Patents, Copyrights, and Trade-marks (1913); Graham, Patents, Trade-marks and Copyrights (2d ed. 1921); Law, Copyright and Patent Laws of the United States, 1790–1870 (3d ed. 1870); Copinger, Law of Copyright (7th ed. 1936); Shafter, Musical Copyright (2d ed. 1939) 174.

[8] Wittenberg, Protection and Marketing of Literary Property (1937) 195, 261; Shafter, Musical Copyright (2d ed. 1939) 577; Gordon, Annotated Forms of Agreement (1932) 32; 6 Winslow, Forms of Pleading and Practice (3d ed. 1934) § 8267, pp. 501–02; Birdseye, Encyclopedia of General Business and Legal Forms (1924) 280–81; Amdur, Copyright Law and Practice (1936) 836; Church, Legal and Business Forms (2d ed. 1925) 344.

serve the renewal privilege for the personal benefit of authors and their families. They believe the judgment below should be reversed.

MAZER *v.* STEIN.

Syllabus.

MAZER ET AL., DOING BUSINESS AS JUNE LAMP MANUFACTURING CO., *v.* STEIN ET AL., DOING BUSINESS AS REGLOR OF CALIFORNIA.

CERTIORARI TO THE UNITED STATES COURT OF APPEALS FOR THE FOURTH CIRCUIT.

No. 228. Argued December 3, 1953.—Decided March 8, 1954.

Respondents are engaged in the manufacture and sale of electric lamps. One of the respondents created original works of sculpture, from the models of which china statuettes were made. The statuettes were used as bases for fully equipped electric lamps, which respondents sold. Respondents submitted the statuettes, without any lamp components added, for registration under the copyright law as "works of art" or reproductions thereof. *Held:* The statuettes were copyrightable. Pp. 202–219.

(a) The successive Copyright Acts, the legislative history of the 1909 Act, and the practice of the Copyright Office show that "works of art" and "reproductions of works of art" were intended by Congress to include the authority to copyright such statuettes. Pp. 208–214.

(b) That the statuettes, fitted as lamps or unfitted, may be patentable does not bar their copyright as works of art. Pp. 215–217.

(c) The intended or actual use in industry of an article eligible for copyright does not bar or invalidate its registration. P. 218.

(d) The subsequent registration of a work of art published as an element in a manufactured article is not a misuse of the copyright. Pp. 218–219.

204 F. 2d 472, affirmed.

Respondents sued petitioners for copyright infringement, and the District Court dismissed the complaint. 111 F. Supp. 359. The Court of Appeals reversed. 204 F. 2d 472. This Court granted certiorari. 346 U. S. 811. *Affirmed,* p. 219.

Max R. Kraus and *Robert L. Kahn* argued the cause and filed a brief for petitioners.

George E. Frost argued the cause for respondents. With him on the brief were *Will Freeman* and *Charles F. Barber*.

By special leave of Court, *Benjamin Forman* argued the cause for the Register of Copyrights, as *amicus curiae*, urging affirmance. With him on the brief were *Acting Solicitor General Stern, Assistant Attorney General Burger* and *Paul A. Sweeney*.

MR. JUSTICE REED delivered the opinion of the Court.

This case involves the validity of copyrights obtained by respondents for statuettes of male and female dancing figures made of semivitreous china. The controversy centers around the fact that although copyrighted as "works of art," the statuettes were intended for use and used as bases for table lamps, with electric wiring, sockets and lamp shades attached.

Respondents are partners in the manufacture and sale of electric lamps. One of the respondents created original works of sculpture in the form of human figures by traditional clay-model technique. From this model, a production mold for casting copies was made. The resulting statuettes, without any lamp components added, were submitted by the respondents to the Copyright Office for registration as "works of art" or reproductions thereof under § 5 (g) or § 5 (h) of the copyright law,[1] and certifi-

[1] 17 U. S. C. (Supp. V, 1952) § 4:

"The works for which copyright may be secured under this title shall include all the writings of an author."

Id., § 5:

"The application for registration shall specify to which of the following classes the work in which copyright is claimed belongs:

. . . . .

"(g) Works of art; models or designs for works of art.

"(h) Reproductions of a work of art."

Errors of classification are immaterial. See note 19, *infra*.

cates of registration issued. Sales (publication in accordance with the statute) as fully equipped lamps preceded the applications for copyright registration of the statuettes. 17 U. S. C. (Supp. V, 1952) §§ 10, 11, 13, 209; Rules and Regulations, 37 CFR, 1949, §§ 202.8 and 202.9. Thereafter, the statuettes were sold in quantity throughout the country both as lamp bases and as statuettes. The sales in lamp form accounted for all but an insignificant portion of respondents' sales.

Petitioners are partners and, like respondents, make and sell lamps. Without authorization, they copied the statuettes, embodied them in lamps and sold them.

The instant case is one in a series of reported suits brought by respondents against various alleged infringers of the copyrights, all presenting the same or a similar question.[2] Because of conflicting decisions,[3] we granted certiorari. 346 U. S. 811. In the present case respond-

---

[2] An unreported action, *Stein* v. *Zuckerman and DuBeshter,* was pending in the Eastern District of New York. Note, 66 Harv. L. Rev. 877, 878, n. 8. We are advised that it was dismissed by consent February 24, 1953.

[3] *Stein* v. *Expert Lamp Co.,* 188 F. 2d 611. *Stein* v. *Expert Lamp Co.,* 96 F. Supp. 97, was the first action brought. Through an accident in presentation, the trial court determined the case as though the copyright was on a statuette with lamp attachments. It held the statuettes not copyrightable because this "was evidence of the practical use" intended. *Id.,* at 98. On petition for reconsideration, it held the presence or absence of the attachments immaterial. *Stein* v. *Mazer,* 111 F. Supp. 359, 361; *Rosenthal* v. *Stein,* 205 F. 2d 633, 634. The Court of Appeals for the Seventh Circuit affirmed on the ground that the Copyright Act "does not refer to articles of manufacture having a utilitarian purpose nor does it provide for a previous examination by a proper tribunal as to the originality of the matter offered for copyright . . . ." *Stein* v. *Expert Lamp Co.,* 188 F. 2d 611, 613.

Stein v. *Rosenthal,* 103 F. Supp. 227, was a second infringement case. It was there held "Protection is not dissipated by taking an unadulterated object of art as copyrighted and integrating it into commercially valuable merchandise." *Id.,* at 230. On appeal, the Court

ents sued petitioners for infringement in Maryland. *Stein* v. *Mazer,* 111 F. Supp. 359. Following the *Expert* decision and rejecting the reasoning of the District Court in the *Rosenthal* opinion, both referred to in the preceding note, the District Court dismissed the complaint. The Court of Appeals reversed and held the copyrights valid. *Stein* v. *Mazer,* 204 F. 2d 472.[4] It said: "A subsequent utilization of a work of art in an article of manufacture in no way affects the right of the copyright owner to be protected against infringement of the work of art itself." *Id.,* at 477.

Petitioners, charged by the present complaint with infringement of respondents' copyrights of reproductions of their works of art, seek here a reversal of the Court of Appeals decree upholding the copyrights. Petitioners in their petition for certiorari present a single question:

> "Can statuettes be protected in the United States by copyright when the copyright applicant intended primarily to use the statuettes in the form of lamp

---

of Appeals for the Ninth Circuit affirmed, saying "The theory that the use of a copyrighted work of art loses its status as a work of art if and when it is put to a functional use has no basis in the wording of the copyright laws and there is nothing in the design-patent laws which excludes a work of art from the operation of the copyright laws." *Rosenthal* v. *Stein,* 205 F. 2d 633, 635.

In *Stein* v. *Benaderet,* 109 F. Supp. 364, 365, a district court of Michigan held that it is the "intent and purpose" of the designer which determines whether an object is copyrightable as a work of art. The court said plaintiffs should have applied for a design patent and held for defendants. An appeal is pending now in the Court of Appeals for the Sixth Circuit.

The opinions in the above cases and those of the District Court and the Court of Appeals in the present litigation deserve careful reading.

[4] In this case the Register of Copyrights participated as *amicus curiae* and supported respondents. Through the Solicitor General he has also filed a brief in this Court, and participated in the oral argument. 346 U. S. 882.

> bases to be made and sold in quantity and carried the intentions into effect?
>
> "Stripped down to its essentials, the question presented is: Can a lamp manufacturer copyright his lamp bases?"

The first paragraph accurately summarizes the issue. The last gives it a quirk that unjustifiably, we think, broadens the controversy. The case requires an answer, not as to a manufacturer's right to register a lamp base but as to an artist's right to copyright a work of art intended to be reproduced for lamp bases. As petitioners say in their brief, their contention "questions the validity of the copyright based upon the actions of the respondents." Petitioners question the validity of a copyright of a work of art for "mass" production. "Reproduction of a work of art" does not mean to them unlimited reproduction. Their position is that a copyright does not cover industrial reproduction of the protected article. Thus their reply brief states:

> "When an artist becomes a manufacturer or a designer for a manufacturer he is subject to the limitations of design patents and deserves no more consideration than any other manufacturer or designer."

It is not the right to copyright an article that could have utility under §§ 5 (g) and (h), note 1, *supra,* that petitioners oppose. Their brief accepts the copyrightability of the great carved golden saltcellar of Cellini but adds:

> "If, however, Cellini designed and manufactured this item in quantity so that the general public could have salt cellars, then an entirely different conclusion would be reached. In such case, the salt cellar becomes an article of manufacture having utility in addition to its ornamental value and would therefore have to be protected by design patent."

It is publication as a lamp and registration as a statue to gain a monopoly in manufacture that they assert is such a misuse of copyright as to make the registration invalid.

No unfair competition question is presented. The constitutional power of Congress to confer copyright protection on works of art or their reproductions is not questioned.[5] Petitioners assume, as Congress has in its

---

[5] We do not reach for constitutional questions not raised by the parties. *Chicago & G. T. R. Co.* v. *Wellman,* 143 U. S. 339, 345; *New York ex rel. Rosevale Realty Co.* v. *Kleinert,* 268 U. S. 646, 651; *C. I. O.* v. *McAdory,* 325 U. S. 472, 475. The fact that the issue was mentioned in argument does not bring the question properly before us. *Herbring* v. *Lee,* 280 U. S. 111, 117.

No question of our jurisdiction emerges. *Chicot County Dist.* v. *Bank,* 308 U. S. 371. Compare *Kalb* v. *Feuerstein,* 308 U. S. 433, and *Continental Illinois Nat. Bank & Trust Co.* v. *Chicago, R. I. & P. R. Co.,* 294 U. S. 648, 667.

Compare on the constitutional question the following: *Burrow-Giles Lithographic Co.* v. *Sarony,* 111 U. S. 53, upheld the copyright of a photograph unanimously. It was said: "By writings in that clause is meant the literary productions of those authors, and Congress very properly has declared these to include all forms of writing, printing, engraving, etching, &c., by which the ideas in the mind of the author are given visible expression." *Id.,* at 58.

"These findings, we think, show this photograph to be an original work of art, the product of plaintiff's intellectual invention, of which plaintiff is the author, and of a class of inventions for which the Constitution intended that Congress should secure to him the exclusive right to use, publish and sell, as it has done by section 4952 of the Revised Statutes." *Id.,* at 60.

Bleistein v. *Donaldson Lithographing Co.,* 188 U. S. 239, 249–250, upheld a copyright on circus posters. The Court said:

"We shall do no more than mention the suggestion that painting and engraving unless for a mechanical end are not among the useful arts, the progress of which Congress is empowered by the Constitution to promote. The Constitution does not limit the useful to that which satisfies immediate bodily needs. . . . Personality always contains something unique. It expresses its singularity even

enactments and as do we, that the constitutional clause empowering legislation "To promote the Progress of Science and useful Arts, by securing for limited Times to Authors and Inventors the exclusive Right to their

---

in handwriting, and a very modest grade of art has in it something irreducible, which is one man's alone. That something he may copyright unless there is a restriction in the words of the act."

Kalem Co. v. *Harper Bros.*, 222 U. S. 55, 63, involved pirating by motion pictures of the copyrighted dramatic rights of a book. This Court said:

"It is argued that the law construed as we have construed it goes beyond the power conferred upon Congress by the Constitution, to secure to authors for a limited time the exclusive right to their writings. Art. I, § 8, cl. 8. It is suggested that to extend the copyright to a case like this is to extend it to the ideas as distinguished from the words in which those ideas are clothed. But there is no attempt to make a monopoly of the ideas expressed. The law confines itself to a particular, cognate and well known form of reproduction. If to that extent a grant of monopoly is thought a proper way to secure the right to the writings this court cannot say that Congress was wrong."

See also *Schreiber* v. *Thornton,* 17 F. 603, reversed on other grounds, *Thornton* v. *Schreiber,* 124 U. S. 612.

See Fenning, The Origin of the Patent and Copyright Clause of the Constitution, 17 Geo. L. J. 109; 2 Story, Constitution (5th ed.), c. XIX.

Trade-Mark Cases, 100 U. S. 82, 94. Congress had passed a trade-mark act under the Patent and Copyright Clause. A unanimous Court held this effort to protect trade-marks was unconstitutional:

"The ordinary trade-mark has no necessary relation to invention or discovery. . . . If we should endeavor to classify it under the head of writings of authors, the objections are equally strong. In this, as in regard to inventions, originality is required. And while the word *writings* may be liberally construed, as it has been, to include original designs for engravings, prints, &c., it is only such as are *original,* and are founded in the creative powers of the mind. The writings which are to be protected are *the fruits of intellectual labor,* embodied in the form of books, prints, engravings, and the like." The trade-mark does not "depend upon novelty, invention, discovery,

respective Writings and Discoveries," Art. I, § 8, cl. 8, includes within the term "Authors" the creator of a picture or a statue. The Court's consideration will be limited to the question presented by the petition for the writ of certiorari.[6] In recent years the question as to utilitarian use of copyrighted articles has been much discussed.[7]

In answering that issue, a review of the development of copyright coverage will make clear the purpose of the Congress in its copyright legislation. In 1790 the First Congress conferred a copyright on "authors of any map, chart, book or books already printed." [8] Later, designing, engraving and etching were included; [9] in 1831 musical

---

or any work of the brain. It requires no fancy or imagination, no genius, no laborious thought. It is simply founded on priority of appropriation."

See as to commerce, *id.*, at 95–98; Robert, Commentary on the Lanham Trade-Mark Act, 15 U. S. C. A. (§§ 81–1113, 1948) p. 265.

[6] *National Licorice Co.* v. *Labor Board,* 309 U. S. 350, 357, n. 2; *General Talking Pictures Corp.* v. *Western Electric Co.*, 304 U. S. 175; *Crown C. & S. Co.* v. *Ferdinand Gutmann Co.*, 304 U. S. 159, and cases cited; *Gunning* v. *Cooley,* 281 U. S. 90. The policy is incorporated in Rule 38 (2), Revised Rules of the Supreme Court of the United States, and the practice of bringing "additional questions into a case" has been condemned recently in *Irvine* v. *California,* 347 U. S. 128, 129.

[7] Ball, Law of Copyright and Literary Property (1944), 390; Howell, Copyright Law (1952), 130; 1 Ladas, The International Protection of Literary and Artistic Property (1938), 247; Weil, Copyright Law (1917), 227; Derenberg, Copyright No-Man's Land: Fringe Rights in Literary and Artistic Property, 1953 Copyright Problems Analyzed (CCH), 215; Pogue, Borderland—Where Copyright and Design Patent Meet, 52 Mich. L. Rev. 33; Notes, 21 Geo. Wash. L. Rev. 353; 66 Harv. L. Rev. 877; 27 Ind. L. J. 130. See Report of the Copyright Committee, Board of Trade (London, October 1952), Artistic Copyright and Industrial Designs, 82 *et seq.*

[8] 1 Stat. 124.

[9] 2 Stat. 171.

compositions;[10] dramatic compositions in 1856;[11] and photographs and negatives thereof in 1865.[12]

The Act of 1870 defined copyrightable subject matter as:

> ". . . any book, map, chart, dramatic or musical composition, engraving, cut, print, or photograph or negative thereof, or of a painting, drawing, chromo, *statue, statuary, and of models or designs intended to be perfected as works of the fine arts.*" (Emphasis supplied.)[13]

The italicized part added three-dimensional work of art to what had been protected previously.[14] In 1909 Con-

---

[10] 4 Stat. 436.

[11] 11 Stat. 139.

[12] 13 Stat. 540. Between 1789 and 1904, there were in all some twenty-five laws dealing with copyrights. Solberg, Copyright in Congress (1905), 89–93.

[13] § 86, 16 Stat. 212. This Act also vested control of records relating to copyrights in the Librarian of Congress and provided he should administer the law. *Id.*, § 85.

[14] In connection with the phrase in the 1870 Act "intended to be perfected as works of the fine arts," see the 1874 amendatory Act, 18 Stat. 78, and *Bleistein* v. *Donaldson Lithographing Co.*, 188 U. S. 239. Section 3 contained the following provision: "That in the construction of this act, the words 'Engraving,' 'cut' and 'print' shall be applied only to pictorial illustrations or works connected with the fine arts, and no prints or labels designed to be used for any other articles of manufacture shall be entered under the copyright law, but may be registered in the Patent Office."

This was repealed in 1939 and the following enacted:

"Sec. 2. Section 5 (k) of the Act entitled 'An Act to amend and consolidate the Acts respecting copyright' approved March 4, 1909, is hereby amended to read: '(k) Prints and pictorial illustrations including prints or labels used for articles of merchandise.'" 53 Stat. 1142. This was an amendment to § 5 (k) of the Act of 1909, 35 Stat. 1077. It is to be noted, however, that the 1909 Act did not conform to the 1874 language, but the present Act, 17 U. S. C. (Supp. V, 1952) § 5 (k), does contain the amendatory language of the 1939 Act.

gress again enlarged the scope of the copyright statute.[15] The new Act provided in § 4:

> "That the works for which copyright may be secured under this Act shall include all the writings of an author." [16]

Some writers interpret this section as being coextensive with the constitutional grant,[17] but the House Report, while inconclusive, indicates that it was "declaratory of existing law" only.[18] Section 5 relating to classes of writings in 1909 read as shown in the margin with subsequent additions not material to this deci-

---

[15] S. Rep. No. 6187, 59th Cong., 2d Sess. 4:

"The existing statutes attempt specifications which are unfortunate because necessarily imperfect and requiring frequent additions to cover new forms or new processes. The bill in its general definition substitutes a general term, 'all the works of an author.' The term used in the constitution is 'writings.' But Congress has always construed this term broadly, and in doing so has been uniformly supported by judicial decision. It has, for instance, interpreted it as authorizing subject-matter so remote from its popular significance as photographs, paintings, statuary, and dramas, even if unwritten.

"As thus interpreted, the word 'writings' would to-day in popular parlance be more nearly represented by the word 'works;' and this the bill adopts; referring back, however, to the word 'writings' by way of safe anchorage, but regarding this as including 'all forms of record in which the thought of an author may be recorded and from which it may be read or reproduced.' "

Burrow-Giles Lithographic Co. v. *Sarony,* 111 U. S. 53 (1884), has held that photographs were copyrightable in spite of the argument that the Constitution only specified protection for "writings" of an "author." This decision made clear that "writings" was not limited to chirography and typography.

[16] 35 Stat. 1076.

[17] Weil, Copyright Law (1917), 214; Howell, The Copyright Law (3d ed. 1952), 8.

[18] H. R. Rep. No. 2222, 60th Cong., 2d Sess. 10. The report is not very clear on the point, however.

sion.[19] Significant for our purposes was the deletion of the fine-arts clause of the 1870 Act.[20] Verbal distinctions between purely aesthetic articles and useful works of art ended insofar as the statutory copyright language is concerned.[21]

The practice of the Copyright Office, under the 1870 and 1874 Acts and before the 1909 Act, was to allow registration "as works of the fine arts" of articles of the same character as those of respondents now under challenge. Seven examples appear in the Government's

---

[19] "The application for registration shall specify to which of the following classes the work in which copyright is claimed belongs:

"(a) Books including composite and cyclopaedic works, directories, gazetteers, and other compilations;

"(b) Periodicals, including newspapers;

"(c) Lectures, sermons, addresses, prepared for oral delivery;

"(d) Dramatic or dramatico-musical compositions;

"(e) Musical compositions;

"(f) Maps;

"(g) Works of art; models or designs for works of art;

"(h) Reproductions of a work of art;

"(i) Drawings or plastic works of a scientific or technical character;

"(j) Photographs;

"(k) Prints and pictorial illustrations:

"*Provided, nevertheless,* That the above specifications shall not be held to limit the subject-matter of copyright as defined in section four of this Act, nor shall any error in classification invalidate or impair the copyright protection secured under this Act." 35 Stat. 1076.

Subsection (k) was amended by the addition of the words "including prints or labels used for articles of merchandise" in 1939. 53 Stat. 1142. See note 14, *supra*. Two more classes "(l) Motion-picture photoplays" and "(m) Motion pictures other than photoplays" were added in 1912. 37 Stat. 488.

[20] See note 14, *supra,* for repeal of clause defining engraving cuts and prints in terms of "fine art."

[21] Title 17 of the United States Code entitled "Copyrights" was codified into positive law in 1947 without change in the pertinent provisions. 61 Stat. 652, 17 U. S. C. (Supp. V, 1952) §§ 4, 5.

brief *amicus curiae*.[22] In 1910, interpreting the 1909 Act, the pertinent Copyright Regulations read as shown in the margin.[23] Because, as explained by the Government, this regulation "made no reference to articles which might fairly be considered works of art although they might also serve a useful purpose," it was reworded in 1917 as shown below.[24] The *amicus* brief gives sixty examples selected at five-year intervals, 1912–1952, said to be typical of registrations of works of art possessing utilitarian aspects.[25] The current pertinent regulation, published in 37 CFR, 1949, § 202.8, reads thus:

> "*Works of art* (*Class G*)—(a) *In General.* This class includes works of artistic craftsmanship, in so far as their form but not their mechanical or utilitarian aspects are concerned, such as artistic jewelry,

---

[22] *E. g.*, "A female figure bearing an urn in front partly supported by drapery around the head. The figure nude from the waist up and below this the form concealed by conventionalized skirt draperies which flow down and forward forming a tray at the base. Sides and back of skirt in fluted form. The whole being designed as a candlestick with match tray. The figure standing and bent forward from hips and waist."

[23] "*Works of art.*—This term includes all works belonging fairly to the so-called fine arts. (Paintings, drawings, and sculpture.)

"Productions of the industrial arts utilitarian in purpose and character are not subject to copyright registration, even if artistically made or ornamented." Rules and Regulations for the Registration of Claims to Copyright, Bulletin No. 15 (1910), 8.

[24] "Works of art and models or designs for works of art. This term includes all works belonging fairly to the so-called fine arts. (Paintings, drawings, and sculpture.)

"The protection of productions of the industrial arts utilitarian in purpose and character even if artistically made or ornamented depends upon action under the patent law; but registration in the Copyright Office has been made to protect artistic drawings notwithstanding they may afterwards be utilized for articles of manufacture." 37 CFR, 1939, § 201.4 (7).

[25] *E. g.*, "*Lighting fixture design.* By F. E. Guitini. [Bowl-shaped bracket embellished with figure of half-nude woman standing

enamels, glassware, and tapestries, as well as all works belonging to the fine arts, such as paintings, drawings and sculpture. . . ."

So we have a contemporaneous and long-continued construction of the statutes by the agency charged to administer them that would allow the registration of such a statuette as is in question here.[26]

This Court once essayed to fix the limits of the fine arts.[27] That effort need not be appraised in relation to this copyright issue. It is clear Congress intended the scope of the copyright statute to include more than the traditional fine arts. Herbert Putnam, Esq., then Librarian of Congress and aetive in the movement to amend the copyright laws, told the joint meeting of the House and Senate Committees:

> "The term 'works of art' is deliberately intended as a broader specification than 'works of the fine arts' in the present statute with the idea that there is subject-matter (for instance, of applied design, not yet within the province of design patents), which may properly be entitled to protection under the copyright law." [28]

The successive acts, the legislative history of the 1909 Act and the practice of the Copyright Office unite to show

---

in bunch of flowers.] Copyright December 28, 1912. Registration number G 42645. Copyright claimant: Kathodion Bronze Works, New York."

[26] *Great Northern R. Co.* v. *United States,* 315 U. S. 262, 275.

[27] *United States* v. *Perry,* 146 U. S. 71, 74.

[28] Arguments before the Committees on Patents of the Senate and House of Representatives, conjointly, on S. 6330 and H. R. 19853, To Amend and Consolidate the Acts Respecting Copyright, 59th Cong., 1st Sess., June 6–9, 1906, p. 11. The statement is applicable to the 1909 Act since §§ 5 (g) and (h) of the 1909 Act are identical with the same sections of S. 6330 and H. R. 19853. Although there were other hearings and reports (see 51 House Committee Hearings before

that "works of art" and "reproductions of works of art" are terms that were intended by Congress to include the authority to copyright these statuettes. Individual perception of the beautiful is too varied a power to permit a narrow or rigid concept of art. As a standard we can hardly do better than the words of the present Regulation, § 202.8, *supra,* naming the things that appertain to the arts. They must be original, that is, the author's tangible expression of his ideas. Compare *Burrow-Giles Lithographic Co.* v. *Sarony,* 111 U. S. 53, 59–60. Such expression, whether meticulously delineating the model or mental image or conveying the meaning by modernistic form or color, is copyrightable.[29] What cases there are confirm this coverage of the statute.[30]

The conclusion that the statues here in issue may be copyrighted goes far to solve the question whether their intended reproduction as lamp stands bars or invalidates their registration. This depends solely on statutory interpretation. Congress may after publication protect by copyright any writing of an author. Its statute creates the copyright.[31] It did not exist at common law even

---

Committee on Patents (1906–1912), on Consolidating and Revising the Copyright Laws; H. R. Rep. No. 2222, 60th Cong., 2d Sess. 3), this statement of Mr. Putnam is the only explanation of the change in statutory language, though S. Rep. No. 6187, 59th Cong., 2d Sess., p. 11, refers to "works of art" as a new designation and mentioned the deletion of "fine" from the category.

[29] Cf. *H. C. White Co.* v. *Morton E. Converse & Son Co.,* 20 F. 2d 311.

[30] *Burrow-Giles Lithographic Co.* v. *Sarony,* 111 U. S. 53, 60; *Bleistein* v. *Donaldson Lithographing Co.,* 188 U. S. 239, 250; *Louis De Jonge & Co.* v. *Breuker & Kessler Co.,* 182 F. 150, 152; *F. W. Woolworth Co.* v. *Contemporary Arts,* 193 F. 2d 162, 164; see same case, 344 U. S. 228; *Yuengling* v. *Schile,* 12 F. 97, 100; *Schumacher* v. *Schwencke,* 25 F. 466; *Pellegrini* v. *Allegrini,* 2 F. 2d 610.

[31] *Wheaton and Donaldson* v. *Peters and Grigg,* 8 Pet. 591, 661; *Fox Film Corp.* v. *Doyal,* 286 U. S. 123, 127.

though he had a property right in his unpublished work.[32]

But petitioners assert that congressional enactment of the design patent laws should be interpreted as denying protection to artistic articles embodied or reproduced in manufactured articles.[33] They say:

> "Fundamentally and historically, the Copyright Office is the repository of what each claimant considers to be a cultural treasure, whereas the Patent Office is the repository of what each applicant considers to be evidence of the advance in industrial and technological fields."

Their argument is that design patents require the critical examination given patents to protect the public against monopoly. Attention is called to *Gorham Co.* v. *White,* 14 Wall. 511, interpreting the design patent law of 1842, 5 Stat. 544, granting a patent to anyone who by "their own industry, genius, efforts, and expense, may have invented or produced any new and original design for a manufacture . . . ." A pattern for flat silver was there upheld.[34] The intermediate and present law differs

---

[32] Lord Brougham and Lord St. Leonards in *Jefferys* v. *Boosey,* IV H. L. C. 815, 968, 979, 10 Eng. Rep. 681, 741, 745.

[33] Two cases are relied upon to support the position of the petitioners. *Taylor Instrument Companies* v. *Fawley-Brost,* 139 F. 2d 98, and *Brown Instrument Co.* v. *Warner,* 82 U. S. App. D. C. 232, 161 F. 2d 910. These cases hold that the Mechanical Patent Law and Copyright Laws are mutually exclusive. As to overlapping of Design Patent and Copyright Laws, however, a different answer has been given by the courts. *Louis De Jonge & Co.* v. *Breuker & Kessler Co.,* 182 F. 150, affirmed on other grounds in 191 F. 35, and 235 U. S. 33; see also cases cited in note 37, *infra.*

[34] This Court said, p. 525: "It is a new and original design for a manufacture, whether of metal or other material; . . . to be either worked into, or on, any article of manufacture; or a new and original shape or configuration of any article of manufacture—it is one or all of these that the law has in view. And the thing invented or pro-

little. "Whoever invents any new, original and ornamental design for an article of manufacture may obtain a patent therefor, . . ." subject generally to the provisions concerning patents for invention. § 171, 66 Stat. 805. As petitioner sees the effect of the design patent law:

> "If an industrial designer can not satisfy the novelty requirements of the design patent laws, then his design as used on articles of manufacture can be copied by anyone."

Petitioner has furnished the Court a booklet of numerous design patents for statuettes, bases for table lamps and similar articles for manufacture, quite indistinguishable in type from the copyrighted statuettes here in issue.[35] Petitioner urges that overlapping of patent and copyright legislation so as to give an author or inventor a choice between patents and copyrights should not be permitted. We assume petitioner takes the position that protection for a statuette for industrial use can only be obtained by patent, if any protection can be given.[36]

---

duced, for which a patent is given, is that which gives a peculiar or distinctive appearance to the manufacture, or article to which it may be applied, or to which it gives form. . . . It therefore proposes to secure for a limited time to the ingenious producer of those appearances the advantages flowing from them. . . . It is the appearance itself, therefore, no matter by what agency caused, that constitutes mainly, if not entirely, the contribution to the public which the law deems worthy of recompense."

[35] *E. g.*, Design Patent 170.445 Base for table lamps, a fanciful statuette of a girl standing in front of a high rock in bathing costume.

[36] The English Copyright Act, 1911, § 22, 4 Halsbury's Statutes of England (2d ed.), p. 800, does not protect designs registrable under the Patents and Designs Act (now the Registered Designs Act, 1949, 17 Halsbury's Statutes of England (2d ed.)) unless such designs are not used or intended to be used as models or patterns to be multiplied by any industrial process. The Board of Trade has ruled that a design shall be deemed to be used as a model or pattern to be multi-

As we have held the statuettes here involved copyrightable, we need not decide the question of their patentability. Though other courts have passed upon the issue as to whether allowance by the election of the author or patentee of one bars a grant of the other, we do not.[37] We do hold that the patentability of the statuettes, fitted as lamps or unfitted, does not bar copyright as works of art. Neither the Copyright Statute nor any other says that because a thing is patentable it may not be copyrighted. We should not so hold.[38]

Unlike a patent, a copyright gives no exclusive right to the art disclosed; protection is given only to the expression of the idea—not the idea itself.[39] Thus, in *Baker* v. *Selden,* 101 U. S. 99, the Court held that a copyrighted book on a peculiar system of bookkeeping was not infringed by a similar book using a similar plan which achieved similar results where the alleged infringer made a different arrangement of the columns and used different headings. The distinction is illustrated in *Fred Fisher, Inc.* v. *Dillingham,* 298 F. 145, 151, when the court speaks of two men, each a perfectionist, independently making

---

plied by industrial process within the meaning of § 22 when the design is reproduced or intended to be reproduced in more than fifty single articles. The Copyright (Industrial Designs) Rules, 1949, No. 2367, 1 Statutory Instruments 1949, p. 1453.

[37] See *Rosenthal* v. *Stein,* note 3, *supra; In re Blood,* 57 App. D. C. 351, 23 F. 2d 772; *Korzybski* v. *Underwood & Underwood, Inc.*, 36 F. 2d 727; *William A. Meier Glass Co.* v. *Anchor Hocking Glass Corp.*, 95 F. Supp. 264, 267; *Jones Bros. Co.* v. *Underkoffler,* 16 F. Supp. 729; *Louis De Jonge & Co.* v. *Breuker & Kessler Co.*, 182 F. 150; 66 Harv. L. Rev. 884; 52 Mich. L. Rev. 33; cf. *Taylor Instrument Companies* v. *Fawley-Brost,* 139 F. 2d 98.

[38] See, Pogue, Borderland—Where Copyright and Design Patent Meet, 52 Mich. L. Rev. 33, 58.

[39] *F. W. Woolworth Co.* v. *Contemporary Arts,* 193 F. 2d 162; *Ansehl* v. *Puritan Pharmaceutical Co.*, 61 F. 2d 131; *Fulmer* v. *United States,* 122 Ct. Cl. 195, 103 F. Supp. 1021; *Muller* v. *Triborough Bridge Authority,* 43 F. Supp. 298.

maps of the same territory. Though the maps are identical, each may obtain the exclusive right to make copies of his own particular map, and yet neither will infringe the other's copyright. Likewise a copyrighted directory is not infringed by a similar directory which is the product of independent work.[40] The copyright protects originality rather than novelty or invention—conferring only "the sole right of multiplying copies." [41] Absent copying there can be no infringement of copyright.[42] Thus, respondents may not exclude others from using statuettes of human figures in table lamps; they may only prevent use of copies of their statuettes as such or as incorporated in some other article. Regulation § 202.8, *supra,* makes clear that artistic articles are protected in "form but not their mechanical or utilitarian aspects." See *Stein* v. *Rosenthal,* 103 F. Supp. 227, 231. The dichotomy of protection for the aesthetic is not beauty and utility but art for the copyright and the invention of original and ornamental design for design patents. We find nothing in the copyright statute to support the argument that the intended use or use in industry of an article eligible for copyright bars or invalidates its registration. We do not read such a limitation into the copyright law.

Nor do we think the subsequent registration of a work of art published as an element in a manufactured article, is a misuse of the copyright. This is not different from

---

[40] *Sampson & Murdock Co.* v. *Seaver-Radford Co.,* 140 F. 539. See, Anno. 26 A. L. R. 585.

[41] *Jeweler's Circular Pub. Co.* v. *Keystone Publishing Co.,* 281 F. 83, 94.

[42] *White-Smith Music Pub. Co.* v. *Apollo Co.,* 209 U. S. 1; *Bleistein* v. *Donaldson Lithographing Co.,* 188 U. S. 239, 249; *Arnstein* v. *Porter,* 154 F. 2d 464, 468–469; *Alfred Bell & Co., Ltd.* v. *Catalda Fine Arts, Inc.,* 191 F. 2d 99, 103; *Ansehl* v. *Puritan Pharmaceutical Co., supra; Christie* v. *Cohan,* 154 F. 2d 827.

the registration of a statuette and its later embodiment in an industrial article.

"The copyright law, like the patent statutes, makes reward to the owner a secondary consideration." *United States* v. *Paramount Pictures,* 334 U. S. 131, 158. However, it is "intended definitely to grant valuable, enforceable rights to authors, publishers, etc., without burdensome requirements; 'to afford greater encouragement to the production of literary [or artistic] works of lasting benefit to the world.'" *Washingtonian Co.* v. *Pearson,* 306 U. S. 30, 36.

The economic philosophy behind the clause empowering Congress to grant patents and copyrights is the conviction that encouragement of individual effort by personal gain is the best way to advance public welfare through the talents of authors and inventors in "Science and useful Arts." Sacrificial days devoted to such creative activities deserve rewards commensurate with the services rendered.

Affirmed.

Opinion of MR. JUSTICE DOUGLAS, in which MR. JUSTICE BLACK concurs.

An important constitutional question underlies this case—a question which was stirred on oral argument but not treated in the briefs. It is whether these statuettes of dancing figures may be copyrighted. Congress has provided that "works of art," "models or designs for works of art," and "reproductions of a work of art" may be copyrighted (17 U. S. C. § 5); and the Court holds that these statuettes are included in the words "works of art." But may statuettes be granted the monopoly of the copyright?

Article I, § 8 of the Constitution grants Congress the power "To promote the Progress of Science and useful Arts, by securing for limited Times to Authors . . . the exclusive Right to their respective Writings . . . ." The power is thus circumscribed: it allows a monopoly to be granted only to "authors" for their "writings." Is a sculptor an "author" and is his statue a "writing" within the meaning of the Constitution? We have never decided the question.

Burrow-Giles Lithographic Co. v. *Sarony*, 111 U. S. 53, held that a photograph could be copyrighted.

Bleistein v. *Donaldson Lithographing Co.*, 188 U. S. 239, held that chromolithographs to be used as advertisements for a circus were "pictorial illustrations" within the meaning of the copyright laws. Broad language was used in the latter case, ". . . a very modest grade of art has in it something irreducible, which is one man's alone. That something he may copyright unless there is a restriction in the words of the act." 188 U. S., at 250. But the constitutional range of the meaning of "writings" in the field of art was not in issue either in the *Bleistein* case nor in *Woolworth Co.* v. *Contemporary Arts*, 344 U. S. 228, recently here on a writ of certiorari limited to a question of damages.

At times the Court has on its own initiative considered and decided constitutional issues not raised, argued, or briefed by the parties. Such, for example, was the case of *Continental Bank* v. *Rock Island R. Co.*, 294 U. S. 648, 667, in which the Court decided the constitutionality of § 77 of the Bankruptcy Act though the question was not noticed by any party. We could do the same here and decide the question here and now. This case, however, is not a pressing one, there being no urgency for a decision. Moreover, the constitutional materials are quite meager (see Fenning, The Origin of the Patent and Copyright Clause of the Constitution, 17 Geo. L. J. 109 (1929)); and much research is needed.

The interests involved in the category of "works of art," as used in the copyright law, are considerable. The

Copyright Office has supplied us with a long list of such articles which have been copyrighted—statuettes, book ends, clocks, lamps, door knockers, candlesticks, inkstands, chandeliers, piggy banks, sundials, salt and pepper shakers, fish bowls, casseroles, and ash trays. Perhaps these are all "writings" in the constitutional sense. But to me, at least, they are not obviously so. It is time that we came to the problem full face. I would accordingly put the case down for reargument.

SEARS, ROEBUCK & CO. *v.* STIFFEL COMPANY.

CERTIORARI TO THE UNITED STATES COURT OF APPEALS FOR THE SEVENTH CIRCUIT.

No. 108. Argued January 16, 1964.—Decided March 9, 1964.

Respondent, whose design and mechanical patents are invalid for want of invention, cannot under a state unfair competition law obtain an injunction against copying its product or an award of damages for such copying, as such use of state law conflicts with the exclusive power of the Federal Government to grant patents only to true inventions, and then only for a limited time. An unpatented article, being in the public domain, may be freely copied, though labeling or other precautions may be required by state law where appropriate to prevent deception as to source. Pp. 225–233.

313 F. 2d 115, reversed.

Will Freeman argued the cause for petitioner. With him on the briefs were *Frank H. Marks, D. D. Allegretti* and *George B. Newitt.*

Warren C. Horton argued the cause for respondent. With him on the brief was *Max R. Kraus.*

Solicitor General Cox, Assistant Attorney General Orrick, Daniel M. Friedman and *Lionel Kestenbaum* filed a brief for the United States, as *amicus curiae,* urging reversal.

MR. JUSTICE BLACK delivered the opinion of the Court.

The question in this case is whether a State's unfair competition law can, consistently with the federal patent laws, impose liability for or prohibit the copying of an article which is protected by neither a federal patent nor a copyright. The respondent, Stiffel Company, secured design and mechanical patents on a "pole lamp"—a vertical tube having lamp fixtures along the outside, the tube being made so that it will stand upright between the floor and ceiling of a room. Pole lamps proved a decided commercial success, and soon after Stiffel brought them on the market Sears, Roebuck & Company put on the market a substantially identical lamp, which it sold more cheaply, Sears' retail price being about the same as Stiffel's wholesale price. Stiffel then brought this action against Sears in the United States District Court for the Northern District of Illinois, claiming in its first count that by copying its design Sears had infringed Stiffel's patents and in its second count that by selling copies of Stiffel's lamp Sears had caused confusion in the trade as to the source of the lamps and had thereby engaged in unfair competition under Illinois law. There was evidence that identifying tags were not attached to the Sears lamps although labels appeared on the cartons in which they were delivered to customers, that customers had asked Stiffel whether its lamps differed from Sears', and that in two cases customers who had bought Stiffel lamps had complained to Stiffel on learning that Sears was selling substantially identical lamps at a much lower price.

The District Court, after holding the patents invalid for want of invention, went on to find as a fact that Sears' lamp was "a substantially exact copy" of Stiffel's and that the two lamps were so much alike, both in appearance and in functional details, "that confusion between them is likely, and some confusion has already occurred." On these findings the court held Sears guilty of unfair competition, enjoined Sears "from unfairly competing with [Stiffel] by selling or attempting to sell pole lamps identical to or confusingly similar to" Stiffel's lamp, and ordered an accounting to fix profits and damages resulting from Sears' "unfair competition."

The Court of Appeals affirmed.[1] 313 F. 2d 115. That court held that, to make out a case of unfair competition under Illinois law, there was no need to show that Sears had been "palming off" its lamps as Stiffel lamps; Stiffel had only to prove that there was a "likelihood of confusion as to the source of the products"—that the two articles were sufficiently identical that customers could not tell who had made a particular one. Impressed by the "remarkable sameness of appearance" of the lamps, the Court of Appeals upheld the trial court's findings of likelihood of confusion and some actual confusion, findings which the appellate court construed to mean confusion "as to the source of the lamps." The Court of Appeals thought this enough under Illinois law to sustain the trial court's holding of unfair competition, and thus held Sears liable under Illinois law for doing no more than copying and marketing an unpatented article.[2] We granted certiorari to consider whether this

---

[1] No review is sought here of the ruling affirming the District Court's holding that the patent is invalid.

[2] 313 F. 2d, at 118 and nn. 6, 7. At least one Illinois case has held in an exhaustive opinion that unfair competition under the law of Illinois is not proved unless the defendant is shown to have "palmed off" the article which he sells as that of another seller; the court there said that "[t]he courts in this State do not treat the 'palming off' doctrine as merely the designation of a typical class of cases of unfair competition, but they announce it as the rule of law itself—the test by which it is determined whether a given state of facts constitutes unfair competition as a matter of law. . . . The 'palming off' rule is expressed in a positive, concrete form which will not admit of 'broadening' or 'widening' by any proper judicial process." *Stevens-Davis Co.* v. *Mather & Co.*, 230 Ill. App. 45, 65–66 (1923). In spite of this the Court of Appeals in its opinions both in this case and in *Day-Brite Lighting, Inc.*, v. *Compco Corp.*, 311 F. 2d 26, rev'd, *post*, p. 234, relied upon one of its previous decisions in a trade-name case, *Independent Nail & Packing Co.* v. *Stronghold Screw Products*, 205 F. 2d 921 (C. A. 7th Cir. 1953), which concluded that as to use

use of a State's law of unfair competition is compatible with the federal patent law. 374 U. S. 826.

Before the Constitution was adopted, some States had granted patents either by special act or by general statute,[3] but when the Constitution was adopted provision for a federal patent law was made one of the enumerated powers of Congress because, as Madison put it in *The Federalist* No. 43, the States "cannot separately make effectual provision" for either patents or copyrights.[4] That constitutional provision is Art. I, § 8, cl. 8, which empowers Congress "To promote the Progress of Science and useful Arts, by securing for limited Times to Authors and Inventors the exclusive Right to their respective Writings and Discoveries." Pursuant to this constitu-

---

of trade names the *Stevens-Davis* rule had been overruled by two subsequent Illinois decisions. Those two cases, however, discussed only misleading use of trade names, not copying of articles of trade. One prohibited the use of a name so similar to that of another seller as to deceive or confuse customers, even though the defendant company did not sell the same products as the plaintiff and so in one sense could not be said to have palmed off its goods as those of a competitor, since the plaintiff was not a competitor. *Lady Esther, Ltd.*, v. *Lady Esther Corset Shoppe, Inc.*, 317 Ill. App. 451, 46 N. E. 2d 165 (1943). The other Illinois case on which the Court of Appeals relied was a mandamus action which held that under an Illinois statute a corporation was properly denied registration in the State when its name was "deceptively similar" to that of a corporation already registered. *Investors Syndicate of America, Inc.*, v. *Hughes*, 378 Ill. 413, 38 N. E. 2d 754 (1941). The Court of Appeals, by holding that because Illinois forbids misleading use of trade names it also forbids as unfair competition the mere copying of an article of trade without any palming off, thus appears to have extended greatly the scope of the Illinois law of unfair competition beyond the limits indicated in the Illinois cases and beyond any previous decisions of the Seventh Circuit itself. Because of our disposition of these cases we need not decide whether it was correct in doing so.

[3] See I Walker, Patents (Deller ed. 1937), § 7.

[4] The Federalist (Cooke ed. 1961) 288.

tional authority, Congress in 1790 enacted the first federal patent and copyright law, 1 Stat. 109, and ever since that time has fixed the conditions upon which patents and copyrights shall be granted, see 17 U. S. C. §§ 1–216; 35 U. S. C. §§ 1–293. These laws, like other laws of the United States enacted pursuant to constitutional authority, are the supreme law of the land. See *Sperry* v. *Florida,* 373 U. S. 379 (1963). When state law touches upon the area of these federal statutes, it is "familiar doctrine" that the federal policy "may not be set at naught, or its benefits denied" by the state law. *Sola Elec. Co.* v. *Jefferson Elec. Co.,* 317 U. S. 173, 176 (1942). This is true, of course, even if the state law is enacted in the exercise of otherwise undoubted state power.

The grant of a patent is the grant of a statutory monopoly; [5] indeed, the grant of patents in England was an explicit exception to the statute of James I prohibiting monopolies.[6] Patents are not given as favors, as was the case of monopolies given by the Tudor monarchs, see *The Case of Monopolies* (*Darcy* v. *Allein*), 11 Co. Rep. 84 b., 77 Eng. Rep. 1260 (K. B. 1602), but are meant to encourage invention by rewarding the inventor with the right, limited to a term of years fixed by the patent, to exclude others from the use of his invention. During that period of time no one may make, use, or sell the patented

---

[5] Patent rights exist only by virtue of statute. *Wheaton* v. *Peters,* 8 Pet. 591, 658 (1834).

[6] The Statute of Monopolies, 21 Jac. I, c. 3 (1623), declared all monopolies "contrary to the Laws of this Realm" and "utterly void and of none Effect." Section VI, however, excepted patents of 14 years to "the true and first Inventor and Inventors" of "new Manufactures" so long as they were "not contrary to the Law, nor mischievous to the State, by raising Prices of Commodities at home, or Hurt of Trade, or generally inconvenient . . . ." Much American patent law derives from English patent law. See *Pennock* v. *Dialogue,* 2 Pet. 1, 18 (1829).

720-509 O-65—19

product without the patentee's authority. 35 U. S. C. § 271. But in rewarding useful invention, the "rights and welfare of the community must be fairly dealt with and effectually guarded." *Kendall* v. *Winsor,* 21 How. 322, 329 (1859). To that end the prerequisites to obtaining a patent are strictly observed, and when the patent has issued the limitations on its exercise are equally strictly enforced. To begin with, a genuine "invention" or "discovery" must be demonstrated "lest in the constant demand for new appliances the heavy hand of tribute be laid on each slight technological advance in an art." *Cuno Engineering Corp.* v. *Automatic Devices Corp.,* 314 U. S. 84, 92 (1941); see *Great Atlantic & Pacific Tea Co.* v. *Supermarket Equipment Corp.,* 340 U. S. 147, 152–153 (1950); *Atlantic Works* v. *Brady,* 107 U. S. 192, 199–200 (1883). Once the patent issues, it is strictly construed, *United States* v. *Masonite Corp.,* 316 U. S. 265, 280 (1942), it cannot be used to secure any monopoly beyond that contained in the patent, *Morton Salt Co.* v. *G. S. Suppiger Co.,* 314 U. S. 488, 492 (1942), the patentee's control over the product when it leaves his hands is sharply limited, see *United States* v. *Univis Lens Co.,* 316 U. S. 241, 250–252 (1942), and the patent monopoly may not be used in disregard of the antitrust laws, see *International Business Machines Corp.* v. *United States,* 298 U. S. 131 (1936); *United Shoe Machinery Corp.* v. *United States,* 258 U. S. 451, 463–464 (1922). Finally, and especially relevant here, when the patent expires the monopoly created by it expires, too, and the right to make the article—including the right to make it in precisely the shape it carried when patented—passes to the public. *Kellogg Co.* v. *National Biscuit Co.,* 305 U. S. 111, 120–122 (1938); *Singer Mfg. Co.* v. *June Mfg. Co.,* 163 U. S. 169, 185 (1896).

Thus the patent system is one in which uniform federal standards are carefully used to promote invention while at the same time preserving free competition.[7] Obviously a State could not, consistently with the Supremacy Clause of the Constitution,[8] extend the life of a patent beyond its expiration date or give a patent on an article which lacked the level of invention required for federal patents. To do either would run counter to the policy of Congress of granting patents only to true inventions, and then only for a limited time. Just as a State cannot encroach upon the federal patent laws directly, it cannot, under some other law, such as that forbidding unfair competition, give protection of a kind that clashes with the objectives of the federal patent laws.

In the present case the "pole lamp" sold by Stiffel has been held not to be entitled to the protection of either a mechanical or a design patent. An unpatentable article, like an article on which the patent has expired, is in the public domain and may be made and sold by whoever chooses to do so. What Sears did was to copy Stiffel's design and to sell lamps almost identical to those sold by Stiffel. This it had every right to do under the federal patent laws. That Stiffel originated the pole lamp and made it popular is immaterial. "Sharing in the goodwill of an article unprotected by patent or trade-mark is the exercise of a right possessed by all—and in the free exercise of which the consuming public is deeply interested." *Kellogg Co.* v. *National Biscuit Co., supra,* 305 U. S., at 122. To allow a State by use of its law of unfair competition to prevent the copying of an article which rep-

---

[7] The purpose of Congress to have national uniformity in patent and copyright laws can be inferred from such statutes as that which vests exclusive jurisdiction to hear patent and copyright cases in federal courts, 28 U. S. C. § 1338 (a), and that section of the Copyright Act which expressly saves state protection of unpublished writings but does not include published writings, 17 U. S. C. § 2.

[8] U. S. Const., Art. VI.

resents too slight an advance to be patented would be to permit the State to block off from the public something which federal law has said belongs to the public. The result would be that while federal law grants only 14 or 17 years' protection to genuine inventions, see 35 U. S. C. §§ 154, 173, States could allow perpetual protection to articles too lacking in novelty to merit any patent at all under federal constitutional standards. This would be too great an encroachment on the federal patent system to be tolerated.

Sears has been held liable here for unfair competition because of a finding of likelihood of confusion based only on the fact that Sears' lamp was copied from Stiffel's unpatented lamp and that consequently the two looked exactly alike. Of course there could be "confusion" as to who had manufactured these nearly identical articles. But mere inability of the public to tell two identical articles apart is not enough to support an injunction against copying or an award of damages for copying that which the federal patent laws permit to be copied. Doubtless a State may, in appropriate circumstances, require that goods, whether patented or unpatented, be labeled or that other precautionary steps be taken to prevent customers from being misled as to the source, just as it may protect businesses in the use of their trademarks, labels, or distinctive dress in the packaging of goods so as to prevent others, by imitating such markings, from misleading purchasers as to the source of the goods.[9] But because of the federal patent laws a State may not, when the article is unpatented and uncopyrighted, prohibit the

---

[9] It seems apparent that Illinois has not seen fit to impose liability on sellers who do not label their goods. Neither the discussions in the opinions below nor the briefs before us cite any Illinois statute or decision requiring labeling.

copying of the article itself or award damages for such copying. Cf. *G. Ricordi & Co.* v. *Haendler*, 194 F. 2d 914, 916 (C. A. 2d Cir. 1952). The judgment below did both and in so doing gave Stiffel the equivalent of a patent monopoly on its unpatented lamp. That was error, and Sears is entitled to a judgment in its favor.

Reversed.

[For concurring opinion of MR. JUSTICE HARLAN, see *post*, p. 239.]

COMPCO CORPORATION *v.* DAY-BRITE LIGHTING, INC.

CERTIORARI TO THE UNITED STATES COURT OF APPEALS FOR THE SEVENTH CIRCUIT.

No. 106. Argued January 16, 1964.—Decided March 9, 1964.

Design which is not entitled to design patent may be copied at will even though it identifies maker to trade, and injunction against such copying or an accounting for damages for copying is in conflict with federal patent laws. *Sears, Roebuck & Co.* v. *Stiffel Co., ante,* p. 225, followed. Pp. 234–239.

311 F. 2d 26, reversed.

Jerome F. Fallon argued the cause for petitioner. With him on the briefs were *Horace Dawson* and *John H. O. Clarke.*

Owen J. Ooms argued the cause for respondent. With him on the brief was *Roy A. Lieder.*

Solicitor General Cox, Assistant Attorney General Orrick, Daniel M. Friedman and *Lionel Kestenbaum* filed a brief for the United States, as *amicus curiae,* urging reversal.

MR. JUSTICE BLACK delivered the opinion of the Court.

As in *Sears, Roebuck & Co.* v. *Stiffel Co., ante,* p. 225, the question here is whether the use of a state unfair competition law to give relief against the copying of an unpatented industrial design conflicts with the federal patent laws. Both Compco and Day-Brite are manufacturers of fluorescent lighting fixtures of a kind widely used in offices and stores. Day-Brite in 1955 secured from the Patent Office a design patent on a reflector having cross-ribs claimed to give both strength and attractiveness to the fixture. Day-Brite also sought, but was refused, a mechanical patent on the same device. After Day-Brite had begun selling its fixture, Compco's predecessor[1] began making and selling fixtures very similar to Day-Brite's. This action was then brought by Day-Brite. One count alleged that Compco had infringed Day-Brite's design patent; a second count charged that the public and the trade had come to associate this particular design with Day-Brite, that Compco had copied Day-Brite's distinctive design so as to confuse and deceive purchasers into thinking Compco's fixtures were actually Day-Brite's, and that by doing this Compco had unfairly competed with Day-Brite. The complaint prayed for both an accounting and an injunction.

The District Court held the design patent invalid; but as to the second count, while the court did not find that Compco had engaged in any deceptive or fraudulent practices, it did hold that Compco had been guilty of unfair competition under Illinois law. The court found that the overall appearance of Compco's fixture was "the same, to the eye of the ordinary observer, as the overall appearance" of Day-Brite's reflector, which embodied the design of the invalidated patent; that the appearance of Day-Brite's design had "the capacity to identify [Day-Brite] in the trade and does in fact so identify [it] to the trade"; that the concurrent sale of the two products was "likely to cause confusion in the trade"; and that "[a]ctual confusion has occurred." On these findings the court adjudged Compco guilty of unfair competition in the sale of its fixtures, ordered Compco to

[1] The sales of which Day-Brite complained in this action had actually been made by the Mitchell Lighting Company. However, by the time the complaint was filed, Mitchell had been acquired by Compco, which was therefore the defendant in the action and is the petitioner here. For simplicity we shall throughout the opinion refer only to Compco even though the transactions for which Compco was sought to be held liable were those of the predecessor company, Mitchell.

account to Day-Brite for damages, and enjoined Compco "from unfairly competing with plaintiff by the sale or attempted sale of reflectors identical to, or confusingly similar to" those made by Day-Brite. The Court of Appeals held there was substantial evidence in the record to support the District Court's finding of likely confusion and that this finding was sufficient to support a holding of unfair competition under Illinois law.[2] 311 F. 2d 26. Although the District Court had not made such a finding, the appellate court observed that "several choices of ribbing were apparently available to meet the functional needs of the product," yet Compco "chose precisely the same design used by the plaintiff and followed it so closely as to make confusion likely." 311 F. 2d, at 30. A design which identifies its maker to the trade, the Court of Appeals held, is a "protectable" right under Illinois law, even though the design is unpatentable.[3] We granted certiorari. 374 U. S. 825.

To support its findings of likelihood of confusion and actual confusion, the trial court was able to refer to only one circumstance in the record. A plant manager who had installed some of Compco's fixtures later asked Day-Brite to service the fixtures, thinking they had been made by Day-Brite. There was no testimony given by a purchaser or by anyone else that any customer had ever been misled, deceived, or "confused," that is, that anyone had ever bought a Compco fixture thinking it was a Day-Brite fixture. All the record shows, as to the one instance cited by the trial court, is that both Compco and Day-Brite fixtures had been installed in the same plant, that three years later some repairs were needed, and that

---

[2] The Court of Appeals also affirmed the holding that the design patent was invalid. No review of this ruling is sought here.

[3] As stated in *Sears, Roebuck & Co.* v. *Stiffel Co., ante,* at p. 228, n. 2, we do not here decide whether the Court of Appeals was correct in its statement of Illinois law.

the manager viewing the Compco fixtures—hung at least 15 feet above the floor and arranged end to end in a continuous line so that identifying marks were hidden—thought they were Day-Brite fixtures and asked Day-Brite to service them.[4] Not only is this incident suggestive only of confusion *after* a purchase had been made, but also there is considerable evidence of the care taken by Compco to prevent customer confusion, including clearly labeling both the fixtures and the containers in which they were shipped and not selling through manufacturers' representatives who handled competing lines.

Notwithstanding the thinness of the evidence to support findings of likely and actual confusion among purchasers, we do not find it necessary in this case to determine whether there is "clear error" in these findings. They, like those in *Sears, Roebuck & Co.* v. *Stiffel Co., supra,* were based wholly on the fact that selling an article which is an exact copy of another unpatented article is likely to produce and did in this case produce confusion as to the source of the article. Even accepting the findings, we hold that the order for an accounting for damages and the injunction are in conflict with the federal patent laws. Today we have held in *Sears, Roebuck & Co.* v. *Stiffel Co., supra,* that when an article is unprotected by a patent or a copyright, state law may not forbid others to copy that article. To forbid copying would interfere with the federal policy, found in Art. I, § 8, cl. 8, of the Constitution and in the implementing federal statutes, of allowing free access to copy whatever the federal patent and copyright laws leave in the public domain. Here Day-Brite's fixture has been held not to be entitled to a design or mechanical patent. Under the federal pat-

[4] The only testimony about this incident was given by a sales representative of Day-Brite, who said that the plant manager had climbed up on a forklift truck to look at the fixtures. The manager was not called as a witness.

ent laws it is, therefore, in the public domain and can be copied in every detail by whoever pleases. It is true that the trial court found that the configuration of Day-Brite's fixture identified Day-Brite to the trade because the arrangement of the ribbing had, like a trademark, acquired a "secondary meaning" by which that particular design was associated with Day-Brite. But if the design is not entitled to a design patent or other federal statutory protection, then it can be copied at will.

As we have said in *Sears*, while the federal patent laws prevent a State from prohibiting the copying and selling of unpatented articles, they do not stand in the way of state law, statutory or decisional, which requires those who make and sell copies to take precautions to identify their products as their own. A State of course has power to impose liability upon those who, knowing that the public is relying upon an original manufacturer's reputation for quality and integrity, deceive the public by palming off their copies as the original. That an article copied from an unpatented article could be made in some other way, that the design is "nonfunctional" and not essential to the use of either article, that the configuration of the article copied may have a "secondary meaning" which identifies the maker to the trade, or that there may be "confusion" among purchasers as to which article is which or as to who is the maker, may be relevant evidence in applying a State's law requiring such precautions as labeling; however, and regardless of the copier's motives, neither these facts nor any others can furnish a basis for imposing liability for or prohibiting the actual acts of copying and selling. Cf. *Kellogg Co.* v. *National Biscuit Co.,* 305 U. S. 111, 120 (1938). And of course a State cannot hold a copier accountable in damages for failure to label or otherwise to identify his goods unless his failure is in violation of valid state statutory or decisional law requiring the copier to label or take other precautions to prevent confusion of customers as to the source of the goods.[5]

Since the judgment below forbids the sale of a copy of an unpatented article and orders an accounting for damages for such copying, it cannot stand.

Reversed.

MR. JUSTICE HARLAN, concurring in the result.*

In one respect I would give the States more leeway in unfair competition "copying" cases than the Court's opinions would allow. If copying is found, other than by an inference arising from the mere act of copying, to have been undertaken with the dominant purpose and effect of palming off one's goods as those of another or of confusing customers as to the source of such goods, I see no reason why the State may not impose reasonable restrictions on the future "copying" itself. Vindication of the paramount federal interest at stake does not require a State to tolerate such specifically oriented predatory business practices. Apart from this, I am in accord with the opinions of the Court, and concur in both judgments since neither case presents the point on which I find myself in disagreement.

---

[5] As we pointed out in *Sears, Roebuck & Co.* v. *Stiffel Co., ante,* p. 232, n. 9, there is no showing that Illinois has any such law.

*[This opinion applies also to No. 108, *Sears, Roebuck & Co.* v. *Stiffel Co., ante,* p. 225.]

CHAPTER 22

COPYRIGHT & TAXES

2201. Tax law and copyright law touch bases in several respects.

2202. The copyright creator (writer, painter, sculptor) may be an amateur hobbyist or a professional businessman. Both the hobbyist and the professional have to report income; the professional is allowed to deduct his ordinary and necessary business expenses.

2203. Business expenses may include: trade books and magazines; professional groups' dues and dinners and conventions; transportation; telephone; rent; utilities; depreciation; office supplies; publicity; promotion; advertising; travel; skill level maintenance.

2204. Producers and distributors of the three dimensional products (books, records, magazines, newspapers, films, etc) which contain copyright protected works (writings, recordings, songs, etc.) may be able to utilize:

(a) investment credit,
(b) depreciation rules (concerning certain expensive purchases for cash or made on credit),
(c) cash method of accounting, and
(d) other tax consideration to raise money to produce and distribute copyright protected works.

2205. Copyright creators and exploiters can investigate current tax publications concerning:

(a) income averaging,
(b) installment method of reporting gains,
(c) differences between tax rates for ordinary income and for capital gains,

(d) theoretical and practical aspects of legitimately structuring transactions so that gain is taxed at the lower capital gain rates,
(e) donating rights and products to certain organizations and obtaining tax deductions for such donations,
(f) sharing copyrights and income with family members who made contributions to the creation of the copyrighted work,
(g) other tax shelters, and legal "loopholes" that may allow the taxpayer to keep more of his gross income.

2206. WARNING: There may be a conflict between your interests as a copyright owner (who wants to control his rights, limit the duration of licenses, etc.) and your interests as a legal tax avoider.

CHAPTER 23

THE RETURN OF COPYRIGHT RIGHTS.

2301. Sometimes the COPYRIGHT CREATOR <u>wants</u> the RIGHTS USER to return RIGHTS to the CREATOR under circumstances such as:

(a) A play producer fails to open a play before a certain date.
(b) A song given to a music publisher is not recorded at a union session before a certain date.
(c) A movie producer fails to pick up an option to buy a script.
(d) A book publisher fails to keep the book in print for six months.
(e) A movie distributor twenty year period of dis-distribution rights terminates.
(f) Or other circumstances.

2302. The COPYRIGHT OWNER should consider factors such as:

(a) Prohibiting the RIGHTS USER from transferring any rights in the copyright (as distinguished from mere licenses to use the work on a limited bases).
(b) Providing for automatic assignment by the RIGHTS USER to the COPYRIGHT CREATOR of all rights to receive money from THIRD PARTIES who promised to pay the RIGHTS USER for the use of the copyright.
(c) Receiving (for free?) the right to reproduce something paid for by the RIGHTS USER. For example, an author may want the right to reproduce the type-set pages of a book; the publisher paid for the type-setting; the author may be able to persuade another publisher to pay for a printing of the author's work if the new publisher has the free right to photocopy pages of the book printed by the first publisher.

CHAPTER 24

SOURCES OF INFORMATION - LAW REVIEWS

2401. Researchers may find answers to copyright questions in law reviews. The following clipping is part of a law review article which is in the public domain:

PAMPHLET No. 27—100—74

HEADQUARTERS
DEPARTMENT OF THE ARMY
WASHINGTON, D.C., *Fall 1976*

MILITARY LAW REVIEW—VOL. 74

Articles:

Ever since 1895, statutory provisions have prohibited the assertion of copyright in any publication of the United States Government.[1] Although the interaction of the statutory provisions contained in the printing law and in the copyright law, and the provisions themselves raise almost as many questions as the provisions answer,[2] the major issue of what constitutes a publication of the United States Government has been largely settled by administrative practice,[3] the courts[4] and the interpretations of commentators.[5] Nonetheless, questions regarding the rights of military authors in works produced in the course of their duties still arise, and little readily available military authority is available to quickly resolve these issues.[6]

Three other questions of varying degrees of importance are alive in the area, although two may be neatly resolved by the Congress in the near future. The two easily resolved questions concern the common law rights of the Government in unpublished works and the ability of the Government to secure a copyright in works that are not "publications" in the sense that they are not printed documents. The third question is somewhat more complex. It is whether the prohibition against copyright

* The opinions and conclusions presented in this article are those of the author and do not necessarily represent the views of The Judge Advocate General's School or any other governmental agency.

** JAGC, U.S. Army. Editor, *Military Law Review*. B.A., 1970, Washington & Lee University; J.D., 1973; LL.M., 1976, University of Virginia School of Law. Member of the Bars of Virginia and the U.S. Court of Military Appeals.

in government publications should extend to materials produced under government funded grants or contracts. This issue has not been litigated in recent years and has emerged only in the congressional hearings considering the revision of the copyright laws. The committee proceedings have provided a forum for advocates on either side of the question[7] and have produced little in the way of balanced commentary. Most of the presentations have ignored the historical basis for the copyright prohibition as well as two programs which have explicitly authorized copyright in government subsidized materials for several years.

This article will trace the development of the American common law and statutory prohibitions on copyright in government publications and synthesize the various reasons the courts first, and then the Congress, determined that governmental works should not be copyrighted. This discussion will illustrate situations in which the courts have found the restriction applicable and will consider some of the other problems typically associated with the publication of materials created by government authors. Using the historical and theoretical bases for the prohibition of copyright in government publications, the article will then address two questionable and probably incorrect provisions of the Army regulation; whether the Government may assert common law copyright in unpublished government materials; and whether materials produced under government contracts are the proper subject of copyright. The discussion of these issues will draw upon the published congressional hearings considering the various bills to revise the copyright law and will note proposed legislative alterations where appropriate.

II. AMERICAN COMMON LAW ORIGINS

A. EARLY SUPREME COURT CASES

Even before Congress enacted the first statutory prohibition of copyright in government publications, the Supreme Court, first in a casual aside, and later in a more clearly articulated holding, determined that on public policy grounds there could be no copyright in the written judicial opinions of the courts.

[7] As a general rule, book publishers and researchers have sought an exception to the statute which would permit them the opportunity to publish government sponsored material with copyright protection, and news media representatives have opposed any such exemption with equal vigor. *See* Discussion and Comments on the Report of the Register of Copyrights (Committee Print Feb. 1963). There Mr. Rosenfield of the Public Affairs Press advocated strict adherence to the principles of noncopyrightability, *id.* at 203, while Mr. Frase of the American Book Publishers Council extolled the advantages of private publication and copyright. *Id.* at 204.

CHAPTER 25

MULTIPLE COPYRIGHT NOTICES

2501. Sometimes, more than one copyright notice is required.

2502. For example, persons who are releasing phonograph record albums may need:

(a) A Ⓟ notice on the record label to protect the sound recordings. For example: Ⓟ MCMLXXVII Seven Arts Tape Library.
(b) A © notice on the record label to protect the literary or musical content. For example: © MCMLXXVII by Room Seven Music. (This is rarely done as a matter of practice. We take the controversial position that it is advisable and safer to add on copyright notice for each song.)
(c) A © notice on the front and on the back of each LP cover and each reproduction of the cover in other media (tape boxes, Tee Shirts, advertisements). For example: © MCMLXXVII by Seven Arts Tape Library. That © notice is intended to cover the art work, photographs, liner notes and other visible material.
(d) In the event lyrics are reproduced on the LP jacket cover, inside sleeve, or enclosed lyric sheet, use a © notice for each song just above or below the lyrics. For example: © 1977 by Suite Seven Music (ASCAP) may be under one song, while © 1940, 1968 by Room Seven Music (BMI) may be under another song.
(e) On each enclosure (sleeve, lyric sheet, advertisement of other LPs of the company, fan club membership and material) add an appropriate © notice. For example, © 1979 by the William Storm Hale Fan Club.
(f) On each advertisement, poster, photograph, etc. publizing the company, artist, record, etc.

CHAPTER 26

NEW MEDIA

2601. How many recording company-artist contracts provide for payment to the artist by the record company based upon money received by the record company from a Tee Shirt manufacturer for the right to sell Tee Shirts containing copies of album covers?

2602. Tee Shirts are (1) an advertising gimmick and (2) a commercial media.

2603. A record company may pay money to buy Tee Shirts or for "transfers" for advertising reasons. A record company may receive money from a Tee Shirt manufacturer or a "transfer" manufacturer for a license to reproduce the cover.

2604. A so-called "new media" may be an old media, such as piano rolls.

2605. A copyright creator may be able to learn enough about a new media to (1) find the big companies which may pay royalties, (2) start a company to exploit the commercial possibilities of the new media.

2606. For example, the road from the original creation to the Tee Shirt reproduction may be:

(a) The live entertainer is photographed (in black and white or color).
(b) The photograph is placed on a Xerox (or other appropriate reproduction machine). Also placed in proper position so that it is reproduced, is a © notice.
(c) The reproduction is made on the appropriate "transfer" or "pre-transfer" special paper.
(d) If there is a "pre-transfer" the appropriate picture reproduciton or heat method is used to carry the image to a transfer.
(e) The "transfer" is ironed on to a Tee Shirt. In that way, a piece of art can be created (the photograph), reproduced, and placed on the media

(the Tee Shirt) in a matter of minutes.

2607. A record store (which had appropriate licenses from record companies) could reproduce one LP cover at a time for customers who specifically request such service.

2608. Any entertainer could experiment with a small supply of Tee Shirts by preparing advertising material concerning himself on Tee Shirts, and offering them for sale.

2609. The creative copy (picture, etc.) on the Tee Shirt can be reproduced in other ways such as silk screening for medium size numbers and by printing presses. In each case, appropriate papers and inks must be used.

2610. Ideas may be borrowed from other media. For example, the idea of limited editions of numbered and individually signed prints can be experimented with.

2611. A copyright creator can dream wildly: imagine a service for parents which provides large pictures of parents on appropriate clothing of children who might get lost. Busybodies can help match lost children wearing such picture Tee Shirts with frantic parents.

2612. Book store salesmen can wear Tee Shirts containing covers of books, contents or table of contents of books.

2613. This chapter has explored several concepts: Using new media for advertising; selling new media items; operating a tiny creator-reproducer-direct sale to customer company; attempting to interest big reproducers-distributors in paying fees or royalties for use of the copyright creation; applying the copyright notice.

CHAPTER 27

SOURCES OF INFORMATION

Copyright Decisions - Cumulative Index 1909-1970

2701. Bulletins containing: "Decisions of the United States courts involving copyright" and a bulletin containing "Cumulative Index 1909-1970" may be ordered from the Superintendent of Documents.

2702. TABLE OF CASES contain names of plaintiffs (who complain that the other guy wronged the plaintiff), defendants who defend their actions and sometimes their failures to pay), appellants (who appeals and attacks from the decisions of trial courts to appealate courts), appellees (who defends his trial court victories).

2703. The citation includes the volume number, the law book series, the page number in which the case is reported. For example, 186 F. Supp. 443 means Volume 186, the law book series known as Federal Supplement, Page 443.

2704. The last 2 columns of TABLE OF CASES show the Volume and Page of the BULLETINS containing COPYRIGHT DECISIONS at which the case appears.

2705. On the next page is a reproduction of page 1 of the CUMULATIVE INDEX 1909-1970 which covers cases in BULLETINS Nos. 17-35 (Stock No. 3002-00137, Superintendent of Documents).

TABLE OF CASES

A

The Works Involved In Litigation

2706. A researcher may want to read how similar classes of works were treated in different cases.

2707. The CUMULATIVE INDEX 1909-1970 contains many pages listing SOME OF THE WORKS INVOLVED IN COPYRIGHT AND RELATED LITIGATION. Some of the subheadings are:

(a) BOOKS, INCLUDING CONTRIBUTIONS TO PERIODICALS AND UNPUBLISHED MANUSCRIPTS
(b) COMMERCIAL PRINTS AND LABELS
(c) DESIGNS
(d) DRAMATIC AND DRAMATICAL-MUSICAL COMPOSITIONS
(e) DRAWINGS OR PLASTIC WORKS OF A SCIENTIFIC OR TECHNICAL CHARACTER
(f) MOTION PICTURES
(g) MUSICAL COMPOSITIONS
(h) PERIODICALS
(i) PHOTOGRAPHS
(j) PICTORIAL PRINTS
(k) RADIO AND TV SCRIPTS
(l) SLOGANS
(m) SOUND RECORDINGS
(n) TRADEMARKS AND TRADE NAMES
(0) WORKS OF ART

2708. The Volume and Page refer to the Volume Number of the BULLETIN OF DECISIONS OF THE UNITED STATES COURTS INVOLVING COPYRIGHT, in which the respective case can be found.

2709. To illustrate the contents of the WORKS INVOLVED IN LITIGATION, we are reproducing on the next page of this book page 172 of the CUMULATIVE INDEX 1909-1970.

RADIO AND TV SCRIPTS–Continued

SLOGANS

SOUND RECORDINGS

Subject Index

2710. SUBJECT INDEX OF CASES PRINTED IN BULLETINS NOS. 17-35 provides major subjects, phrases, volume and page numbers of cases which concern the major subjects and phrases.

2711. Some major subject headings are procedural: INJUNCTIONS, SEIZURE AND DESTRUCTION, DAMAGES AND PROFITS.

2712. Other major subject headings are by media: COMIC BOOKS, MUSICAL, LABELS, COMPOSITIONS.

2713. State subject headings: CALIFORNIA, NEW JERSEY, NEW YORK.

2714. The next several pages are reproduced for illustration purposes, for teaser purposes, to tease you into ordering the book from the Superintendent of Documents. The title is:

DECISIONS OF THE UNITED STATES COURTS INVOLVING COPYRIGHT, CUMULATIVE INDES 1909-1970. COPYRIGHT OFFICE BULLETINS NOS. 17-37.

CHAPTER 28

A COPYRIGHT CRIMINAL CASE

2801. The following was clipped from the Metropolitan New, A Daily Legal Newspaper, April 26, 1977. Neither the newspaper nor the column displayed a copyright notice.

Statute Proscribing Copyright Infringement Not Vague; Gov't Failed to Show No First Sale

Woodrow Wise, Jr. appealed his conviction of criminal copyright infringement in violation of 17 U.S.C. 104. He was charged with seven counts of criminal copyright infringement by willfully and for profit vending copyrighted feature-length motion pictures, and with seven counts of interstate transportation of stolen and converted property. On appeal Wise challenged the constitutionality of 17 U.S.C. 27 and 104, contested the sufficiency of the evidence to sustain the conviction, and argued that his conviction was precluded by collateral estoppel.

Citing **United States v. Wells**, 176 F.Supp. 630, 633 (S.D. Tex.1959), the USCA stated that the copyright statute is sufficient to put one on notice that the unauthorized vending of copyrighted works constitutes infringement. The two central requirements of collateral estoppel-identity of issues and identity of parties - are absent in this case. Appellant was not a party in either of the prior cases upon which he relied. To prove infringement by vending, the Government must also prove the absence of a first sale as to those articles sold by defendant. In this case, the Government failed in its burden of proving the absense of first sale of one of the films. The USCA also concluded that even if prints of the photoplays involved in this case were sold for salvage, the Government's evidence proved that the prints sold by appellant were not films which had been sold for salvage. No sale was effected under agreements whereby film was loaned to actors for personal use.

The judgment was part affirmed and part reversed.

United States v. Wise. USCA, 9th Cir, No.76-1141, March 28, 1977. (gg)

2802. Defendants have the right to request rehearings and can try to have the United States Supreme Court:

(a) consider the case,
(b) reverse the conviction.

2803. Readers of copyright cases should consider that past cases may provide guidance for judges considering future cases.

TRADEMARKS

Q. **What is a trademark?**

A. A trademark is a word, name, symbol, or device, or any combination of these, adopted and used by a manufacturer or merchant to identify his goods and distinguish them from those manufactured or sold by others. In short, it is a brand name used on goods moving in the channels of trade.

Q. **What is the function of a trademark?**

A. The primary function of a trademark is to distinguish one person's goods from those of another; but a trademark also serves to indicate to purchasers that the quality of the goods bearing the mark remains constant, and it serves as the focal point of advertising to create and maintain a demand for the product.

Q. **How are trademark rights established?**

A. Rights in a trademark are established by adoption and actual use of the mark on goods moving in trade, and use ordinarily must continue if the rights are to be maintained. No rights exist until there has been actual use; and a trademark may not be registered until the goods bearing the mark have been sold or shipped in interstate, foreign or Territorial commerce.

Q. **Who may own a trademark?**

A. A trademark may be owned by an individual, a firm or partnership, a corporation, or an association or other collective group.

Q. **Is there any time limitation within which an application should be filed?**

A. No. An application may be filed at any time after the mark has been used on the product and the product is sold or shipped in interstate, foreign or Territorial commerce.

Q. **What has to be done by the trademark owner in order to qualify for federal registration of a trademark?**

A. The mark must be applied in some manner to goods or their containers and the goods sold or shipped in interstate, foreign or Territorial commerce.

Patents & Inventions:

What Is a Patent?

A patent is a grant by the United States to an inventor of the right to exclude others for a limited time from making, using, or selling his invention in this country. It is a printed document in which the invention is fully disclosed and the rights of the inventor are defined. When an inventor secures a patent he has the opportunity to profit by manufacture, sale, or use of the invention in a protected market or by charging others for making or using it. In patents granted for invention of new and useful processes, machines, manufactures, compositions of matter or plants, the patent rights run for 17 years from the date when the patent is granted. A patent for a new, original and ornamental design for an article of manufacture may run for 3½, 7, or 14 years, as desired by the patentee.

The Importance of Patents

It is natural to ask why the Government makes this offer of protection under the patent law. The answer is in the Constitution itself, which provides that Congress may secure this right to inventors *in order to promote the progress of the useful arts.* The public benefits from this system for three reasons:

First, by offering patent protection, *it induces the inventor to make the invention.*

Second, if the inventor succeeds with the help of the patent in developing and marketing the invention, *this gives the public the opportunity to use it.*

Third, since the inventor must describe the invention in the patent, and copies of the patent may be purchased by the public for 50 cents each, *the knowledge of the invention is made available to everyone.*

If it were not for the patent law many inventors would be unable to develop their inventions and would abandon their ideas instead of going forward with them, and many others would keep them secret as long as they could, *instead of publishing them in patents which stimulate others to make still further inventions.*

LAW LIBRARY JOURNAL

Law Library Journal is published quarterly by the American Association of Law Libraries. In the May 1976, issues, an article commencing on page 203, states: "The Copyright Law was intended to provide incentive to authors so that they might be instructive, informative and entertaining to readers. The library is an institution intended to store this information and disseminate it to readers, serving as a middleman between authors and users created an arbitrary status for the library...As the need for copyright revision became more evident, the library abandoned its arbiter status and created something of a feud between the copyright owner and the library."

WIPO'S COPYRIGHT

Copyright is a monthly review of the World Intellectual Property Organization. It reports on its activities, bilateral agreements, national legislations, correspondence, the Universal Copyright Convention (1952), the Universal Copyright Convention (1971), other conventions. The follwing quote comes from the April 1976 "Letter from the U.S.S.R." on pages 96-111: "The Soviet Union has concluded a number of treaties and agreements that are directly concerned with copyright questions. Multilateral agreements include the Universal Copyright Convention in its version of 1952, which came into force in the USSR on May 27, 1973, and the Convention Establishing the World Intellectual Property Convention of July 14, 1967, ratified by the USSR on September 19, 1968."

PUBLISHERS WEEKLY

Publishers Weekly is a trade publication aimed at publishers. Its coverage of the 1976 Copyright Act at final bill stage stated "Representing more than 20 years of legislative effort, the bill (S.22) provides the first complete revision of the federal copyright law - Title 17 of the U.S. Code, since 1909...Written in a time of dynamic technologial change, S.22 represents a delicate balance between the interests of copyright owners and the public's right of access to information, arrived at after prolonged and agonizing negotiations among the affected parties."
October 11, 1976, page 22.

BULLETIN OF THE COPYRIGHT SOCIETY OF THE U.S.A.

Bulletin of the Copyright Society of the U.S.A. is published six times a year by The Society at the Law Center of New York University, 40 Washington Square South, New York, N.Y. 10011. Bulletins contain: I Articles. II Legislative and Administrative Developments. III Conventions, Treaties and Proclamations. IV Judicial Developments in Literary and Artistic Property. V Bibliography. In an article, "COPYRIGHT IN THE 1980's", Barbara Ringer, United States Register of Copyrights, wrote, "I believe that the courts and Congress will continue to expand the subject matter protected by copyright and to cover the new uses of copyrighted works made possible by the expanding technology".
23 BULL. CR. SOC. page 303 (1976)

CHAPTER 29

PLAGIARISM & CREDITS

2901. "And people who...plagiarized without giving credit...got a reaction from a Kirlian".

....A. E. Van Vogt, THE ANARCHIST COLOSSUS

2902. "PLAGIARISM. The act of appropriating the literary composition of another, or parts of passages of his writings, or the ideas or language of the same, and passing them off as the product of his own mind."

....BLACK'S LAW DICTIONARY

2903. A vast amount of public domain material (material not protected by copyright) has been used in this book.

2904. Two scholarly chapters concerning the history and evolution of copyright were lifted from a book "THE QUESTION OF COPYRIGHT" published by G. P. Putnam's Sons so long ago that the period of copyright protection expired.

2905. The new copyright act was copied from a free U.S. government publication distributed by the Copyright Office.

2906. Questions and answers concerning the new copyright act were furnished by the American Society of Composers and Authors in a pamphlet which was published without a copyright notice; as a matter of courtesy we asked and received permission from ASCAP to copy their publication.

2907. Supreme Court copyright decisions were copied from public domain reports published by the Superintendent of Documents.

2908. PATENTS AND TRADEMARKS information comes from public domain government documents.

2909. Illustrations by Don Rico were furnished by him in the copyright law status as "employee-for-hire".

2910. Photography by Nona Rae was furnished by her in her copyright law status as "employee-for-hire".

2911. Other persons made contributions as "employee-for-hire" under the 1909 act and as "worker-for-hire" under the 1976 act. We thank them all.

2912. You, who are interested in copyright, may at various times be a creator.

2913. Creators tend to take a little here, a little there, add a little, mix well and shake.

2914. Try to avoid taking from works protected by copyright. The public domain is a fertile and legitimate source.

2915. (NOTE: The quote from A. E. Van Vogt copyright protected book is allowed as "fair use". For leads to more information concerning "fair use" see the index.)

BIBLIOGRAPHY

AMERICAN COPYRIGHT LAW-Arthur W. Weil. Chicago: Callaghan, 1917

BIBLIOGRAPHY ON DESIGN PROTECTION-Barbara A. Ringer. U.S. Copyright Office

BULLETIN. Copyright Society of the U.S.A. New York: New York University Law Center, 1953-to date. (published bimonthly)

CASES AND MATERIALS ON COPYRIGHT AND OTHER ASPECTS OF LAW PERTAINING TO LITERARY, MUSICAL AND ARTISTIC WORKS-Melville B. Nimmer (American Casebook Series) St. Paul: West Publishing Co., 1971

CASES ON COPYRIGHT, UNFAIR COMPETITION, AND OTHER TOPICS BEARING ON THE PROTECTION OF LITERARY, MUSICAL, AND ARTISTIC WORKS-Benjamin Kaplan & Ralph S. Brown, Jr. 2d ed. by Ralph S. Brown, Jr. Mineola, New York: Foundation Press, 1974

COPYRIGHT AND RELATED TOPICS-A CHOICE OF ARTICLES Los Angeles Copyright Society and the UCLA School of Law. Berkeley: University of California Press, 1964

COPYRIGHT GUIDE, A-Harriet F. Pilpel & Morton Goldberg. 4th ed. New York: Bowker, 1969

COPYRIGHT IN HISTORICAL PERSPECTIVE-Lyman Ray Patterson. Nashville: Vanderbilt University Press, 1968

COPYRIGHT LAW AND PRACTICE-Leon H. Amdur. New York: Clark Boardman, 1936

COPYRIGHT LAW SYMPOSIUM-Nathan Burkan Memorial competition, sponsored by the American Society of Composers, Authors, and Publishers. New York: Columbia University Press, 1939-. (The essays contained in each volume are selected annually for inclusion)

COPYRIGHT LAWS AND TREATIES OF THE WORLD-Bureau of National Affairs. Washington, BNA. 2v.

COPYRIGHTS-Barbara A. Ringer & Paul Gitlin. Rev ed. New York: Practising Law Institute, 1965

DECISIONS OF THE UNITED STATES COURTS INVOLVING COPY-RIGHT-U.S. Copyright Office. Bulletin No. 17-34

ENTERTAINMENT, PUBLISHING AND ARTS; AGREEMENTS AND THE LAW-Alexander Lindey. New York: Clark Boardman, 1963-(loose-leaf)

FILM-TV LAW (YOUR INTRODUCTION TO FILM - TV COPYRIGHT CONTRACTS AND OTHER LAW)-Johnny Minus & William Storm Hale. Entertainment Industry Series, Vol. 7. Los Angeles: Seven Arts Press, Inc., 1973

HOW TO BE A MUSIC PUBLISHER-Walter E. Hurst & Don Rico. Los Angeles: Seven Arts Press, Inc., 1976

HOW TO SELL YOUR SONG-Walter E. Hurst & Don Rico. Los Angeles: Seven Arts Press, Inc., 1961

HOWELL'S COPYRIGHT LAW-Revised and edited by Alan Latman. 4th ed. Washington: Bureau of National Affairs, 1962

LEGAL PROTECTION FOR THE CREATIVE MUSICIAN-Lee Eliot Berk, Boston: Berklee Press

LEGAL PROTECTION OF LITERATURE, ART AND MUSIC-Stanley Rothenberg, New York: Clark Boardman, 1960

LITERARY PROPERTY-Richard Wincor. New York: Clarkson N. Potter, 1967

MANUAL OF COPYRIGHT PRACTICE FOR WRITERS, PUBLISHERS, AND AGENTS, A-Margaret Nicholson. 2d ed. New York: Oxford University Press, 1956

MORE ABOUT THIS BUSINESS OF MUSIC-Sidney Shemel & M. William Krasilovsky. New York: Billboard Publishing Co., 1971

MOTION PICTURE DISTRIBUTION (BUSINESS AND/OR RACKET?!?)-Walter E. Hurst & William Storm Hale. Los Angeles: Seven Arts Press, Inc., 1975

MOVIE INDUSTRY BOOK, THE-Johnny Minus & William Storm Hale. Entertainment Industry Series, Vol. 5. Los Angeles: Seven Arts Press, Inc., 1970

MR. INFORMATION BATTLES FOR THE TAXPAYER-Walter E. Hurst & Don Rico. Los Angeles: Seven Arts Press, Inc., 1976

MUSIC INDUSTRY BOOK, THE-Walter E. Hurst & William Storm Hale. Entertainment Industry Series, Vol. 2. Los Angeles: Seven Arts Press, Inc., 1963

(MUSIC) PUBLISHER'S OFFICE MANUAL (HOW TO DO YOUR PAPERWORK IN THE MUSIC PUBLISHING INDUSTRY)-Walter E. Hurst & William Storm Hale. Entertainment Industry Series, Vol. 3. Los Angeles: Seven Arts Press, Inc., 1966

MUSIC/RECORD BUSINESS & LAW (YOUR INTRODUCTION TO MUSIC/RECORD COPYRIGHT, CONTRACTS AND OTHER BUSINESS & LAW)-Walter E. Hurst & William Storm Hale. Entertainment Industry Series, Vol. 9. Los Angeles: Seven Arts Press, Inc., 1974

MUSICAL COPYRIGHT-Alfred M. Shafter. 2d ed. Chicago: Callaghan, 1939

NIMMER ON COPYRIGHT-Melville B. Nimmer. Albany: M. Bender, 1963-(loose-leaf)

PATENT, TRADEMARK & COPYRIGHT JOURNAL-Washington, D.C.: Bureau of National Affairs 1970-to date. (Beginning with November 5, 1970, published every Thursday except the Thursday following July 4 and the last Thursday in December)

PERFORMING ARTS MANAGEMENT AND LAW-Joseph Taubman. New York: Law-Arts Publishers, 1972. Vol. 1-2

PROTECTION OF LITERARY PROPERTY, THE-Philip Wittenberg. Boston: The Writer, Inc., 1968

RADIO AND TELEVISION RIGHTS-Harry P. Warner. Albany: M. Bender, 1953

RECORD INDUSTRY BOOK, THE-Walter E. Hurst & William Storm Hale. The Entertainment Industry Series, Vol. 1. Los Angeles: Seven Arts Press, Inc., 1961, 1971

RIGHTS AND WRITERS - A HANDBOOK OF LITERARY AND ENTERTAINMENT LAW-Harriet F. Pilpel & Theodora Zavin. New York: Dutton, 1960

RISKS & RIGHTS IN PUBLISHING, TELEVISION, RADIO, MOTION PICTURES, ADVERTISING AND THEATRE-Samuel Spring. 2d ed. New York: W. W. Norton & Co., 1956

STUDIES ON COPYRIGHT-Copyright Society of the U.S.A. Compiles and edited under the supervision of the Copyright Society of the U.S.A. 2v. Arthur Fisher Memorial Edition. South Hackensack, N.J.: F. B. Rothman and Indianapolis: Bobbs-Merrill Co., 1963

TECHNOLOGY AND COPYRIGHT: ANNOTATED BIBLIOGRAPHY AND SOURCE MATERIALS-George P. Bush. Mt. Airy, Md: Lomond Systems, Inc., 1972

THIS BUSINESS OF MUSIC-Sidney Shemel & M. William Krasilovsky. Edited by Paul Ackerman. Rev and enl. ed. New York: Billboard Publishing Co., 1971

TREATISE ON THE LAW OF PROPERTY IN INTELLECTUAL PRODUCTIONS IN GREAT BRITAIN AND THE UNITED STATES-Eaton S. Drone. Boston: Little, Brown, 1879

U.S. MASTER PRODUCER'S & BRITISH MUSIC SCENE BOOK-Walter E. Hurst & William Storm Hale. Entertainment Industry Series, Vol. 4. Los Angeles: Seven Arts Press, Inc., 1968

UNHURRIED VIEW OF COPYRIGHT, AN-Benjamin Kaplan. (James S. Carpentier Lectures, 1966) New York: Columbia University Press, 1967

PROVING THAT YOU CREATED YOUR WORK

You may decide to wait a while before registering your work with the Copyright Office.

You may consider the advantages of registering your work as soon as legally possible, thus being able to prove with a U.S. Government certificate that as of a certain date you did file your claim to copyright, and probably (possibly) being able to prove (with a photocopy of the item registered) the work in which copyright protection was claimed.

On the other hand, you may be too lazy, too poor, too unprofessional, too something or other (prolific, etc.) to register every complete work. You may also be working on incomplete versions of your work.

Therefore, you may wish to use a DECLARATION or AFFIDAVIT from someone you know, someone who will probably be available to be a witness if you ever have to prove the contents of the declaration in court.

The declarant may be able to (at a later time) refresh his recollection be re-reading the declaration he signed at an earlier time.

On the next page is a form you may want to use to guide yourself in preparing the declaration for your witness.

On the left hand side in one style of type is the form; on the right side, in italics, is a sample illustration of information a witness may provide.

PROOF OF COPYRIGHT CREATION

WITNESS' DECLARATION

I, the undersigned WITNESS declare:

On the following date:	*April 35, 197X*
at the home (office) of:	*Sharon*
at the following address:	*1234 Main Street*
city, state, zip:	*Somewhere, CA 90086*
I did read (see, hear):	*read hear*
the song (manuscript, picture, etc.):	*song*
tentatively entitled:	*Sharon's Song*
written (lyrics, music) by:	*Kyle*
address:	*1234 Main Street*
city, state, zip:	*Somewhere, CA 90086*
social security No:	*111-11-1111*
driver's license state & No:	*CA 1111111*
telephone:	*(213)444-4444*

The work was on: *a lyric sheet on 8 1/2 x 11 paper*
a lead sheet on 10 x 14 music paper
an audio cassette

My name is:
My address is:
city, state, zip:
social security No:
driver's license state & No:
telephone:
My relationship to the copyright creator is:
My occupation is:

I declare under penalty of perjury that the above is true and correct.

Executed on ________________ at (city & state) __________

Signed: ____

I N D E X

COPYRIGHT CREATORS/EXPLOITERS

TAX-SAVING RECORD-SAVING FORMS

On the next few pages are forms you may want to duplicate and use.

You may wish to duplicate all four forms on the front and back of 8 1/2" x 11" sheets.

You can then fill in the pertinent details as you incur the respective expense.

You can use as many forms each day as you need.

Try to staple or tape receipts to forms.

You may be able to use the collected information to save yourself a lot of money by reducing your income taxes.

(A set of 200 forms can be ordered for $5.00, payable with the order, from SEVEN ARTS PRESS, INC., P.O. Box 649, Hollywood, California 90028)

COPYRIGHT OWNERS/EXPLOITERS
ENTERTAINMENT EXPENSE FORM

I declare that today I entertained for business reasons:

Person Entertained:	*Tom Maruzzi*
Occupation:	*Songwriter, Publisher*
Company:	*Maruzzi Music (ASCAP)*
Place:	*Musso & Franks*
Expense for (food, drink, etc.):	*Food & Drink*
How Much:	*$24.00*
Business Reason:	*To discuss Tom's publishing & my song entitled "Art of Love"*

DATE: ______________________

TAXPAYER: JACK SHAPIRO

COPYRIGHT OWNERS/EXPLOITERS LIST OF EXPENSES

DATE:	*4/1/19xx*
AMOUNT:	*$4.55*
ITEM PURCHASED:	*Trade papers*
NAME OF BUSINESS PAID:	*7 Arts Bookstore*
IF BY CHECK, CHECK NUMBER:	*#123*
IF BY CHARGE, CARD COMPANY"	*---*
IF ITEM IS BUSINESS GIFT, RECIPIENT:	*Al*
OCCUPATION OF RECIPIENT:	*Gofer*
COMPANY OF RECIPIENT:	*Gofer Does All*
BUSINESS REASON FOR GIFT:	*To educate Al so he can understand his work better & will service my account better.*

COPYRIGHT OWNERS/EXPLOITERS TELEPHONE CALLS

AMOUNT:
DATE:
PERSON CALLED:
TELEPHONE NUMBER:
COMPANY:
BUSINESS PURPOSE:
NOTES DURING CONVERSATION:

COPYRIGHT OWNERS MILEAGE RECORD

I, the undersigned taxpayer declare that I went the following miles for business reasons:

DATE:	*4/19/19xx*
FROM: (My home, my office, studio):	*office*
TO: (newsstand selling trade papers, record store);	*Bookstore, Book City*
MILEAGE AT START:	*10000*
MILEAGE AT DESTINATION:	*10005*
TOTAL MILES:	*5*
BUSINESS REASON FOR TRIP:	*buy MUSIC INDUSTRY BOOK*
RELATED EXPENSES:	*Bought gas $5.00 Bought THE MUSIC INDUSTRY BOOK $25*

COPYRIGHT OWNERS/EXPLOITERS TRAVEL EXPENSE FORM

	DATE	AMOUNT*	PAYEE	BUSINESS PURPOSE
TAXI				
RENTAL CAR				
OWN CAR				
BUS				
HOST'S CAR				
PLANE				
GAS				
PARKING				
TOLLS				
HOTEL				
FOOD				
DRINK				
LAUNDRY				
TIPS				

AMOUNT* - Use initials: K for Cash
for Check
CH for Charge

Seven Arts Press, Inc.
Book and Music Publishers
6605 HOLLYWOOD BOULEVARD
HOLLYWOOD, CALIFORNIA 90028
(213) 469-1095

4 CASSETTE COURSE - $40.00 - ARTIST-RECORDING COMPANY CONTRACT AND RELATIONSHIP.
2 CASSETTE COURSE - $20.00 - THE SONGWRITER AS A BUSINESSMAN.
4 CASSETTE COURSE - $40.00 - RECORDING SESSION BUDGET & CHECKLIST.
1 CASSETTE COURSE - $10.00 - TAX AUDIT GUIDELINES & TECHNIQUES.
1 CASSETTE COURSE - $10.00 - OVERVIEW OF TAX SHELTERS.
1 CASSETTE COURSE - $10.00 - HOW TO PROTECT YOUR SONG.
20 CASSETTE COURSE - $200.00 - COPYRIGHT & THE MOVIE BUSINESS I.
20 CASSETTE COURSE - $200.00 - COPYRIGHT & THE MUSIC BUSINESS I.
20 CASSETTE COURSE - $200.00 - CONSTITUTIONAL LAW I.
20 CASSETTE COURSE - $200.00 - BLACK STUDIES
20 CASSETTES - $200.00 - SHOW BUSINESS I.
20 CASSETTES - $200.00 - CRIMINAL LAW I.
20 CASSETTES - $200.00 - HIGH FINANCE LAW I.
100 CASSETTES - $1,000.00 - RECENT U.S. SUPREME COURT DECISIONS (1970 to Present).
100 CASSETTES - $1,000.00 - U.S. SUPREME COURT LANDMARK DECISIONS (1790 to 1969).

Entertainment Law

THE U.S. MASTER PRODUCERS & BRITISH MUSIC SCENE BOOK. By Walter E. Hurst and William Strom Hale. Hollywood: 7 Arts Press, 1968. Pp. 373. $25. Written by a lawyer working in the music and recording business, this book deals with the legal problems of record promotion, business and money promotion, recording contracts, and advertising. In addition, it includes sample contracts for all phases of dealings among artists, master producers, recording companies, fan clubs, record clubs, motion picture producers, talent scouts, music publishers, and television producers. Special attention is given to description of the music industry in England. Excerpts from British law books, the Performing Right Society Limited publications, and other trade publications are presented to inform the American artist or producer of his business rights in England and generally to acquaint him with the British industry. The book is thorough in its coverage and the table of contents and index are well designed.

. . . *SOUTHERN CALIFORNIA LAW REVIEW*

CALIFORNIA WESTERN LAW REVIEW

MOTION PICTURE DISTRIBUTION. By Walter E. Hurst and William Storm Hale. Seven Arts Press: Hollywood. 1974. Pp. 158. $10.00. The authors have prepared an easy to read review of the various aspects of motion picture distribution; its theory and practice. Various problem areas and pitfalls, as well as basic aspects of the subject area, are set forth in alphabetical sequence for easy reference and are intricately detailed through the use of definitional statements and practical forms and examples.

MOTION PICTURE DISTRIBUTION: (BUSINESS AND/OR RACKET?!?), by Walter E. Hurst and William Storm Hale. Seven Arts Press, Hollywood, CA; 1975; $10.00 paper; 158 pp.; illus.; index; biblio. What every film producer always wanted to know about distribution but was afraid to ask. Detailed handbook covers a wide variety of producer-distributor-exhibitor conflicts.

Educational Film Library
Association, Inc.

Browsing the Book Stalls •

HOW TO BE A MUSIC PUBLISHER; by Walter E. Hurst & Don Rico; Seven Arts Press Inc.; 125 pages (paperback); $10.

The authors, a top Hollywood music attorney and a leading artist/illustrator and writer, have collaborated to produce a primer which covers the main principles of the music publishing business for songwriters, artists, musicians, distributors, teachers, students, accountants, attorneys, publicists and anyone else seeking to understand the rudiments of this multimillion-dollar industry.

While it is by no means a comprehensive guide to this end of the music business (and anyone seeking to enter it would be well advised to use this book merely as a point of departure for further research), nevertheless it does manage to provide a good overflow of the fundamentals which must be mastered.

It covers some of the basics of copyright law, contracts, licensing agreements, acquiring and selling song rights, etc. It also covers key principles of musical composition. It is an excellent companion volume to Hurst's earlier work (with William Storm Hale): "Introduction to Music/Record Copyright, Contracts and Other Business and Law."

There is much to learn about the business and legal aspects of the music and record industry — and this book is a welcome addition to available books on these subjects. — **John Charnay**

CALIFORNIA TOWN & COUNTRY

BOOK REVIEW
BY CAROLINE HALL

THE MANAGERS, ENTERTAINER AND AGENTS BOOK
JOHNNY MINUS & WILLIAM STORM HALE

I have spent a quarter of a century as an entertainer, agent, booking agent, talent scouting and as a manager and last but not least as a personal manager. I have worked with many managers, entertainers agents, lawyers, promoters songwriters, publishers and others in show business, some I have also worked against. I have booked many stars and aspiring stars. I have lenared one thing-show business brings out the best or the worst in a person, but it allows both stars and associates an exciting and full life. Most young people, who read fan magazine and day-dream about themselves as a great singer, actor, singer, performer and all the glamor is there so they start out in a neighborhood or school event to become the leading lady or man. Sometimes fond parents cheer them on or force them, encourage their offsprings, but only until the point when the parents worry about the horrible temptations and dangers that they face when they enter show business. The parents are afraid that they will become bums with a unpredictable future. There are books and courses for youngsters who want to prepare themselves for any number of careers. There has never been a book written that will guarantee you success, but this book **THE ENTERTAINEMTN INDUSTRY SERIES, AND THE MANAGER'S, ENTERTAINERS and AGENTS BOOK** is probably the best guideline for you to follow. If you were an entertainer and are looking for a manager to manage your career and a stranger told you that he was a manager and would like to manage you how would you qualify him. If you wanted to be or were a manager or agent, and a singer, songwriter, group and a performer wanted you to manage them how would you qualify the performer, etc. I have not had the book available to me, but **THE MANAGERS', ENTERTAINERS' and AGENTS BOOK**, I am glad that the book exist, however, if you do purchase this book for fun, profit and help to guide you in your career remember one thing it is a guide and do not for one minute buy it for instant success, but use it as a reference and a guide and it will help you in the business of the **STARS, SHOW PEOPLE** and the people around them. You also will probably reap the harvest that is there.

THE CHRISTIAN SCIENCE MONITOR

The World Beyond the Turntable

By Louis Chapin

The writing, promoting, recording, and publishing of popular songs is usually estimated in one of three ways. Either it is (a) something any fool can make a mint of money out of, or (b) something only a fool would risk his shirt in, or (c) well worth considering. The authors of **"The Record Industry Book,** Volume One (How to Make Money in the Record Industry)" are given, naturally, to opinion (c); yet they have written it so as at least to entertain, if not convert, the adherents of the other opinions.

These two authors are Walter E. Hurst and William Storm Hale—the former a lawyer and the latter apparently a figure of some prominence disguised by a pen name. Their bulky book has been published by Seven Arts Press in Hollywood in letter-size monolith at $25. In spite of unpromising typography, "The Record Industry Book" is written with a conversational style that almost reads itself.

Practical Guide

It is specifically informative, with a sprinkling of tables, charts, diagrams, comic-strip expositions, and sample documents (such as contracts and copyright forms). It should be a thoroughly practical guide to those concerned with the writing, playing, recording, publishing, selling, and otherwise exploiting of popular music. It might encourage the timid, and temper the overconfident.

Moreover, leavened as it is with free-wheeling anecdotal illustrations, "The Record Industry" may well be read and enjoyed by some who merely listen—and make the whole business possible. They will find breezy, conversational stretches of Americana, as "case histories" are leafed through, with both actual and fictitious names to document the rough and smooth sides of the pop music coin. They will find a busy, palpitating, apparently self-sufficient world of downbeats, takes, and royalties.

Pennies Add Up

They may be surprised, too, to learn of the tremendous volume on which record profits are predicated. The "artist" may realize only three or four cents a record, but when sales are "snowballed" up to 500,000 or 1,000,000 he'll need something bigger than a penny bank. And he may need to learn how to give his copyrights to charity, so that he can take home three times as much after taxes.

There are certain questions the reader will not find discussed in "The Record Industry." Among them: whether the whole operation represents the greatness of American enterprise with a song on its lips, or (conceivably) a colossal cultural short circuit. Or both.

Another question: whether the writing, performing, recording, and publishing of symphonies, operas, and other such "long-hair" items should be excluded from "the record industry" by definition. A front-page story in a recent Wall Street Journal was headlined "Opera Recordings Sell Briskly. . . . Birgit Nilsson's Turandot Outsells Hit Crosby Album." Apparently those other songwriters Mozart, Verdi, Puccini — even Kurt Weill — had some profitable skills.

It is significant, of course, that most of these booming opera records are made outside the United States, in countries where musicians' costs are still invitingly low. But where such a domestic market obviously exists, what enterprising man of industry is going to turn his back on possibilities (however remote) of domestic production?

"The Record Industry," it appears, is a thought-provoking book. And since a new and larger edition is already being contemplated, its authors may still take the opportunity of reconsidering their terms. And judging by the book in hand, they will do so good-naturedly and readably.

THE Hollywood REPORTER

The Managers, Entertainers, and Agents Book; Johnny Minus and William Storm Hale; Seven Arts Press, $35.

In "The Managers, Entertainers, and Agents Book," the sixth and latest volume to join the Seven Arts Press Entertainment Industry Series, authors Johnny Minus and William Storm Hale (pseudonyms) provide thorough coverage on—to borrow their subtitle—"how to plan, plot, scheme, learn, perform, avoid dangers, and enjoy your career in the entertainment industry." Using typewriter-script text, many duplications of contracts and related forms and applications, and cartoon-strip illustrations of legal cases, this 732-page compilation of guidelines includes almost all situations that would affect the trio of the title. The examination and exposé of business "insides" — rarely available to tyro and civilian, and the probable reason for the pseudonymous authorship — makes this unique, local publication a sound investment, worthy of the $35 price tag, and a definite must for those needing solid and accurate "How To-" information on these occupational divisions of the business.

DAILY VARIETY DAILY

WHAT'S THE SCORE?

By JOHN G. HOUSER

★ ★ ★

WORDS AND MUSIC: "THE RECORD INDUSTRY." AUTHORS Walter E. Hurst and William Storm Hale have contributed a massive, monumental and authoritative work that is as comprehensive a study of an intricate industry as it is possible to reveal. The material included in the invaluable work is a compendium and a textbook for neophyte and journeyman in all facets of the disk biz. It will be classed (as is Blackstone and Gray's Anatomy in the legal and medical professions) as the supreme authority for those in the recording industry. The price, $25, will be an investment many times recovered if the purchaser makes use of the lessons to be learned (the easy way). Authors have made "the lessons" an exciting panorama of case histories from artist to copyright and promotion to payola. Published by 7 Arts Press, the book should be at the right hand of every a&r man, musician, songwriter and publisher . . .